£10 –

# MGB

## The Racing Story

# MGB
## The Racing Story

**John Baggott**

**Foreword by Paddy Hopkirk**

The Crowood Press

First published in 2002 by
The Crowood Press Ltd
Ramsbury, Marlborough
Wiltshire SN8 2HR

**British Library Cataloguing-in-Publication Data**
A catalogue record for this book is available from the British Library.

ISBN 1 86126 530 1

Typeset by Florence Production Ltd, Stoodleigh, Devon

Printed and bound in Great Britain by
Bookcraft, Midsomer Norton

# Contents

Foreword *by Paddy Hopkirk*     6

Introduction and Acknowledgements     7

1    MGB Enters the Fray     9

2    Long Distance Races at Home and Abroad     39

3    Take to the Hills     50

4    Historics     57

5    The MG Car Club BCV8 Championship     62

6    The MG Owners Club/BARC Championship     99

7    Barry Sidery-Smith     115

8    Sports and Grand Touring Cars with MGB Power     123

9    The MGC GTS Project     155

10    Taming the MGB GT V8     171

11    The MGC     180

Bibliography     188

Index     189

# Foreword

**by Paddy Hopkirk**

Most people who remember anything about my fifteen years of professional motor sport career (1955–70), associate me with Minis and rallying in the sixties. Actually I competed in many races too, which won me the accolade of becoming a member of the British Racing Drivers Club, of which I am now honoured to be a Director too.

I raced on most of the best-known circuits on the British Isles as well as on the Continent, including Le Mans, Nürburgring, Targa Florio, Zandvoort, and many more. In the USA I also competed at Sebring, Riverside and Bridge-hampton.

Although I have to say that the Mini Cooper played the biggest part in my life's motoring career, the MGB comes a close second and cer-tainly rates number one for racing at venues like Le Mans, Sebring, Targa Florio, Bridgehampton and many more.

Certain cars become cult cars and the MGs of that era are no exception. Many enthusiasts like to own these classic models and still use them today.

Aren't I the lucky one to have been a part of that classic history? The MGB was so well designed and such a simple and reliable car with straightforward handling. It will always bring back many happy memories for me and the co-drivers I shared it with during those wonderful times.

# Introduction and Acknowledgements

Over the last forty years, MGBs and their variants have competed in just about every form of motor sport. To attempt to detail every driver and outing would be impossible, but this book tells the stories of some of the competitors, the majority amateur, who have derived a great deal of pleasure from racing, hill climbing, sprinting and, in one case, Rallycrossing their particular examples. In certain instances, details are based solely on drivers' recollections and, whilst believed to be accurate, are not guaranteed.

Many competitors, past and present, MGB enthusiasts, mechanics, tuners and others have either provided me with information or put me in touch with someone who could. My sincere thanks to the following:

Don Adams, John Aley, Graham Ash, Jill & Steve Ashby, Keith Ashby, Roy Ashford, Dr Mark Ashworth, Clive Baker, Andre Baldet, Warwick Banks, Tony Barnard, Paul Barnes, Jim Baynham, Dave Beecham, Malcolm Beer, Rod Begbie, John Belsey, Derek Bentley, Dave Beresford, Lawrence Bescoby, Tony Bianchi, Steve Bicknell, Anthony Binnington, Mike Bird, Bob Birrell, Don Bishop, Piers Blankney-Edwards, Jimmy Blumer, Fred Boothby, Sylvia Boothby, Dr Tom Boyce, Andrew Bradshaw, Cliff Bray, Mike Breedon, Len Bridge, Cedric Brierley, Terry Briggs, Gerry Brown, Peter Brown, Peter Browning, Don Bunce, Graham Burrows, Arnold Burton, Paul Butler, Brian Cakebread, Paul Campfield, Christabel Carlisle, Barry Cartmell, Bruce Casey, Mike Chalk, John Chatham, Paul Chudecki, Bob Clare, Tony Claydon, David Cleverdon, Norman Cochrane, Henry Cole, Nick Cole, Derek Colebourne, Peter Collis, Judith Condon, Mike Connor, Barry Cooper, John Cotton, Peter Cottrell, Tom Coulthard, Jim Cox, Alistair Crawford, Bob Curl, Grahame Davis, Rae Davis, Arthur Debenham, Jeremy Delmar-Morgan, John and Pauline Dignan, Ray Dilley, Bob Dixon, Roger A. Dunbar, Stuart Eddy, Kit Edwards, Roger Edwards, David Ellison, Tommy Entwhistle, Bev Fawkes, Carol Folkard, Roger Fowler, Roger Frankland, David Franklin, Rob Gammage, Ivan Garner, Mark Garner, Mike Garton, Jim Garvey, Mike Gaston, Geoff Gear, Danny Gladwin, Edna Glynn, Robbie Gordon, Tim Goss, Rob Grant, Robb Gravett, Den Green, Ben Grub, Martin Hadwen, Tony Hansford, Cliff Hatcher, Mike Hawke, John Haynes OBE, Jackie Hayter, Andrew Hedges, Jean Henderson, Bill Hewitt, John Hewitt, David Hives, Phil Hooper, Paddy Hopkirk, Richard Horn, Paul Howard, Roy Hunnisett, Richard Hurl, Alan Hutcheson, Brian Hutchinson, Martin Ingall, Jenny Ives, Philip Ivimey, Peter Jackson, Sue Jamieson, Dave Jarvis, David Jeffrey, Terry Johnstone, Nigel Jordan, Paul Jordan, Tony Kember, Bob Kemp, John Kempton, Brian and Pat Kenyon, Alan Kingwell, Edward Kirkland, Brian Lambert, John Lane, Amanda Langton, Liz Langton, Mervyn Larner, Kevin Law, Malcolm Lawrence, Rod Leach, Nick Lees, Bunny Lees-Smith, Stan Leithead, Mike Lewis, Martin Lilley, Jack Lloyd, Jill Lloyd, John Lodge, Andrew Longden, Dr Rod Longton, Jim Loveday, Bob Luff, Nova Mahon, Geoff Mansell, Graham Marchant, Len Marchant, Carol Marks, Gerry Marshall, Richard Martin-Hurst, Ian Massey-Crosse, Roy and Pam McCarthy, John McDonald, Alistair McHardy, Derek McMahon, Loraine Mercury, John Mew, Peter Mew, Ron Middleton, Alan Miles, Terry Mitchell,

Chris Montague, Anita Morrell, Bob Neville, Jim Nicholson, Garo Nigogosian, Peter Noad, Andy Nott, Terry Osborne, Chris Painter, Dr Terry Parker, Malcolm Parsons, Graham Pearce, John Pearson, Graeme Perkins, Ian Perrett, Nigel and Sandra Petch, Terry Pigott, Robin Pinkerton, Jonathan Playfoot, Alec Poole, Arnie Poole, Phil Price, Trevor Pyman, Christopher Raithby-Veall, Steve Reid, Ailsa Richardson, Paul Richardson, Carl Ripley, Martin Ripley, Andrew Roberts, Donna Robertson, Pete Robertson, Brian Roland, Les Ryder, Gerry Sagerman, Simon Saye, Richard Scantlebury, Dr Paul Scott, Chris Seaman, Peter Sharp, Barry and Pam Sidery-Smith, Graham Smeeton, Barry and Jo Smith, Chris Smith (Gilbern Garage), Chris Smith (Westfield), Colin Smith, Doug Smith, Enid Smith, Terry Smith, Derek Spall, Chris Steel, Roy Stephenson, Brian Stern, Jerry Sturman, John Tadman, Stuart Tallack, Huw Taylor, Neil Taylor, Jonathan Thomson, Tom Threlfall, Julius Thurgood, James Tiller, Josie Tolhurst, Piers Townsend, Jerry Trace, John Trace, Malcolm Trewhitt, Jenny Tudor-Owen, Ernie Unger, Sean Valentine, Roy Venness, Julian Vernaeve, John Vernon, Paul Vincent, Phil Walker, Mike Walton, Russ Ward, Colin Wareham, Keith Warner, Steve Watkins, John Watson, Geoff Webb, Barrie Weller, Vivien West, Mary Wheeler, Richard Wileyman, Ray Wilkinson, Bernard Williams, Steve Williams, Douglas Wilson-Spratt, Tony Wilson-Spratt, Martyn Wise, Barry Wood, Nigel Woolcott, Ted Worswick, Richard Worts, Dick Wright, Maureen Wyatt, Malcolm Young, Neville Young, Vic Young, Alan Zafer.

The MG Car Club, the MG Owners Club, Elva Racing & Owners Club, the Gilbern Owners Club and TVR Car Club have all assisted with information from their archives and in forwarding correspondence to their members. My wife Jane has again put her proof-reading skills to good use and assisted me with research.

Information has been obtained from the BARC press archive, Motor Racing Archive and the National Motor Museum Library. Peter Cope and Dave Woodgate have readily made material, from periodicals not in my own collection, available to me. I have consulted back issues of: *Autocar, Autosport, Cars and Car Conversions, Classic Car Weekly, Classic and Sportscar, Collectors Car, Enjoying MG, Historic Race and Rally, Motoring News, Motor Sport, Safety Fast, Small Car, Sports Car World, Thoroughbred & Classic Cars.* To their past and present editors, reporters and contributors, thank you.

Many photographers have made a contribution to this book. Not all the prints I have been lent bear the name of the person behind the lens and some were copies, but they include: Harold Barker, Ron Cover, Ray Dilley, John Gaisford, Graphic Images (UK) Ltd, Chris Green, Frank E. Hall, Chris Harvey, Mary Harvey, Roger Harvey, Derek Hibbert, Piers Hubbard, Steve Jones, Edward Kirkland, Diana Lucas, John March, Neville Marriner, Eric Metcalfe, Andrew Roberts, Fred Scatley, Evan Selwyn-Smith, Julius Thurgood, John Whitmore and Sue Williams.

**John Baggott**
*2002*

# 1  MGB Enters the Fray

Launched in September 1962, the MGB had a unitary body construction. The 'B' series engine bored out to 3.16in (80.3mm) gave a capacity of 1,798cc and produced 95bhp; thus in standard form, the unladen 2,050lb (930kg) sports car had a top speed of 103mph (165km/hr).

Terry Mitchell, chassis designer at MG's Abingdon works, says that the MGB was not originally designed with competition in mind. During the development process, they may well have thought certain parts of it would suit competition use but their brief was to build a production model to replace the MGA.

Many Motor Show new models often made their track debut at one of the then traditional Boxing Day meetings, but not the MGB, which had to wait until 1963 to make its race debut. This was in America when Ronnie Bucknum took two Sports Car Club of America victories at Riverside in February. He went on to win Class D in twenty of the twenty-four rounds and took the Championship.

## Alan Hutcheson

The earliest MGB home success was a Class win for Alan Hutcheson at the BARC Goodwood Easter Meeting on Monday 15 April 1963. Driving 7 DBL, the works car that failed to finish at Sebring, in the Sussex Trophy Race for GT Cars, he beat the AC Bristols of Bob Burnard and John Nicholson by thirty-nine seconds and set joint-fastest lap. Graham Hill's E Type Jaguar was the overall winner. Alan chalked up another Class victory in the same vehicle at Silverstone on 7 May 1963. He found the B particularly

*Driving 6 DBL in a 1963 Marque Sports race, Alan Hutcheson looks in his mirror to check on the train of cars behind him. Famous E-Type, CUT 7, is in third place.*

competitive on shorter circuits and scored outright wins at Brands, Crystal Palace and Mallory Park.

Alan, who also drove for BMC in European races, is probably best known for his (in)famous trip into the Mulsanne sand trap during the 1963 Le Mans 24-Hour Race. His MGB outings were all in works-owned cars, which were lent to him so that he could compete as a private entrant. He mainly drove 7 DBL, in which he took a Class win at Spa, but also competed in 6 DBL, which he eventually destroyed after a lurid roll in front of the television cameras at Woodcote on lap one, during the Silverstone British Grand Prix meeting on 26 July 1963. Hutcheson finished second in Class C in the 1963 Autosport Championship. After a brief time with Elva early in 1964, he went on to join Lotus.

## Bill Nicholson

A former Jaguar development engineer, Bill Nicholson started his competitive days riding a motor cycle for his previous employers BSA. In 1961 he had his first circuit race in a Sunbeam Alpine. His MGB, 286 FAC, was probably one of the most famous racing MGBs of all time. Known as 'Old Girl', the brand-new car was a forty-fourth birthday present from his wife Ros on 7 January 1963, though he had to wait until 12 February to collect it from Abingdon. It could have been a different story had Lotus delivered the Elan he originally ordered in time for him to prepare it for the 1963 season.

Once run in, the B was stripped and rebuilt for racing. There was very little available by way of tuning parts for such a new model but, with

*Bill Nicholson in 286 FAC, known as 'Old Girl', (54) at Silverstone in August 1968.*

advice from Syd Enever, Bill made his own, including lowered springs. He fitted a Twin Cam clutch plate in order to utilize a close-ratio gear set. After resolving early tyre problems the car was run in Group 3, and later Group 4, where regulations allowing fibreglass panels enabled him to reduce the weight by 1.5cwt (76kg). Later in the development programme, Bill changed the Weber for larger SU carburettors, relocated the front wishbone mounting points and fitted stronger springs front and rear.

Bill first raced his B on 15 April 1963 and retired in 1981. During that period, he took 251 race, plus fourteen sprint and hill-climb wins; the car also had five wins in other hands. His MGB consistently held its own against Lotus Elans, Healey 3000s and, on occasion, E Type Jaguars. Bill attributed his success to the power-to-weight ratio and the fact that basically it was a forgiving car. The name Nicholson became the byword for MGB tuning with many owners visiting his premises at Wellingborough Road, Weston Favel in Northamptonshire, a business he set up in 1965.

'MG Bill' as he became known, chalked up ten victories during the 1967 season, along the way taking the Silverstone Club Circuit lap record at 1min 10.4sec. He also set the fastest lap in an MGB at Croft (1min 24.4sec) and Crystal Palace (1min 7.4sec). His other notable outing that year was at Bishopscourt where, after a terrific battle, he beat Irishman Alec Poole on his home turf. Running costs for thirty-two events that year were around £500.

Bill was noted as a Silverstone specialist; amongst many wins at this circuit he took the Marque Sports race at the Maidstone and Mid-Kent MC meeting on 25 April 1964 where he beat J. McKechnie's Morgan and John Sharp's MGB, which finished in third place. Despite claiming he did not like racing with what he described as the 'hoi polloi' who competed at Brands, he had a particularly good outing around the Grand Prix Circuit there on 19 October 1968. The exotic machinery at the front of the field either fell off or retired and he found his dice for sixth place with fellow 'B' drivers

Anthony Binnington and Charles Dawkins had suddenly become the race for the lead. Bill kept in front to head Anthony and Charles home for an MGB overall 1, 2, 3.

Nicholson's most exciting race in 1969 was at Zandvoort, where he lapped a Porsche 911 S twice and finished eleventh overall, amongst the GT 40s. Many remember his performance at Silverstone in September when he swapped places five times on the last lap. Although well known as a racing driver, few are aware of Bill's success in showing Alsatians – he usually had five in a run at the side of his home and took many awards. Nicholson, an out-and-out racer, sadly died in 1994, but will be remembered for his MGB tuning prowess and fine dices with Roy Ashford, Don Bunce, David Franklin and, of course, John Gott in the Big Healey.

## Les Ryder

On 10 March 1969, one of Nicholson's former Jaguar colleagues, Les Ryder, joined him to do the cylinder heads, his hand-written contract of employment giving him a weekly wage plus a royalty of £2 for each cylinder head he produced. Les had already established a reputation for heads at Beta Cars and Hartshill Engine Developments. Ryder, who worked sixty hours a week, has kept records of all the heads he has ever modified and calculates that, in his time, he did 428 for MGBs alone!

Bill Nicholson Tuning moved to new premises at Towcester in 1970, taking a workshop with a Texaco petrol forecourt, right opposite the police station. Tipped off by Brian Reece at Morris Motors that the Coventry engine department was selling off a dynamometer, they snapped it up. Having arranged to draw water from the canal to the rear of the premises to cool engines on test, the equipment was installed, only for the landlords to tell them to take it out as it was contrary to their lease.

Les commuted from his home in Coventry to Towcester each day in his 1963 MGB, which he replaced with a Cooper S in 1971. As you would expect, the engine was to full race-spec and most of his journeys to work were 'pretty quick'. One day he was travelling down the M1 at around 100mph, wanting to get in a bit early as on the back seat he had a very special cylinder head to deliver to the police station for John Gott, the racing Chief Constable of Northamptonshire. Les glanced in the mirror to see that there was a black Cooper S following him; he speeded up and so did the other Mini. He pulled off the motorway one junction early and the other car followed, overtaking him at the roundabout, when the 'Police Stop' sign popped up in the back window.

Duly pulling over, Les waited and was amazed when Gott himself emerged from the passenger door of the unmarked police car, one of two such Ss on the force, and walked back to have words with him. Wagging his finger, Gott suggested that Les had really dropped him in it. What would his driver think if he failed to book a motorist with such a blatant disregard for the speed limit? Continuing to wag his finger, Gott eyed the gleaming Big Healey cylinder head on the back seat before walking back to his own car and ordering his driver to proceed. Les later learnt that the PC had been told his superior

considered that in this instance a reprimand would be more effective than a prosecution.

In 1972, Les moved on with Mini racer and former workmate Roger Edwards to R E Engineering, 13 Gunnery Terrace, Leamington Spa, an end-of-terrace property with a two-car garage on the side where Roger worked on customers' cars. They dug out the cellar for Les to use as his cylinder-head workshop.

## Don Bunce

Eventually to become the driver of 'the other Nicholson MGB', Don Bunce started his motor racing at the Snetterton-based Jim Russell Racing Drivers School and did two seasons in single seaters with them. Through a work colleague, Don met Richard Worts who offered him the drive in his MGB, 94 HJJ, for the 1965 season. This was red with a black hardtop, a white stripe and wire wheels, was prepared by Barwell and had previously been raced by Barry Sidery-Smith.

Richard sold HJJ at the end of the season and bought a brand-new MGB, JYH 770D, from Wilsons, the BMC dealer in Tooting. It was in a

*Both Barry Sidery-Smith and Don Bunce drove 94 HJJ for Richard Worts. Barry later bought the car himself and raced it in his own right. Here Don races the car at Brands Hatch, complete with wire wheels.*

*Nigel Jordan in 94 HJJ at MGCC Silverstone, June 1968. The car was used for sprints, races and his daily journey to work.*

similar colour scheme to the old one, again with 5½ J × wire wheels. At the same time, he purchased a Bedford Utilibrake, painted in matching livery and trailer as it was felt it would be more professional to tow the MGB to meetings. Richard and Don ran the new car in on the road, then took it to Bill Nicholson to be race prepared.

Following Don's first sports car race at Mallory Park, the B was returned to Bill's original workshop in Market Harborough. It was stolen overnight, but the thieves, obviously unaware of the car's speed, went straight on at a corner about five miles away; the remains were found abandoned at the scene. Fortunately, the car was insured and when the new body shell arrived, Don took time off work to assist Bill with the re-shell.

The Bunce car was shod with Dunlop Green Spot tyres, which ran at 45psi, and he liked his suspension set up very stiffly with the adjustable Armstrongs on the rear virtually solid, whereas Nicholson preferred his own car a little softer and favoured White Spots. Don considers Dr Rod Longton's TVR his main rival, though he also had some close dices with Bill, competing against each other at Crystal Palace on 5 August 1967. On occasions, Don managed to get in front

of Bill during a race but never recalls beating him over the finish line.

On 9 May 1966 Don Bunce and Bill Nicholson shared 286 FAC in the Ilford Films 500-mile race at Brands Hatch. Don spent several laps following Gerry Marshall in the TVR and was getting increasingly frustrated at being unable to pass him. He was pleased when the TVR performed its now familiar wheel-shedding trick yet again, but for a moment, joy turned to concern as he wondered where the errant wheel might land. It missed the B and the pair went on to finish seventh overall, third in class.

Having gone into partnership in a garage business near Gatwick, Richard Worts decided that he would no longer have time for racing. He sold the MGB to Don who financed the purchase by changing jobs to release the funds from his superannuation fund. In 1972 Don gave up racing JYH and Bill Nicholson sold it to an American who continued to compete in the car.

## Nigel Jordan

When Richard Worts sold 94 HJJ it became a road car, but as a result of an advertisement in *Autosport*, it was to return to racing in the hands of Nigel Jordan during 1968. He arranged to meet the seller in the car park of The Highwayman at Dunstable in December 1967 and, following a test drive, paid £695 for the wire-wheeled car plus a set of wide racing wires and tyres. He always drove to the track on the standard wheels and tyres and carried the racing ones on board: two on the passenger seat, one in the boot, the fourth on a boot rack. Nigel's first outing was in January 1968 in the Brands Hatch season opener, the Tunbridge Wells Motor Club Sprint, where he recorded a class second.

Encouraged, Nigel who had previously done events in an Austin Healey 3000, raced the MGB for two years, taking in events at Brands Hatch, Lydden Hill and Silverstone. In July 1969 he had one outing at Thruxton, but recalls the car was under geared for that particular circuit; despite this, he finished second in class. Nigel gained a first class award in the High Speed Trial at Silverstone in May 1969. He had non-finishes due to a broken fan belt and loose plug leads, and bitterly remembers the clutch springs breaking as he changed down for Paddock Hill Bend at Brands. These problems apart, he had an enjoyable time in HJJ, competing in his last race in September 1969 before selling the car, which was by now getting a little tired, in the summer of 1970.

## John Sharp

A development engineer at Abingdon, John Sharp raced an MGA Twin Cam, ORX 885, which he later converted to MGB power. It was in this form that he raced it throughout the 1963 season, taking nearly forty awards. At Mallory Park on 23 June, he did well to deprive the more powerful Skailes Aston Martin of third place in the ten-lap unlimited GT race. He always went well at Aintree, taking outright wins at the circuit on 11 May and 7 September, and again finished first overall at the London MC race meeting at Snetterton on 7 July.

During the season, he also took eleven Class wins and seven second-places in races, sprints and the occasional hill climb at Firle. He was never beaten by any other MG throughout the year and set faster times at all venues than any other type of MGA. His best times at the principal tracks were: Aintree 72.4sec, Brands 63sec, Silverstone Club 73.6sec and Mallory 60.3sec.

The grey car was later sold to Sussex estate agent Michael Warrard, who raced and hill climbed the MGA/B. It was looked after by Roy Hunisett at South Coast Racing, who had occasional race outings in the car. Roy recalls that he used to wait until midnight, then take the untaxed vehicle, in full race trim, out on road test along the Brighton to Saltdean coast road and was never stopped by the police.

Early in 1964, John Sharp apparently bought, for a very nominal sum, the remains of 7 DBL which Andrew Hedges and John Sprinzel had crashed on the Tour de France in September 1963. A new 7 DBL was built for the Morley brothers to win the GT category in the following January's Monte Carlo Rally. John rebuilt his car, which came with its smashed Le Mans 'droop snoot nose' but without its famous registration number, in the Development Department and then used the car, now painted blue, for circuit racing.

Jim Cox, who joined the Development Department in 1952 – where, amongst other projects, he built the engines for the MG record-breaking cars – prepared John's power units for both the A and B in his 'spare time'. Jim considered them every bit as good as those he built for the works cars. John's were based on test-bed engines, which had been rejected for one reason or another, then sold off. He took the rebuilt units back to his home on the outskirts of Dorchester, where he completed final assembly of his racers.

Jim always thought highly of the early three-bearing MGB engines, which he found maintained good oil pressure. The early five-bearing units had problems in this area that were eventually traced to the oil pump which had been designed for it. Following a meeting with Syd Enever, Jim cured the issue by grafting a three-bearing pick-up onto the longer-nosed pump from the transverse 1800 engine. Once proved, the manufacturers produced pumps to the new

*Jenny Tudor-Owen with 665 FXF and her winner's bouquet at Denmark's Roskildering in 1963.*

design. This was supposed to be an interim measure, but apparently continued until the end of MGB production.

John Sharp had a good day in his 'new MGB' at the BARC meeting at Goodwood on 14 March 1964, when he beat Brian Kendall in the ex-Dence Morgan Plus Four by 0.6sec to win the damp Marque race at an average speed of 77.98mph (124.77km/hr). At the same track, on 30 May 1964, he again beat Kendall (by 0.2sec) to record another win. He took a Class win at Mallory Park on 18 July.

## Jenny Tudor-Owen

In 1963, Jenny Tudor-Owen, who had started racing in a Mike Parkes-prepared 850 Mini, bought a brand-new red MGB, 665 FXF, from a Fulham showroom. It cost her £800 and had a distinctive bulbous white hardtop. It was race tuned by Barwell of Chessington. She enjoyed a good finish to her season with an enjoyable dice against T. N. Crisp's Daimler Dart, which won on handicap, in the last race of 1963 at Goodwood on 21 September.

At the end of the season, FXF was sold to George Konig, brother of Mark – noted for his exploits in the Nomad. It was subsequently raced by Barry Sidery-Smith, Freddie Yhapp, Neville Marriner, Colin Pearcy, Gerry Marshall, and Geoff Moyer. Malcolm Young, who now owns her, has successfully used FXF in historic races and rallies since he bought the car back in 1995. Malcolm and co-driver Paul Chudecki won their Class in the 2001 Modena Cento Ore Classic.

Having failed to get to grips with an Elan in 1964, Jenny bought another B for 1965. Red, this time with a works hardtop, the car was again Barwell tuned. A much quicker car than her previous example, Jenny took a number of class wins in it. She remembers dicing with Jean Denton at Silverstone and was on the row behind Jean and Gabriel Konig the day they had their big coming together at Castle Combe in August, narrowly missing getting involved in the accident herself. Jenny drove both the Bs to the race circuits, the open exhaust system occasionally attracting the attention of 'Mister Plod'. She competed at Nürburgring, where practice problems precluded a race, but fared better at Denmark's Roskildering where she was placed third overall.

Impressed with her driving, the JCB Team offered Jenny some races in their lightweight MGB, but these did not prove as successful as the outings in her own car. The gearbox broke during practice at the Sevenoaks & District Motor Club meeting at Brands Hatch on 12 November 1967. The following year she shunted it badly at Oulton Park. Running with the wrong 'diff' ratio for Oulton, she clicked down from overdrive third to third for Cascades, the switch came off in her hand and the car cart-wheeled down the track. Fortunately it came to rest on its wheels without any harm to the driver. The same could not be said of the car and Peter Brown had the unenviable task of ringing Anthony Bamford to inform him of the damage.

In 1968, Jenny moved on to a rapid E Type that, unlike the Bs, had to be trailered to the track. At the end of the year she was part of a Volvo crew on the London to Sydney Marathon. Having arrived in Australia she travelled the world, not returning to England until 1985.

## Ray Dilley

In 1965, MG suggested to Ray Dilley, who had raced a Fraser Nash Ray since 1959, that he ought to be competing in an MGB. He was, after all, the proprietor of the local MG dealers Rays of Hove, who had showrooms in Church Road. Ray was due to get one of the lightweight MGBs that had gone to Sebring, but they never returned to England. Having sold the Fraser Nash, his garage took in a 40,000 mile, 1963 pull-handle MGB, 6594 AP, which it had supplied new, and modified it for racing. Len McCormack, his mechanic, went to Abingdon in January 1966 to collect the various special tuning parts required and, whilst there, assimilated as much insider knowledge from the works mechanics as he could. Brighton motor cycle ace, Gordon Thompson, built the three-bearing

*Ray Dilley's MGB, 6594 AP, had unique front wings that he had specially made by a glass-fibre specialist on the Isle of Wight.*

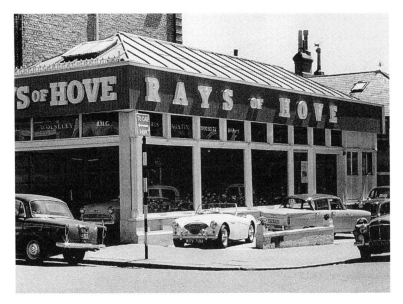

Local BMC dealers Rays of Hove was owned by MGB racer Ray Dilley.

engine which had a 100-ton steel crank, gave power to 6,500rpm and revved to 7,000rpm.

Unable to obtain a set of aluminium front wings from the factory, who were out of stock, Ray had to make alternative arrangements. He had previously had dealings with Mr D. Finlay, a fibreglass specialist from the Isle of Wight, and got him to mould a pair of special front wings and a hardtop for the car. The cutaway wings were designed to take E Type Jaguar-style recessed headlamps, for which Ray made his own Perspex covers. He further personalized his B by fixing the 'V'-shaped chrome trim from the Ford Consul Mk 2, facing forward on the front wings, like an arrow head. These had the purpose of holding the wing in place at high speed. The unique hardtop had a vent above the rear window to release the air pressure. The car was actually built at Dilley's other premises, Palace Pier Garage, Brighton and the preparation costs totalled £773 7s (£773. 35p). At the time, a brand-new MGB was £825 on the road.

The car was painted Jaguar dark racing green and used for races at Brands Hatch, Goodwood and Silverstone. Ray's first outing was at the 1966 Goodwood International Easter Meeting on 11 April, where he finished third in class behind Chris Lawrence's 2.2 litre Morgan and

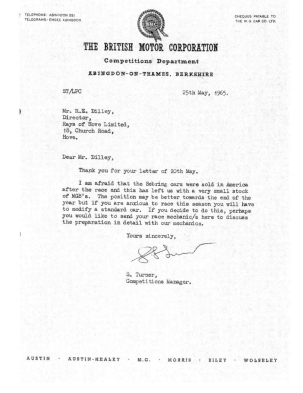

The letter that Ray Dilley received from Stuart Turner in response to his request to buy one of the ex-works Bs after the 1965 Sebring race.

winner Bob Burnard in a Simca Abarth 2000. Whilst Roger Enever's works development car beat him at Silverstone, Ray invariably had the upper hand at Goodwood. 6594 AP was never trailered anywhere, always driven. A typical racing weekend would see Ray and his wife leave home on Friday afternoon with the children in the back and drive to Abingdon where they booked into a hotel. On Saturday he would race at Silverstone, then, after another Abingdon stop-over, drive to Brands for two or three races on the Sunday. He took a Class win at MGCC Brands on 3 April 1967.

He raced the car until 1970 and sold it in 1972 to a young man whose father wanted him to race something safe. The new owner took the MGB to a test day at Brands and succumbed to the temptation when someone offered him a quick profit on the well-known car.

## Julius Thurgood

In 1979, Glen Dudley sold Julius Thurgood 6594 AP and he raced it at Spa in August 1980. He also competed in the car at VSCC Silverstone and MGCC events at Snetterton and Mallory Park. The distributor broke at Mallory and Bob Luff collected the stalled car coming out of the Devils Elbow, whereupon it mounted the Armco and ran along the top on one wheel, as if on rails. Roy McCarthy repaired it, going to great lengths to make good the unique front wing. Gerry Marshall and Terry Nightingale were amongst subsequent owners. During the early 1990s Bob Fleet raced it in the BCV8 series and John Target now campaigns this MGB in American historic events.

*Julius Thurgood stops 6594 AP in the soaking pit lane at Spa in August 1980.*

## Roy Ashford

Bristol MG dealers Windmill and Lewis, of Marchants Road, Clifton, had already enjoyed racing success in 1961 when they ran a Midget for Roy Ashford, their workshop foreman, who had also raced an MGA. The Midget was sold and the firm bought, at a good price, a brand-new MGB, which Roy and his colleagues built up to racing spec over the winter of 1963–4. As well as an aluminium bonnet, standard on early Bs, it had front wings, doors and boot lid in the same material. The engine was rebuilt in accordance with the homologation papers – Roy reckons it was not far off full factory spec. During the period 1964 to 1971, the partnership of MGB 222 WAE and Roy Ashford were to prove one of the most prolific award winners for the marque in those early years. From 1967 onwards he nearly always picked up a top-three placing, despite admitting it was not the easiest car to get off the line.

The car started off in British Racing Green with a white hardtop, which was later black, the B eventually ending up BRG all over. Later, one of the workshop apprentices who helped out at race meetings suggested they paint it green and orange; Roy said that was fine by him provided the bosses agreed, which they did. Given that advertising was not permitted on cars at the time, this distinctive scheme was the next best thing and the MGB became well known throughout the country. It ran on 5.5in wires until 1966, then they changed the wheels to 6.5in knock-on Minilites, for which they managed to get a couple of sets of the star pattern Firestone tyres, retaining the original wires and tyres for the wet.

Roy recalls the first outing being at Castle Combe, his local circuit, early in 1964. Though he predominantly competed in the Chevron, Freddie Dixon STP race championships, Roy also did a couple of local hill-climbs each year, just to keep the Windmill and Lewis name before the Bristol enthusiasts. Peter Robinson the MD enjoyed his racing but running the car was taken very seriously, with each department of the garage contributing to the overall budget. If a race meeting happened to clash with Roy's

*Roy Ashford at the wheel of the Windmill and Lewis MGB.*

*Roy Ashford in the Windmill and Lewis showroom with 222 WAE and some of the trophies that he won with the car.*

annual holiday, he was expected to return for the weekend to compete. Strangely, he found, possibly because of their relative lack of power, the original three-bearing engines were quite reliable, but he did blow up a couple of the five-bearing versions. On one occasion he went to Robinson's office on Monday morning to report a detonated engine, only to be told not to waste time telling the boss about it until he had ordered all the parts for the rebuild, so they could be out again the next weekend! They would supply all the parts for the bottom end to Downton Engineering, who then built it up and fitted their own cylinder head. Amongst his results, Roy found a bill for such a rebuild, the cost £108!

By 1968, the MGB was blue and the wheel arches had been flared to take the new 8in-wide J. A. Pearce alloy wheels now back on Dunlop tyres. Roy's most enjoyable race was at Thruxton on 24 May 1970 when he finished second, splitting two AC Cobras. Shaun Jackson won in his 7.4-litre model with a race time of 12min 42.2sec, Roy's time was 12min 44.0sec, whilst Ian Richardson, whose car had a 5.4-litre engine,

was third having completed the ten laps in 12min 47.0sec. This was an excellent achievement for the 2-litre MGB at Thruxton, which has always been regarded as a 'power circuit'. *Motoring News* described it as 'The hairiest Modsports race for many a frantic day'.

Over the years, Bill Nicholson and Roy had many head-to-heads in their respective MGBs, and whilst Roy had his fair share of victories at most tracks, he invariably lost out to his rival at Silverstone, where Bill was faster in the run up to Club Corner. Try as he might Roy would spin off at Stowe, the corner before, trying to keep his speed up. Prior to the Nottingham Sports Car Club Silverstone meeting on 3 August 1969, Roy carried out modifications to the car to make it more competitive at that circuit. He changed the 'diff' and replaced his usual 649 'Race' camshaft with a 'Sprint' cam. Sure enough it worked, he got ahead of Bill early on and stayed there. On lap four, having failed to get ahead of him, Nicholson retired to the paddock.

The pair had another run in at Silverstone on 19 September 1970, where they were dicing nose to tail for eight laps. On lap nine, Jim Loveday's

MGB burst its oil cooler and Roy spun on the contents, which effectively ended his challenge. He got going again and finished fifteen seconds behind Nicholson.

During the period Roy raced the B, fire extinguishers, which had hitherto been optional, were beginning to become obligatory at some meetings. At one of the wettest races he ever competed in at Thruxton, he was told he could not race unless he had one. An extinguisher was hastily removed from the tow car and bolted onto the inner sill. Following an indiscretion during the race, he spun off into a water-filled ditch and as he undid his seat belt and scrambled out of the car he watched the extinguisher slowly disappear under the muddy liquid and thought 'that was a lot of good!'.

## Terry Osborne

In September 1970, Windmill and Lewis were taken over by Lex, who, after a year, decided not to continue running the car. Peter Robinson asked Roy if he would like to buy it. He declined but, at his suggestion, 222 WAE was sold to his friend Terry Osborne in November 1971.

Over the winter, it was resprayed Fiat Mediterranean Blue at the firm where Terry worked and from 1972 to 1998 he competed in the car. The first race in Terry's ownership was the Chevron Oils Championship round at Mallory Park in March 1972. Initially Terry shared the driving with Roy, one doing the Modsports race, the other driving in the GT event. However, after Terry failed to get a drive at two meetings

*Despite having a reputation as a persistent practical joker, Terry Osborne took his motor racing very seriously and won many awards in 222 WAE between 1971 and 1993. Here he races the car, in one of its modified forms, at Thruxton in November 1976.*

following problems during Roy's race, Roy decided to leave the driving to his friend.

During the early seventies, Terry mainly did Modsports races at Castle Combe, Silverstone, Mallory Park and Brands Hatch, and always entered the MGCC Wiscombe Hill Climb. He joined the BCV8 Championship in its inaugural year, 1977, when it included races, sprints and hill climbs, winning the Modified Championship in 1978 and 1979. He invariably enjoyed good racing against the likes of Barry Sidery-Smith, Bob Luff, Rod Longton, John Hewitt and Colin Pearcy.

His best race was the BCV8 Championship MGCC round at Brands Hatch on 14 September 1980, where he had a race-long dice with Bob Luff, during which they ran side by side for a complete lap! At the finish, the two cars crossed the line virtually as one but Bob was adjudged to have anticipated the start and the ten-second penalty gave the victory to Terry, who rubbed salt into the wound by beating Bob's 1,800cc lap record, getting it down to 56.3 seconds. They were at it again during the BARC meeting at the same circuit on 5 October. After another hectic race, Terry took the chequered flag, beating Barry by 1.3 seconds with Bob third, 0.9 seconds behind him.

At the end of the 1982 season the MGB was fitted with Sebring front wings, rear wheel

*Rob Shellard (130) leads a group of cars off the Silverstone start line in his Bill Nicholson-prepared BRG Roadster, CEV 205B.*

*Having passed Max Payne's Elan, John Cotton (50) climbs the Mountain at Cadwell Park on the way to his maiden Modsports victory 25 June 1972.*

arches and a spoiler. Richard Longman always did the engines and the car was maintained by Roy Ashford, along with David Franklin at Huntsman Garage. Terry also set records at the old Castle Combe circuit on 6 July 1985 (1min 12.0sec) and Wiscombe hill on 15 September 1990 (46.86sec). He raced seven times at Zolder, where his best lap was 2min 1.0sec, at Zandvoort (1min 56.9sec) twice and Spa (3min 13.91sec) twice.

Terry has always had a reputation as a practical joker and became known as 'Ozzie the Winder' because of his fondness of winding people up. One day, when he collected his car from the Huntsman Garage, he found the mechanics had stuck this nickname on it. Having retired from racing, Terry sold it to prolific MG-racer Colin Pearcy who has converted the car back to its original spec, complete with the Ashford green and orange colour scheme, obtained FIA papers and now races it in historic events.

## Rob Shellard

BRG Roadster CEV 205B had a red hardtop and was a Nicholson-prepared car raced by Rob Shellard from 1965 to 1969, when he acquired an ex-works MGB. Although it did not look very radical, without wide wheels and arches, it was quick. Rob became a Brands specialist and enjoyed considerable success with his car before selling it to former Mini racer John Cotton. Anthony Binnington and Rob Shellard came fourth overall in the three-hour Archie Scott-Brown Trophy Race at Snetterton on 20 September 1970. In 1985, Shellard found CEV and bought it back. He restored it to 1960s racing spec but sadly died before he could race it again.

## John Cotton

John drove CEV in the 1970 three-hour race at Snetterton, which he started from the third row, where Minister for Sport, Eldon Griffiths MP, spoke to him on the grid. He had decided to play himself into the race fairly gently and so was surprised to find that he was third on the opening lap. However, his race was about to end.

At the Hairpin on lap two, Mini driver Jim Colbrook braked and his foot went to the floor. Overtaking groups of cars slowing for the corner, he eventually crashed into the boot of Cotton's MGB, before gouging the side of it, then veering off into the banking. It was not over yet: the car bounced off the earth and landed, on its roof, across the MGB's bonnet. After the race, Colbrook, supported between his mechanic and girlfriend, hobbled over to John to apologise. He suggested that hitting the MGB had probably saved his life.

The car was repaired and lived to fight another two seasons. John remembers beating Max Payne's Elan, to take his first win at a wet Cadwell Park meeting on 25 June 1972. Terry Carpenter's B, which started from the back of the grid with a ten-second penalty, was second, having passed the Elan on lap six. John also had an enjoyable dice with John Gott's Big Healey at Silverstone. The MG had fuel starvation problems; he passed the Healey when he had full fuel then it came past him when the supply faltered.

After the race John came over and suggested that he needed to sort out the handling – apparently through some corners the near-side front wheel was one foot in the air. At the end of 1972, John sold the car to someone who used it to take his girlfriends to the pub and apparently wrecked it before his first race. John went on to race in Sports 2000 Production Saloons and an MG Midget.

## Jim Loveday

Looking to buy an MGB, Jim Loveday called in to a local dealers in Gloucestershire to see if they had any for sale. There were no salesman about, but a helpful mechanic told him that a really nice one was due in the following week, furthermore it had been well looked after by its titled lady owner. The lady in question was known to Jim, one of the many local customers of the family furnishing and removal business. He went home, telephoned her and agreed to pay the £600 which the garage had offered in part exchange, suggesting she could then get a cash buyer's discount on her new vehicle. But a week after he got the MGB, ADD 880B, the dealer rang him, most upset at what he had done – they had had the car lined up for one of their directors!

*Driving ADD 880B, Jim Loveday splashes his way along the main straight at MGCC Silverstone on 27 May 1979.*

Jim started competing in the Players Number Six Autocross and got into the 1967 finals at High Wycombe. Prior to racing his MGB, he had already come up against Bill Nicholson when they both rode in motor cycle trials. Jim's first circuit race was the MGCC Castle Combe meeting in September 1968, when he won an all-comers handicap event, beating the MGBs of Ian Polley and P. Williams.

The MGB, green when Jim bought it, was later sprayed in the blue-and-white livery of his removal firm's lorries. He also had a quantity of liveried model lorries made and always had some in his pocket when he went to quote for a job. He would give one to each child in the house-hold, instructing them that when father came home they must show him their new toy and tell him that was the firm that were going to move them. More often than not it worked. The MGB was maintained by Michael Webb at Cherry Tree Lane Garage, Cirencester, who still looks after Jim's cars today. The three-bearing engine was replaced by a Downton-tuned five-bearing version.

Amongst his many successes, Jim won his class and set the fastest lap for race-modified MGBs, 1min 13.4sec and 78.87mph (126.2km/hr), at the MGCC Silverstone meeting in May 1974, and savoured an outright win at Brands Hatch. Having decided to give up racing when he reached sixty, Jim took to trials on four wheels, winning the 1983 BTRDA series in an MG Midget which he still owns. The following year he took the RAC Championship driving a Panther Lima.

## Gerry Brown

In 1982, Gerry Brown of Brown and Gammons bought ADD 880B and raced it at MGCC Silverstone that year. He did not find the hand-ling to his liking, so put the car away and it was not until 1990, when his friend Mike Berry sug-gested they do the Coppa D'Italia, that the car re-emerged. Rebuilt to FIA spec, the pair drove it to nineteenth overall, second in Class, in the four-day event, which turned out to be the last ever run. At one stage, they were running in the

*Gerry Brown and Mike Berry in ADD 880B on the 1990 Coppa D'Italia, a four-day event that comprised ten hill climbs and three races. They finished second in Class.*

*Gerry Brown pits John Target's MGB, AMF 48H, against a Morgan 4/4 in the 1976 BARC Production Sports Car Championship. The cars raced in classes based on the recommended retail price, not the cubic capacity of the engine.*

top ten. Later that year, Gerry was second in Class at the Eifel Klassik GT Race.

Stirling Moss drove it to third place in the 1990 Monte Carlo Challenge, then Gerry used ADD for tarmac and stage historic rallies. Recently he has done two or three FIA races each year; he finished fifth in the Abingdon Trophy race at the 1996 Coys Festival.

In 1976, John Target had asked Gerry to look after his racing MGB, AMF 48H, whilst he went to America. Gerry agreed, provided he could race the car in the 1976 BARC Prodsports Championship. Oliver and Rix Garages of Luton, who sponsored his T type, backed his effort and the car, which had Dawson suspension, was painted in their blue-and-yellow livery. Racing in Class B for cars priced between £2,000 and £3,000, the main opposition came from Chris

Alford's Marcos 1600M, David Beams' Ginetta G15, Morgans and the other MGB of Doc Griffiths. Gerry took one second, two thirds, five fourths, three fifths including one fastest lap, one sixth and crashed to retirement once. Eventually repaired, Gerry briefly ran the Target MGB in Class B of the 1981 BCV8 Championship.

## Anthony Binnington

The first right-hand drive MGB to come off the production line has a continuous racing history since 1967, when Anthony Binnington started competing in MG Car Club events. Originally registered 523 CBL, the Iris Blue car went straight into the Show Shop at Abingdon where, under the direction of Tim Binnington, Anthony's father, it was then prepared for the

*Anthony Binnington has his first ever race in OMO 70 at MGCC Silverstone 1967. This MGB was the first right-hand-drive version off the production line and was originally used as a press car. Anthony regularly races it to this day.*

motoring press to road test. In 1963, Tim purchased the MGB for personal transport, transferring the registration OMO 70 from his MGA. Four years later, Anthony started racing it and enjoyed some factory support.

In 1967, Anthony started racing the car, now Basilica Blue, which had been unofficially prepared in the Show Shop, where they were used to such work as they helped out when the Competition Department was busy. After three wins from three races that season, John Thornley agreed to backing on a more formal basis, with the Competition Department supplying aluminium body panels and an ex-Sebring race engine with close-ratio gearbox. From Anthony's sixteen outings in 1968, he secured fourteen top-three places.

The factory prepared OMO for the 1969 Mugello 500km, which would prove to be the last car prepared by the Competition Department before it was closed down. Mini Cooper racer, Martin Ridehalph, joined Tony as co-driver for an enjoyable, though not entirely successful outing: Martin spun off and Anthony had a puncture on the rough circuit. Nevertheless they finished thirty-sixth. Anthony competed in Marque Sports, then Modsports races in OMO, until 1970. He recorded an outright win in his swansong race at Brands Hatch on 19 April. In 1972 the B was sold and he turned his attention to Formula 3 in an ex-James Hunt March 713M. This he found was a different ball game and he only managed six European races before the money ran out.

All was not lost though as, in 1975, he managed to buy back OMO and resume club racing, competing in Production Sports and MGCC events, and moving into historic racing in 1985. Outings have included four Eifel Klassiks, one of which produced the only top-ten finish for an MGB.

## Jean Denton

Despite only passing her driving test at the age of twenty-six, Jean Denton was keen to compete and within ten months of getting her licence she had her first race. She soon decided that you needed big money to succeed in single seaters and looked to production-based racing. After racing a Cooper Formula 3 car and a brief flirtation with a Mini Cooper, which Jean found

*Jean Denton in her racing MGB, which ran with the notional registration number JDR 1. The power bulge and the low-slung side-exit exhaust system identify that the car was running supercharged.*

too skittish, she settled for an MGB. Dr Tom Boyce, who was her MGB co-driver when it was the only sports car to finish the London to Sydney Marathon in December 1968, also helped to build and prepare the racer. Tom, a mechanical engineer who specialized in combustion, applied his knowledge of fuels to maximize on the MGB's power. Jean's husband Tony also assisted in the preparation and drove on occasions, though his business partners were none too happy.

Having had an accident in the F3 car, Tony's run of bad luck continued when he bent the MGB at both Oulton Park and Snetterton, where he demolished a marshal's post. However, things went better at the Ilford Films 500 Mile Race at Brands Hatch on 9 May 1966. Sharing the driving, Jean and Tony Denton finished twelfth overall having covered 147 laps of the soaking wet Grand Prix Circuit. The conditions were so bad that the race was stopped after six hours, when the winning David Piper/Bob Bondurant Shelby American Cobra had only completed 464 miles 175 laps.

Tom Boyce used the facilities at Imperial College London, where he was teaching, to gas flow the head and develop the suspension to be ready for the 1967 season, which initially went very well for Jean. However, late in August 1967, her racing MGB was written off at Castle Combe's notorious Quarry corner, after Jean and Gabriel Konig had their infamous coming together, which wrecked both cars. The impact was such that the inlet manifold on Gabriel's Sebring Sprite snapped and her Weber was found in the remains of Jean's B, having smashed its way through the fibreglass front wing.

Tom was abroad, so Tony Denton and Peter Smith bought a second-hand MGB and, using the salvageable parts from the original racer, re-shelled it for the next race. Driving the car, now bearing the contrived plates JDR 1 and affectionately known as 'The Beast', Jean Denton, secured the 1967 British Women Racing Drivers Club Championship.

Having got his students to analyse the various available pump fuels, Tom had established that

*Jean Denton and Tom Boyce with UMD 534F and some of the spares and equipment they packed into it for the London to Sydney Marathon. This was a publicity shot taken for Nova magazine, their main sponsor.*

Esso Golden Five Star had an octane rating of 102.5. He carried out tests to establish the highest useful compression ratio and combined the two to obtain a 50 per cent increase in top-end power per unit of fuel. The choice of fuel was kept secret within the team, but towards the end of the season it came out in conversation with Bill Nicholson, who glibly replied that having tried various brands in his MGB, he was also using Esso Golden.

Tom concluded that the high octane would allow the engine to be run with a supercharger. So after she had secured the championship, he convinced Jean that supercharging was the way to go for 1968 and started work on the conversion. He used an Arnott Model 5600 blower, which Carburettor Systems of Ealing Road Wembley marketed for a four-litre engine. The bottom end of an MGB engine was strengthened with a 60-ton, cross-drilled Nitrided steel crankshaft held in with specially made steel main caps. By machining the offset, he was able to utilize the stronger MGA Twin Cam con rods and opted

for an MGB 3/4 race cam. The head had standard inlet valves with over-size exhausts and, so as to eliminate hot spots, Tom machined 'bath tub' combustion chambers. It was secured with MGA Twin Cam studs, torqued down to 70lb (the standard Twin Cam setting). The block's ³⁄₄in-thick deck gave adequate purchase.

Using a cylinder-head gasket as a pattern, he made a number of decompression plates and experimented with them to find the best compression ratio. The ½in plate gave 7 to 1 whilst the ³⁄₁₆in version resulted in 8.5 to 1, which surprisingly gave the best power. The engine revved to 6,000rpm and, by adjusting the pulley size, the blower ran at 5,000rpm; the resulting 14lb boost produced a phenomenal 200bhp at the rear wheels. Adding the RAC's 40 per cent supercharger handicap figure to the 1,798cc engine meant that the car, now rated at 2,517cc, was directly up against the Austin Healey 3000.

Jean again secured the BWDC Championship in 1968. She was presented with the Embassy Trophy by Sheila Scott, the aviatrix, during a

*Jean Denton and Tom Boyce on the Crystal Palace starting ramp for the 1968 London to Sydney Marathon.*

reception held at the Café Royal in London. Tom Boyce and Bill Nicholson were also present at the ceremony. On 19 May, Jean and co-driver Natalie Goodwin took the car to Germany to compete in the Nürburgring 1,000 Kilometres. The pair qualified seventy-second on the grid but failed to finish, setting a best lap of 11min 48.0sec.

For 1969, they looked to international racing. Tom, who had now established a good working relationship with Sidney Enever at Abingdon, got hold of titanium rods and special pistons, and built up a new engine that ran a compression ratio of 11 to 1. He discarded the usual single Weber in favour of a pair of 2in SU carburettors, to get the inlet tract shorter. Combined with a

set of high-lift rockers, which he made in the university's machine shop, Tom eventually tuned this engine, which revved to 7,400, to produce 168bhp, un-supercharged!

Mike Garton co-drove in the A.D.A.C. 1,000 Kilometres Race at the Nürburgring on 1 June 1969. Entered by 'Jean Denton Racing of England', the pair qualified fifty-second on the grid but finished thirty-sixth from the sixty-five starters (fifth in Class). Despite both drivers suffering from carbon monoxide poisoning from fumes sucked in through lightening holes in the rear valance, they covered thirty-two laps in 6hr 21min 37.6sec, during mainly dry conditions. Their fastest lap was 11min 03.1sec.

Garton again shared the driving at Mugello on

20 July 1969. Each lap of this tough road race was 41.1 miles (66.2km) with a total rise and fall of 36,000ft (11,000m), part of the circuit running over the Futa Pass. The rugged circuit took its toll and the MGB retired as the result of a broken half-shaft on lap five, when Mike was lying fourth in Class. He watched the closing stages drinking Chianti with the locals. The pair also retired from the Barcelona Six Hour race at Montjuich on 5 October when the cam gear sheared on lap five. Mike raced the MGB in club meetings at Silverstone (where he finished second after a dice with John Gott) and Brands.

Though not strictly a race, Jean and Tom's finish on the London to Sydney Marathon, in December 1968, was surely her most notable achievement in an MGB. UMD 534F, a car Tom specially built for the event, was forty-ninth from fifty-two finishers out of just over 100 starters and covered 13,000 road miles (20,900km) in twelve days of driving. A remarkable result for what was basically a private entry with a little help from the works. This was achieved despite failing wipers and the overdrive packing up in France, a starter-motor fault in Italy, and the fan going through the radiator, the result of a broken engine-mounting, in Australia. Jean also discovered that she was car sick whilst driving over mountains and suffered a bug for seven out of the nine days of the sea voyage from Bombay to Freemantle.

Having made her mark in motor sport, Jean went on to succeed in commerce and public life. In 1978, she became the first woman to be appointed to the National Executive Committee of the Institute of Management. Two years later she became MD of Herondrive, the car leasing company, moving on to become external affairs director of Austin Rover. In 1991, she was created a life peer as Baroness Denton of Wakefield. She sadly died early in 2001.

## Robbie Gordon and Peter Jackson

In 1966, Robbie Gordon, who had founded Ramsay Racing with fellow Cambridge University students David Wansbrough and the Hon. John Fellowes, acquired 113 DJB, the MGB that Peter Pollard used to campaign. Recently married Peter Jackson returned from Malta with his new wife and was immediately offered the drive in the Marque Sports series. Peter had made his name racing Austin Healey Sprites, in particular his coupé 46 BXN.

Peter recalls that the MGB, which he raced about six times, was a very quick motor car and that whilst he had little problems beating other Bs, Tommy Entwhistle's TVR was a different story. The car was prepared at the Cambridge premises of Newtune, which was close to the legendary Don Moore's workshop. Don 'loaned' Robbie an ex-works head for the car; this, combined with an ST manifold and Weber 45, made it fairly fly.

*Robbie Gordon's MGB, 113 DJB, raced by Robbie, Peter Jackson and David Wansbrough. The car was sold after it was wrecked at Boxing Day Mallory and Douglas Wilson-Spratt re-bodied it as his WSM MGB.*

Peter put it on the front row for the Oulton Park TT, with a time that was the fastest for a B of that era. After practice, Robbie got chatting to Ted Worswick, who was sharing the front row with his Healey 3000 and Ted told him there was not an MGB that could beat his 3000 round Oulton. A £10 wager was made and Jackson won the race by a comfortable margin; he took the trophy and Robbie the tenner.

Robbie himself drove DJB at Castle Combe and the Silverstone Club Championship Finals meeting in October. By now he had formed an association with Bill Nicholson, later going into partnership in his Northampton garage from 1967 to 1969. Nicholson, Don Bunce and Jean Denton were also in the Silverstone race with Denton needing a Class place in order to amass enough points to secure the BWDC title. Robbie managed to pass the rapid WSL Morgan and Nicholson's B but, later in the race, three out of the four Nicholson stable cars retired and Jean secured her title.

Roddy Harvey-Bailey, who usually raced a Jaguar, had an outing in DJB at Silverstone. He set a faster time than Nicholson in practice and was leading the race when the head gasket went, but he still finished third. The car's final outing was in the hands of E type pilot David Wansbrough, who borrowed it for the Mallory Park Boxing Day meeting, where it rolled. He remembers being suspended upside down in the safety harness wondering what to do; on releasing the belts he landed in a heap on the roof. The damaged car was sold to Mike Lewis who got Douglas Wilson-Spratt, of WSM fame, to use it to build his prototype, and only, WSM MGB.

## Peter Brown and the JCB MGBs

In 1967 Stuart Turner, head of BMC Competitions Department, sold 8 DBL to Anthony Bamford of JCB Excavators and the car was repainted in the company's distinctive yellow livery. That year, Peter Brown, son of a local driving school proprietor, used the car to compete in UK club races. Bamford had an outing in it at Oulton Park on 13 May, but unfortunately rolled the car on

the first lap at Knicker Brook. Though the driver walked away unharmed, the car would need a new body shell. The race was won by John Britten's MG Midget and, ironically, Jenny Tudor-Owen drove the first MGB home in fifth place.

At Brands on 16 April 1967, Peter was third in class after fending off the advances of Don Bunce in his MGB. Other outings at Brands and Oulton that year yielded some good class places: one fourth, three thirds and one second. Peter, who ran a car accessories business in Stafford, finished the season in style with second overall and a class win in the penultimate Amasco GT round at Brands on 26 November. This was the yellow car's first outing following the post-roll rebuild by Alan Smith in Derby. It now tipped the scales at just under 16cwt (800kg), had a ZF diff and a 145bhp engine. During the race, which Peter started from third on the grid, he disposed of Alan House, driving the North Motors Morgan +4 and fast-starting Rod Longton's TVR.

*Peter Brown and Anthony Bamford with 8 DBL, the ex-works car that became the JCB MGB for the 1967 and 1968 seasons.*

The following year, Brown continued to campaign 8 DBL in British Club events; he also raced it in Germany and Italy. The home season started well with overall and class third at Brands on 21 January, followed by three seconds at Brands and Mallory Park. Next time out, Oulton again proved to be a bad-luck circuit for 8 DBL, which spluttered to retirement on lap eight whilst leading the class. Back in the Paddock the team discovered that the car was out of petrol, having forgotten to replenish the new four-gallon tank after practice. However, Peter did have the consolation of setting a new lap record at 1min 57.4sec.

Europe produced mixed fortunes for the team. The GT was not ready in time for the trip to Monza and Nürburgring so they took 8 DBL, which, owing to its aluminium bodywork and cross-flow head, had to run in the 2-litre Group 6 Class. The drivers, Peter Brown and Tony Fall, were joined by Anthony Bamford and mechanic Peter Alman for the trip, which took in both races. They towed the racer with a Chevrolet Impala Estate, registered JCB 9. The car went well during practice at Monza but, owing to Vic Elford setting an exceptional fastest lap, was unable to get within the required percentage of his time and failed to qualify for the race on 25 April.

The Targa Florio on 5 May provided a more productive, if eventful, outing. Arriving in Sicily a week before the race, Peter and Tony learnt the

*Peter Brown leads the field round Druids Hairpin at Brands Hatch, 8 February 1968.*

track in the traditional way, thrashing round the road circuit during unofficial practice whilst the roads were still open to the public, in one of Mr Hertz's Fiat 125s. Initially, works Sprite driver Clive Baker led them round in his similar Fiat, but they soon got to grips with it. In order to preserve the MGB, official practice was limited to one lap of the thirty-five-mile circuit per driver.

Having completed this, Peter and Tony returned to their hotel, leaving Alman to drive the MGB back. Despite its bright colour, one of the locals managed to run his Fiat 1500 into the back of it. All was not lost, as the Fiat driver got his friendly local garage to repair what was super-ficial body damage in time for the race. Tony took the start and on his second lap had an off as a result of the road surface breaking up under the heat and the pounding it was taking from the competitors. Using his rally-driving prowess, he decided that a cross-country route would be the best way to rejoin the track. He did not take account of a steep bank, but a 10,000 lira note waved in front of a group of spectators soon saw the car manhandled back onto the road.

After the scheduled four laps, Tony pitted to refuel and hand over to Peter. However, owing to prolonged use of the lights whilst lapping slower cars, the battery failed to restart the engine and eleven minutes were lost while a new one was fitted. Toward the end of his first lap, Peter's concern for the spectators straying onto the track was replaced by worry about noises coming from underneath the car. He decided he must pit to investigate, a wise move as in the final stage of the lap the gear lever started to disappear until he only had just over an inch left to use.

A further fifteen minutes were lost while the offending gearbox cross-member was secured before he could continue. The team had calcu-lated they would do eight laps to the leaders ten but the leaders were having problems as well, meaning Peter had to do nine. On his extra tour, he collected a Lancia Fulvia that was all over the road into a corner, but managed to get to the finish despite the panel damage sustained. The result was twenty-fourth overall and eleventh in

the most hotly contested, Group 6 class. The pair finished fifteenth overall at Mugello on 28 July, but retired with a broken crank at Nürburgring on 20 August.

Another car was ready for the Nürburgring 1,000 Kilometre race on 19 May. The yellow MGB GT was built from a new shell by Alan Smith of Derby. It had a ZF differential, long-range petrol tank, 5.5in Minilite wheels and one of Smith's special 130bhp engines. Brown and co-driver Tony Fall (a BMC works rally driver) finished seventh in class, thirty-eighth overall. The following weekend, Roger Enever shared the driving at Spa for the 1,000km and they came home second in class, fourteenth overall on the fast Belgian circuit. Peter also took the car out in two home races. He non-started at Brands on 2 June with electrical problems but finished eighth overall at Snetterton two weeks later.

Each of the cars was advertised in *Autosport* for £1,500 at the end of the season and sold. The GT went to private owner Graham Parkinson who never sprinted the car as originally in-tended. In 1970, he registered it as XTJ 870H, using the body number as a chassis number for the vehicle. He still owned the car in 2001.

## Charles Dawkins and Rod Eade

Former Morris Motors apprentice Rod Eade and his long-time friend Charles Dawkins first got involved in a racing project together when Rod built a 1,300cc engine for Charles' Mini, which Dawkins drove in his debut race at Lydden in 1966. Come 1967 they were looking to move on and bought a racing MGB, 345 AMO, from Andy Page. The car, which was red with a white stripe, came on specially built 13in by 6in wire wheels. At the time, Alfa Romeos were the only other popular car running 14in rims so there was very little tyre choice. The 13s enabled them to use Dunlop CR70s, the tyres with the star-pattern tread. The pair had the feeling that Alan Hutcheson had previously been involved with AMO, but they were never able to get to the bottom of it.

*The MG Car Club Team, which came third in the 1971 750 Motor Club Six-Hour Relay race at Thruxton. L to R: Phil Axon, Jim Loveday, Charles Dawkins, Rodney Eade, with Dawkins' car on trailer. They also won the Girling Trophy for the first BMC-engined team home.*

They shared the car, competing in both the 1967 and 1968 Amasco and Freddie Dixon series, Charles admitting that Rod was usually just that little bit quicker than him. The B was driven to and from the circuits and they had some enjoyable races, doing reasonably well. Rod had a Marque Sports win at the MGCC Oulton Park meeting on 13 July 1968. With the idea of using it as tow barge, Charles bought a LHD MGB, AGO 341B, from Peter Jackson's garage in Cambridge. It had a number of extras including an HRG cross-flow head. This was tried on 8 DBL with Lucas injection. In the end, AGO was 'ratted for spares'.

Whilst Charles had a good job in computers and Rod, an export technician at Longbridge, obtained all their parts at staff rate, they always needed extra money to fund the racing. At this time, along with other competitors, they began to think they should trailer the MGB to meetings. Charles acquired the Longbridge factory gardener's runabout, a green Austin A55 pick-up BOX 315C, as a more practical tow barge, and now they needed a trailer.

Charles got on to Mike Cannon at Plaxtol near Sevenoaks and discovered customers could buy a complete rolling trailer or just the bed and chassis without the wheels. He ordered one complete and three without wheels, and set off

in his road vehicle, a Downton-engined A35 pick-up, to tow them back, stacking the three chassis on top of the complete trailer. Having got his purchases home, a quick visit to the local breakers for wheels and a can of silver paint and he had three trailers to sell at a profit. As trailers caught on, the exercise was repeated with similar results.

At the end of the 1968 season, they were looking for new pastures and decided that they would like to race in Europe. This change of direction coincided with the JCB MGB, 8 DBL, coming up for sale following its final accident at Oulton. Having competed against it, Rod knew it was a quick car and the deal was done. The A55 pick-up had been replaced by a blue A55 van and they came down the M1 from Leeds, the suspension on the bump stops, with over a ton of spares in the back and 8 DBL on a trailer behind. The car looked a bit sad, with a flattened screen and front wing; the back axle and one stub axle were bent and all the wheel arches were misshapen.

They had a Salisbury bolt-on wheel axle so, as all the wings needed attention, they decided to discard the wire wheels and get Minilite to make them some 15in by 8½in alloys. They believe they were the first to run such wide wheels and big, flared arches on an MGB. The car retained its yellow-and-red livery, though the 45 Weber was discarded in favour of the twin 2in SUs recommended by Bill Nicholson. Unable to get HSs, Rod used HDs which seemed to work just as well, though a sprung sandwich-plate with 'O' rings had to be used to eradicate fuel frothing.

The deadline for the Targa Florio was missed, though Rod and his wife drove down to watch. However, Charles Dawkins and Rod Eade did get an entry for the 1,000 Kilometres of Francorchamps on 11 May 1969. They competed in AMO, fitted with a long-distance spec engine, which Rod built, largely from the van-load of spares that came with DBL. By this time, part of his job included supplying the Abingdon Competition Department with parts from Longbridge, so Peter Browning became a useful contact. Bill Nicholson lent them an ex-factory long-distance fuel tank that sat in the boot and joined with the standard under-floor tank through the hole where the filler rubber usually went.

Rod drove up to Belgium from Sicily, whilst Charles drove the MGB over from England. On arrival at Spa Circuit, despite the appalling visibility in the wet conditions, they qualified within the prescribed 140 per cent of the leading driver's time. After the session, they needed to change the clutch plate, which had oil on it. Aware of their plight, a local garage proprietor offered the use of his workshop nearby and the job was completed in about two hours. The mechanics thought them slightly mad to drive the MGB down to Belgium, race and then drive the same car home again. Rod was delighted that they had qualified as, in those days of the £50 foreign currency restriction, he and his wife had run out of money on their trip to the Targa and needed the start money to get home.

The big day dawned dry but cloudy and a crowd of 70,000 turned out to see the expected Porsche/Ferrari battle for overall honours. The MGB ran like clockwork during the race, with Charles taking the start and finish and Rod the middle section of the four and a half hour race. Rod recalls their pit was next to Australian Paul Hawkins, who was sharing a V8 Lola with D. Prophet. Jo Siffert and Brian Redman won for Ferrari whilst the MGB, which was very well received by the crowd, came home twenty-fourth from thirty-one starters, having covered fifty-one laps and set a race average speed of 102mph (164km/hr). Three Porsches were amongst the retirements.

The start money was handed out at the award ceremony, where Hawkins let off a fire cracker – the officials were definitely not amused. Charles and Rod were invited to a huge party at the Ickx family château, though Jackie had little to celebrate as his Mirage BRM had retired with fuel-system problems.

*Ian Polley with three trophies he won in 8 DBL at the MG Car Club Brands Hatch meeting on 22 July 1975.*

Shortly after returning from Spa, AMO was advertised and Brian Lambert expressed interest in buying, provided it would do a 1min 12sec round Silverstone, and arranged to meet Dawkins and Eade at the next circuit test day. It was a bit of a double-edged sword; they badly wanted to sell but they could not afford to bend it. Charles went out first and got close, then Rod took it round and managed to meet the time, despite the fact that the car still had the long-distance engine fitted. The car was subsequently owned by Chris (Westfield) Smith and John Hewitt.

Charles and Rod did not race in Europe again, but continued to campaign 8 DBL on the British club scene between 1969 and 1971. Charles took the Abingdon Trophy for winning the MGB race at the 1971 MGCC Twenty-First Silverstone weekend. Along with fellow MGB drivers Jim Loveday and Phil Axon, they came third in the 1971 Thruxton Six-Hour Relay and won the Girling Trophy for the first BMC-engined team home.

Later that year, 8 DBL was sold to Ian Polley, in whose hands it continued its winning ways. Amongst his many wins was a victory at the 1973 MGCC early season Brands Hatch meeting, when he beat the highly modified MGB-engined MGA of fellow front-row man Rob Haigh, at an average speed of 73.81mph (118.79 km/hr). He again beat Haigh at Brands in July. Ian won the MGCC Speed Championship that year, beating Phil Axon by ten points.

## David Cleverdon

In 1975, David Cleverdon bought 8 DBL from Bill Nicholson for approximately £1,200 and used it to compete in MG Car Club sprints and race meetings. He finished second in Class at Silverstone on 24 May 1975, beating Terry Osborne, Barry Sidery-Smith and Jim Loveday,

*David Cleverdon shaves the chicane at a Goodwood sprint in 1975.*

*Crowd safety regulations were not very stringent in the 1960s; note the straw bales at Brands Hatch Paddock Hill Bend and spectators dangling from the advertising hoardings. Don Bunce spins away his fourteen-second lead over Bill Nicholson; he got going again to finish second to Bill.*

and later that year took his Class at the Goodwood Sprint. At the very wet 1976 Silverstone meeting, David lost it and damaged the B against the pit-lane wall. It languished in his garage for several years and eventually he bought a front end advertised in his local newspaper, then persuaded a local technical college to do the repairs as one of their engineering projects.

They stitched the new front on and Dave removed the arches and swapped the wide wheels with Anthony Binnington for a set of seventy-two-spoke wires. His intention was to return the car to more standard specification but the job was never completed. Colin Pearcy later bought 8 DBL and it was rebuilt to original works spec, before it was raced in historic events. It now forms part of a private collection and has raced at selected events including the 1996 Coys Historic Festival.

# 2　Long Distance Races at Home and Abroad

Whilst the MGB was not always competitive against other sports cars when raced in ten-lap club events, where it could be eclipsed by the new generation of glass-fibre-bodied sports models like the Lotus Elan, it often excelled in longer endurance races, both in works and private hands.

## Christabel Carlisle

As America had always been a big market for MG, it was decided that the MGB's official competition debut would be in the Sebring 12-Hour Race in March 1963 and two cars, 6 DBL and 7 DBL, were entered. American crew

*BMC always regarded the American race at Sebring as important publicity for their sports cars. This is a team photograph. How many of the MG and Healey personalities can you recognize?*

*Christabel Carlisle wearing the hat she purchased to keep the Sebring sun at bay. The MGB she was due to co-drive retired before she had the chance to get behind the wheel.*

Jim Parkinson and Jack Flaherty were to drive 7 DBL, and BMC Competitions Manager Stuart Turner decided an all-female pairing in the other would gain good publicity. Three British drivers, Christabel Carlisle, Liz Jones and Pauline Mayman, were invited to an MGB evaluation test at Silverstone on 28 November 1962.

Stuart and a couple of mechanics brought the car along with Paddy Hopkirk, who established a control lap time of 2min 15.2sec, on a wet track. The three girls then went out for their fifteen-lap sessions. Christabel, a successful Mini racer, set a time of 2min 17.9sec, whilst Liz and Pauline, who both raced rear-wheel-drive sports cars, did 2min 20.6sec and 2min 27.4sec respectively. American journalist Denise McCluggage was partnered by Christabel at Sebring. The two MGBs were prepared over the bitter winter of 1962–3 but the team had problems in finding a recognized race circuit that was sufficiently clear of snow for testing.

Eventually, a 33ft-long BMC service vehicle was used to melt the snow at Finmere, a World War II airfield test track, and Christabel was able to put in some laps before the cars were shipped out from Liverpool six weeks before the race. It is well recorded that both Ecurie Safety Fast MGBs (Race Nos 47 and 48) retired after about two hours with engine bearing problems, as the result of insufficient testing. As Denise took the Le Mans style start, Christabel, who had put in so much work beforehand, did not get to drive.

## Hedges, Hopkirk & Hutcheson = 3/3 in 24

A single MGB was entered in the Le Mans 24-Hour Race from 1963 to 1965 and finished on each occasion, taking a class win in 1963 and class second the following two years.

Paddy Hopkirk and Alan Hutcheson drove 7 DBL on 15/16 June 1963; the car was backed by the factory but raced as a private entry. The pair finished twelfth overall (from forty-eight starters) and covered 2,207.14 miles (3,552.05km) at an average speed of 92mph (148km/hr) over the twenty-four hours.

It so nearly might not have been: one and a half hours into the race Alan had an off at Mulsanne, ending up in the same piece of sand just vacated by a Lotus Elite. He set to with a shovel, thrown to him by a member of the crowd, and dug the car out. Following ninety minutes of hard labour, he was on his way again, his place in the sand soon being taken by the Deep Sanderson. The B crossed the line just behind the top five, all Ferraris, which had staged a formation finish.

In 1964, Andrew Hedges joined Paddy as co-driver in BMO 541B for the race on 20/21 June, the car running well and without major incident to come home nineteenth out of twenty-five finishers. Just half of the fifty-one cars that set out lasted the distance. The average speed increased to 99.9mph (160.8km/hr), undoubtedly due to the lack of unscheduled stops and the total distance covered was 2,397.73 miles (3858.78km).

*7 DBL, in long-nosed form during a pre-Le Mans test in May 1963, the near-side wing showing signs of damage. That year, Andrew Hutcheson and Paddy Hopkirk won the Two-Litre Class; their fastest lap was 104.14mph (167.6km/hr).*

As the first British-entered, British-built car to finish, they also won the Motor Trophy.

Hedges and Hopkirk were again at the wheel, this time of DRX 255C on 19/20 June 1965, for the MGB's final Le Mans outing. They drove 2,357.64 miles (3,794.26km) and, despite the average speed for the twenty-four hours dropping to 98.2mph (158.04km/hr), they recorded the MGB's best overall position, eleventh out of fourteen finishers from the fifty-one cars that started. Team manager, Peter Browning, had set a target of 288 laps split into ten sessions, the first of twenty-seven laps, the other nine each twenty-nine laps. The objective was to get the average speed for the twenty-four hours over the 100mph mark for the first time.

However, unscheduled pit stops spoilt the plan. After seven and a quarter hours, Andrew had a puncture at Tetre Rouge; he managed to drive to the pits on the rim but lost three minutes whilst the wheel was changed and the wing

repaired. The stewards called the car in after eight hours for the stop-lamp bulb, broken in the off as the result of the puncture, to be replaced – another three minutes lost. The car had qualified on the 1964 spec Dunlop R6 tyres before switching to the slightly wider R7s, specified by Dunlop for the race, during the final practice session. Having already qualified, the drivers took it easy on the new rubber. Following his off, Andrew reported hearing and smelling the near-side rear tyre rubbing on the body. At the next routine stop the car was changed back to R6s.

The puncture caused another five and a half minutes to be lost, when the car was called into the pits after sixteen and a quarter hours for the exhaust system to be wired up, following reports of it grounding on right-hand corners. Yet another thirteen and a half minutes were sacrificed when Paddy was called in after nineteen and three-quarter hours for supposedly baulking Ferraris at Whitehouse – an allegation he

*The 1965 works Le Mans MGB, DRX 255C, on its way to a Class second during the 24-hour race.*

strongly repudiated, given that he could take the corner flat, while the Ferraris had to brake. The lost twenty-five minutes accounted for the car being 1.8mph (2.9km/hr) off the 100mph target.

Paddy had the added handicap of completing the last three and a half laps with no brakes after a piston calliper seal went. In fact, coming into the pits after the finish he nearly ran over the welcoming committee of Browning plus the mechanics Tommy Wellman and Gerald Whiffen, complete with a bottle of bubbly.

All three Le Mans outings had been done using a three-bearing-crankshaft engine that had been bored out to 1,801cc, fitted with high-lift camshaft deep sump, and which ran on a single 45 Weber. The power unit was mated to a close-ratio gearbox by a competition clutch and the cars ran a 3.3:1 diff. They had competition dampers and brake friction-material all round and a twenty-gallon fuel tank. Over the three years, the nose cone, first modified in 1963, was refined to give better aerodynamic advantage.

Was it worth it? Definitely; to finish at all was an achievement – look at the number who failed to complete the distance each year, add to that three class places and the Motor Trophy. The MGB can hold its head up high.

**Later History of DRX 255C**

The 1965 car, DRX 255C, was subsequently used as practice car for European events, before being lent to Alec Poole and Roger Enever for the 1967 Mugello race. The car was damaged before it reached the circuit after Bob Neville, who drove DRX over the St Gothard Pass, hit the rocks whilst avoiding an errant lorry. They managed to get it fixed locally before the race, only for it to crash during practice. It was returned to Ireland to be repaired on the jig at the Poole family business, which assembled BMC cars under licence. Alec then negotiated a purchase from Peter Browning who, tongue in cheek, chastised him for reducing the car's value by damaging it beforehand. Alec and his friend Henry Elliott did several Irish club races, including meetings at Bishopscourt.

Laid up for most of 1968 and 1969, DRX was due out in Alec's hands in Guyana. However, he was not able to go so his brother, Arnie, drove

*Arnie Poole, driving DRX 255C, leads a local MGB out of The Gooseneck at Atkinson Field Circuit, Timehri, Guyana, in November 1969. He went on to win the race.*

the car at the Atkinson Field meeting on 2 November 1969 instead. He took a race win, despite crossing the line with a very tired engine.

Derek McMahon paid Alec £1,000 for DRX; he raced it at Kirkistown, Mondello Park and Ingliston, also taking in local hill climbs at Syonfin and Craigantlet during 1970. He towed it to meetings on an 'A' frame and enjoyed a good many wins with the car. Andrew Neilson purchased DRX for £675 and raced it five times; Derek recalls watching him go off into the bog at the top of Syonfin, though the car was soon rescued by spectators. Laurence Mahon, of Southern Carburettors, had one race in this MGB at Brands in April 1971. Subsequently raced by Bob Shellard, it is now owned and campaigned by Barry Sidery-Smith.

## 1965 Guards Trophy Race

This event, advertised as Britain's longest motor race since pre-war days, brought MGB success on home soil. The 1,000-mile race was run in two 500-mile heats over two days at Brands Hatch on 22/23 May 1965. Factory car 8 DBL was entered by engine tuner and experienced team manager Don Moore, with John Rhodes and Warwick Banks as drivers. Don was also running Paddy Hopkirk and Roger Mac in a Big Healey. The JCB-entered MGB, BRX 853 B, ideal for the event with its long-distance fuel tanks, was driven by brother and sister team Anita and Trevor Taylor. Trevor drove in Formula 1 and had raced other JCB cars, whilst Anita, who drove for Ford, had first experienced a race track when her father had hired Silverstone for the afternoon and she and her brother drove round and round finding their limits. André Baldet/Bill Nicholson (Moto Baldet), John Ralph/Tony Williams and M. J. Donegan/P. P. Cadman were other MGB teams.

Following Friday's practice, when Rhodes had lapped the Brands Grand Prix Circuit in 2min .05sec and kept the revs below 6,200, Don had to decide on a strategy that would allow his drivers to circulate fast enough not to lose concentration yet conserve tyres and fuel to minimize pit stops. He opted for compromise lap speed and Dunlop Green Spot tyres. John Rhodes took the 1pm rolling start, unusual for a

*Andrew Neilson drives DRX 255C at Syonfin Hill Climb in Ireland.*

British event, for the Saturday race, in dry and sunny conditions, as the thirty-five cars went round behind Roy Pierpoint's Ford Mustang. At the end of the first racing lap, John was in seventh place, behind Trevor Taylor in the JCB MGB.

Adhering to his agreed lap times, John followed Trevor for about one and a half hours but on lap forty-two he speeded up and took the other B, elevating himself to sixth. As the result of the first round of pit stops, John was in third place when he came in for his own stop on lap sixty-one. It took 1min 41sec for Warwick to get into the cockpit while the mechanics added fifteen gallons of fuel and topped up the oil. On lap ninety-seven the Healey was black flagged, as one of the rear wheels was breaking up and, as driver Paddy Hopkirk drove into the pits, Warwick Banks stormed into the lead.

The car continued until lap 120, when Banks brought it in for its second routine stop. Rhodes resumed in the lead with the Healey second,

closely followed by the JCB MGB, now driven by Anita Taylor, third. The end of the Saturday section of the race saw an MGB 1, 2, Banks and Rhodes winning at an average speed of 75.23mph (121.07km/hr), with the Taylors second, three laps down. The Jaguar E type of Oliver and Craft was third, one lap behind the second MGB. Unfortunately, the MGB of Baldet and Nicholson was one of the three retirements of the day after pulling out with a broken gearbox.

Having checked 8 DBL over, Don Moore changed the clutch as a preventative measure and the car was ready for another 500 miles on Sunday. Warwick started from pole position but was soon overtaken by the E Type. After one and a half hours the B was 1min 28sec behind. However, Warwick still had his four-lap lead from Saturday in hand, so as far as the overall results went, it still had a three and a half lap advantage, but that was about to change.

*Laurence Mahon racing the ex-Le Mans MGB at MGCC Brands Hatch meeting in April 1971.*

*Warwick Banks puts 8 DBL into a classic four-wheel drift at Stirling's Bend during the 1965 Guards Trophy Race at Brands Hatch. It was the 30-degree slip-angle on the Dunlop 'M'-section tyres that made this possible. Warwick and John Rhodes went on to win the race.*

Warwick Banks pitted for a routine stop and, while John Rhodes took over and the mechanics refuelled, Don, who was checking the oil, noticed a slight oil leak around the filter. To save time, he sent John out again whilst he found a spare sealing ring. John was called in after four laps and lost two laps of his three-lap lead whilst the leak was repaired. He rejoined, still in the lead but only half a lap ahead of the JCB MGB, which was now in second place. With just over 100 laps to go the crowd were faced with the prospect of two MGBs fighting it out for overall victory.

By lap 120, John, who had increased his lead, came in as planned for four new tyres, fuel, oil and a change of driver. Two minutes later Warwick came out of the pit lane just as Anita went past; the overall lead over the JCB car was down to one lap again. Two laps later it was her turn to pit, Trevor took over and decided to go for it. Initially, as the result of his quicker lap times, he closed the gap and the crowd were set for an exciting finish. But on lap 143, the Taylor's hopes of victory evaporated along with the water in their MGB's radiator, the car losing five minutes in the pits whilst a core plug was changed. To add to the team's problems, a rear wheel collapsed during the penultimate lap, due to spoke fatigue. The final tour was driven on three tyres and a mangled wheel rim, which pushed the JCB car down to seventh overall but still second in Class.

Meanwhile, Warwick continued at the head of the field, reducing his pace slightly just in case the oil filter played up again, and went on to win the 1,000-mile event by seven laps, from the Sprite of Mike Garton and Peter Hughes. The two remaining MGBs finished in the top twelve.

## Roger Enever and Alec Poole

Employed in the Development Department at Abingdon, both Roger and Alec had many works outings in all manner of BMC and Leyland machinery, and in addition entered other races in their own cars or vehicles borrowed from the company.

*The 1965 Guards Trophy given to Warwick Banks by Don Moore's family after his death. Don apparently had to shorten the cup after someone dropped it and damaged the rim.*

In May 1965, Roger had co-driven John (Baggy) Sach's MGB, 2 GLL, to eighth overall in the Guards 1000 at Brands. A Shell engineer, Baggy had bought the very early black Roadster, which he ran with an Iris Blue hardtop from BMC's Development Department. He wrote the shell off at Prescott Hill Climb, and following this, it was re-shelled by Development. Enever was third overall behind a brace of E Types and won his class in a ten-lap Marque Sports car race at Brands Hatch, on 7 March 1966.

On 8 May 1966, Roger and Alec raced GLL in the Ilford Films 500 Mile GT Race at Brands; the car was taxed and still had a working radio installed. The grid lined up in engine-capacity order and with many V8s present they were quite well down. The race was held in such appalling, wet conditions that drivers were allowed three acclimatization laps. Another B, driven by Francis Polak and Gordon Council, was pulled off the grid when an alert scrutineer spotted broken spokes on one of the wire wheels. At the end of the first hour, Roger was eighth, the car running well but quietly. After two hours it was leading the up-to-2,500cc Class and had moved up to sixth overall.

Eighty-four laps had elapsed when Roger, still sixth, pitted for fuel and a driver change; this was swiftly executed, with Alec soon back out on the circuit. At the four-hour mark the B was in second place, but after five hours it was passed, on the now drying tack, by the GT40, which had earlier been ordered to pit over an alleged oil leak. The race was won by David Piper and Bob Durrant who covered 175 laps in their seven-litre Shelby Cobra, the GT40 was second (168 laps) and Roger brought the MGB home an amazing third overall and took the Class, after 167 laps of the Brands Grand Prix circuit.

Other classified Bs were Bill Nicholson/Don Bunce, seventh and Class third (159 laps), Jean/Tony Denton, twelfth (147 laps) and Herbert Fernando/Ken Costello, fourteenth (142 laps), the marque making an excellent impression against much more powerful machinery.

The Development Department had used black MGB, BRX 855B, as a test bed for the five-bearing engine which was introduced in 1964. Having covered about 100,000 miles round the MIRA test track it was due to be cut up. However, Roger persuaded his father Syd, who ran Development, to let him convert it for racing. This done, he towed it down to Italy for the June 1966, Monza 3-Hour Race. He and co-driver Clive Baker stayed the weekend in a villa that belonged to innovative motor-cycle race engineer Dr Joe Erlich, of EMC fame. They beat Porsches to win the up-to-two-litre Class; the car ran without a problem, but loading up after the race they spotted that one of the brake discs had cracked.

1967 was to be a hectic year in Europe for Enever and Poole, starting on 25 April with the 1,000 kilometres of Monza, where they finished sixteenth, from forty-one starters, and won the under-2000cc GT Class. One week later they were at Spa for what turned out to be a very wet 1,000 Kilometres of Francorchamps. There were twenty-nine starters for the race and, as ever, the MGB ran reliably throughout, finishing tenth overall and again taking the class.

Nürburgring was the venue for the next 1,000 kilometre race on their calendar, the A.D.A.C. event on 29 May. Sixty-nine cars lined up for the Le Mans-style start, but just thirty-two would take the chequered flag some seven hours later. Once more the MGB's strength was its reliability, with Roger and Alec coming home in sixteenth place just ahead of the other MGB in the race, driven by Clive Baker and Julian Vernaeve. A Porsche 911S took the class.

They again finished sixteenth in the Reims 12-Hour Race on 24/25 June. Without a broken water-pump, which was replaced with one robbed from their tow car, they would undoubtedly have finished higher. Unfortunately, they were unable to repeat their previous year's feat at the now B.O.A.C.-sponsored 500 at Brands Hatch on 25 July. Having qualified thirty-fourth from thirty-six starters the car was settling down during the early stages of the race. After forty-one minutes it was pushed off the track at South Bank, then delayed as an over-zealous official thought water overflowing from the expansion tank was an oil leak. Eventually allowed to continue, it did not cover enough laps to be classified, despite finishing the race.

## The MGB GT Waves the Flag Stateside

On 5 February 1967, the GT showed its promise when two examples driven by Eve/Croucher/Glen and Weaver/Ganger/Goodman had finished respectively seventeenth and twenty-fifth from sixty starters in the gruelling Daytona Continental 24-Hour Race. The highest placed of the two cars covered 493 laps of the 3.81 mile (6.13km) banked circuit.

The GT had its first significant place on the world racing scene in the S.C.C.A.-organized Sebring 12-Hour Race on 1 April 1967. Paddy

*Jeremy Delmar-Morgan and Mike Walton drove Andrew Longden's MGB to ninth overall, fifth in class at the 1966 Ilford Films 500 at Brands Hatch.*

Hopkirk and Andrew Hedges brought the GT, LBL 591E, home eleventh overall and won the Sports Prototype 2,000–3,000cc Class, after covering 189 laps of the 5.2 mile (8.37km) circuit in Connecticut. Timo Makinen and John Rhodes were one lap behind in twelfth overall and took second in class in Roadster GRX 307D.

LBL 591E was back at Sebring the following year, this time in the hands of local drivers G. Rodrigues/R. McDaniel/B. Brack, who claimed eighteenth place overall, and fifth in class.

## Andrew Longden, Jeremy Delmar-Morgan and Mike Walton

HGT 576C was a Roadster that Andrew Longden bought for sprints, hill climbs and the odd circuit race. It was a 100 per cent private effort, though he did get his spark plugs free from his friend John Glover who worked for Champion; thus he was always first to try their latest offering. Andrew finished third overall in the twenty-lap Marque Sports race at Brands Hatch on 8 May 1967. A long-distance race had always appealed, so having asked Jeremy and Mike to drive for him, Andrew was successful in obtaining an entry for the 1966 Ilford Films 500 at Brands Hatch.

Delmar-Morgan lent Andrew a corner of his workshop, where Mini Jems were built, to prepare the MGB for the race and after a week's work it was ready. Andrew ran the team with Ron Parkes as mechanic, and after six hours (153 laps), most of it in the pouring rain, his

*Abingdon Competition and Development Department staff often discussed ideas over lunch. Visiting technicians from companies who supplied items such as sparking plugs and tyres were usually taken to the 'Mister Warrick Arms' in Ock Street, Abingdon. Roger Heavens, son of the landlady, ran a racing team from the garages at the rear. The building has since been converted into flats.*

two drivers brought the car home ninth overall, fifth in class. Although Andrew did one or two other Brands races, the car reverted mainly to sprint and hill-climb use, before he sold it in 1968. Five years later, stopping at a motorway services, he spotted it in the staff car park.

Andrew asked around and was told it belonged to the manager, who came out to see him. The Weber had been replaced with the original SU carburettors, and the owner had no idea of his car's history!

# 3 Take to the Hills

Hill climbs and sprints have traditionally provided an economic way to make a start in motor sport; most competitors in the classes for road-going cars drive them to the event, so an everyday vehicle doubles as competition car. Often drivers would cut their teeth in such events before moving on to circuit racing. Many so much enjoy the intense competition that this discipline of the sport provides, that they continue in speed events.

The original MG Car Club Speed Championship was established by Jeremy Cocker around 1970. Over the years, it progressively became a series for more modified examples of the marque. Jackie Hayter and then Jill Ashby subsequently took the helm, and the championship peaked. To satisfy the demand for more grass roots competitors, club members in the North of England set up the Norwester series, which was aimed at more standard MGs. For 1995 and 1996, things went full circle and the two were combined as the MGCC Moss Europe Open Speed Championship, but it has been run as two series again since 1997.

## Alistair Crawford

Starting with a 1,798cc MGB GT, which was taken out to 1,950cc, Alistair Crawford competed in the MGCC Speed Championship from 1987 to 1993. Following an accident at Knockhill in 1989, the car was re-shelled to become a roadster. Alistair won the MGCC championship.

Preferring the hills, Alistair campaigned the B in the RAC Leaders Championship from 1995 to 2000. Prior to the start of the first season, he went to Alan Staniforth who modified the front suspension by replacing the king pin and trunnion system with Ralt single-seater uprights. This gave much improved geometry at the front, but it was not matched by the standard rear end, which resulted in a body rearranging accident. The repaired car was out again at Harewood in July, where the engine blew. Unbeknown to Alistair, it had been damaged in the accident.

At the end of 1995, he bought an ex-TVR Tuscan Championship, 4.4 litre Rover V8 engine and mated it with a rare ex-works TR8 straight-cut close-ratio gearbox, with uprated bearings. All the extra power meant that the rear suspension now had to be sorted. The live rear axle was retained with coil overs resulting in good geometry all round. Alistair scored points in a couple of rounds of the 1996 RAC Championship, but found it was a huge step up competing against Ferraris, Porsches and V8-powered Westfields.

After constant use it was found that the body shell had suffered stress as a result of the 375bhp it was having to handle, so the car was rebuilt into a Heritage shell. This was strengthened and the suspension mounting points altered so they picked up on the bespoke roll-cage. This altered the geometry yet again, but, because of a miscalculation in respect of the trailing arms, it was for the worse. A change of camber, or the sudden application of throttle or brakes, induced rear wheel steering! Alan Staniforth cured the problem and things began to get better.

The V8 was taken to John Eales who increased the capacity to 5 litres, vastly improving the torque and producing 400bhp. For 1998, Alistair had perfect suspension, maximum power and reliability. The MGB V8 was now running on 10in-wide front wheels with 11in rears. He scored in every round, taking class wins at Harewood (twice), Barbon Manor, Doune and Curborough. Taking his best nine scores from thirteen rounds he won the over-2-litre class RAC Leaders Championship, beating John Lambert's twin-turbo Ferrari 308 and Richard Jones' Porsche 911 Turbo. It was an ideal year and luck was with him almost throughout. His only problem was at Harewood, then his local hill. He broke a half shaft in morning practice, but with twenty friends present there was more than enough help and it was changed in less than an hour.

The following season was not quite so good; there were some engine problems and a broken diff – something that had never happened before. The highlight of the year was Harewood, where he went head to head with Richard Jones. They had three practice runs each on the Saturday and then, knowing it would be close, both stayed late working on their cars. Apparently it was most unusual for Jones to undertake such last-minute preparation. Come Sunday, Alistair took the class by four-tenths of a second, despite the fact that the boost on the Porsche's turbo was up so high that the car was lifting the front wheels. Owing to the earlier problems, Alistair finished the year second in class to Richard.

For 2000, it was difficult to come up with anything to make the car go better. In the end, Alistair decided that the aerodynamics were the only thing that could be improved upon. Paul Wood, who had helped build the car and used to share the driving, had it over the winter and designed a front spoiler which had small winglets on the ends. The total aerodynamic package transformed the car and Alistair describes it going up Shelsey Walsh and Gurston Down like a Go-Kart. At Gurston there is a kink at the finish; in 1999 when he lifted off for this the car lurched about and he crossed the line at 97mph (156km/hr). The new splitter meant the car was stable through the kink and he could cross the line with his foot flat to the floor, at 107mph (172km/hr).

Harewood would again provide the high spot of the season. The production-based classes set their first timed runs in the dry, but by the time the single seaters came out it was raining, so they were setting lower times than usual. As a result the MGB V8 and a Westfield V8 qualified for the top ten run-off, which took place in pouring rain. Alistair beat the Westfield and was within four tenths of a second of the slowest single seater, creating a great deal of excitement for the crowd. He now competes on the hills in a Judd-engined Pilbeam.

## Terry Pigott

In 1984, Terry Pigott paid £900 for a standard 1968 MGB, FXC 18G. For the next twelve years it would be his daily transport and his competition car, driven to and, in most cases, from the event. Whilst it never broke down when actually competing, he had to come home courtesy of the RAC twice when it expired on the homeward journey, once with back axle failure. In 1986 his time round Curborough was 50.40 seconds. Following modification – blue printed + 60 engine, still running on SU carburettors, tubular manifold, suspension lowered to the legal maximum with just 6in ground clearance – his 1997 Curborough time, after eleven years of development, was 40.57 seconds.

In 1992, tiring of the constant welding a twenty-five-year-old MGB requires, Terry bought a Heritage body and got a local garage to re-shell the car for him. This was the last major expenditure as, over the years, virtually everything else had been replaced. Like most drivers who compete in their Bs, he had gone for uprated shock absorbers but found that reconditioned units would not last. So he obtained brand new ones, had them uprated and no longer needs to buy replacements each year.

FXC has phenomenal road holding; the standard wire wheels have been replaced by seventy-two-spoke, 6in-wide rims, originally shod with Avon Turbospeed CR 28S tyres, which were very soft. When these came off the RACMSA A list, permitted for road-going cars, he ended up on Yokohama A 520s. Terry won the MGCC Norwester Speed Championship outright in 1995 and finished either first or second in Class

*Terry Pigott rounds the extremely tight right-hander towards the top of the Pestalozzi Hill Climb in August 2000. He had a big off at the same corner in 1999.*

from 1990 to 1998. In 1995 and 2001, he took the Shirley Cooper Memorial Trophy (fastest MGB).

In 1996, Altringham MG engine-tuner Peter Burgess asked Terry to compete in his V8 Roadster, KWY 762K, which he now runs in the Road Going Specials category. As with the B, Terry drives the car on the road and has use of it as his everyday car throughout the season. For competition use it is shod with Avon CR 28Ss. Success has also come in the V8, with another Championship win in 2001.

## Dave Beresford

Having done some karting, then raced an ex-Alan Woode MG Midget, Dave Beresford had to give up motor sport for family and business reasons. In 1990, he purchased an early MGB Roadster, AEW 432A and rebuilt it to MGCC

BCV8 race championship Road Going specification. Whilst competing in that series, Dave started to do a few sprints and hill climbs, and from 1993 to 1999 became a regular contender in the MGCC Sprint Championship.

In 1994, the first year that the Norwester effectively became the Car Club's national series, Dave took seven wins and six lap records from seven starts to win the championship, the first year that a standard class car had won. His best day on the hills was at Loton Park in July 1997. An idyllic summer's day, it was warm enough to breakfast on the terrace before taking a pleasant two-hour drive in the B to Loton. The meeting went smoothly, allowing each competitor three timed runs. Dave set progressively faster times and ended up recording a run that was on a par with the Modified Class cars, beating his rival Terry Pigott by 0.25 seconds. Partaking of some refreshment whilst waiting for the awards

*Dave Beresford on his way to a Class win in the Thoroughbred Championship race at Oulton Park in April 2001.*
*However, he still enjoys the close competition of regular sprint and hill-climb outings in his MGB.*

ceremony, he chatted to fellow competitors before collecting a splendid trophy, driving home as the sun set. A perfect day of club motor sport.

Dave subsequently modified the car, including a Burgess 1,860cc engine, to race in the MGCC Anglia Phoenix Championship. He enjoyed a good race at Cadwell Park finishing a close second in Class to Richard Evans, and broke the lap record by almost 1.5 seconds. Dave won Class A in the 2001 MGCC Moss Thoroughbred Championship. Despite his racing success, he still gains great satisfaction from the intense driver self-discipline required in speed events, and continues to compete in them.

His son Jonathan Beresford has followed in father's footsteps, winning the novice award in the 1999 MGCC Speed Championship driving his ex-Martin Hall MGB GT, TRO 665M. In 2002 Dave will race the ex-Tom Stewart V8, TJX 3 (now JFT 123N), in BCV8 Class B.

## Jackie Hayter

An MG Car Club member who helped many others go sprinting by running the club's Speed Championship and acting as the secretary of the meeting at the MGCC Goodwood sprint for many years, Jackie Hayter was no mean driver herself. Driving the black MGB Roadster that she shared with husband Charlie, Jackie was well placed in the MGCC Lady's Speed Championship in 1985 and 1986.

## John, Pauline and Peter Dignan

Former 1970s international rally driver and RAF pilot John Dignan has owned his Tartan Red MGB Roadster LPA 786D, for thirty-three years. He drove the car in his formative rallying years and started racing it in the Road Going Modified Class of the 1981 BCV8 Championship, finishing the year third in Class. He was second in 1982 and won his Class the following year.

By 1990, the car sported a race cam with 48 Dellorto and John entered the MG Car Club Norwester Speed Championship. Having contested three hill climbs and three sprints, he won the Road Going MGB Class.

Business commitments the following year meant that only five rounds were entered but John still ended the year second in Class.

The year 1992 was to be a halcyon one. John gave his wife Pauline a speed licence with a set of racing overalls and helmet for her birthday, and she had her first competitive event since the 1970s. The couple shared the car at thirteen events throughout the season, which saw John emerge as Norwester Speed Champion and Pauline take the Shirley Stafford Trophy, the ladies overall award. Amongst the course records

John took, those at Aintree – (2 laps) 136.55sec – and Three Sisters – (1 lap) 53.09sec – still stand.

Business commitments again reduced competitive outings to seven during 1993, but John still managed to hold on to the Norwester Championship and Pauline finished second in the Shirley Stafford points. John's record at Aintree – (1 lap) 57.66sec – still remains current.

A change of job in 1994 saw John take a year off from motor sport but he still found time to buy a red RV8, L39 MWR, which was used to great effect in the Standard Class MGCC Sprint Championship during 1995, and at a wide range of events in 1996. In 1995, he took ten class wins from ten outings and was fastest MG at two events, winning the championship outright. He was also awarded the prestigious Kimber Trophy, which has been presented since 1937, at the Baitings Dam Hill Climb, where John's run set a

*John Dignan on the hill at Harewood in May 1992.*

*John and Pauline Dignan with their RV8 and the array of trophies they won in it during the 1995 season.*

new hill record for MGs. By the end of the season his tally of Class records had risen to seventeen. Pauline, who shared the RV8, again won the Shirley Stafford Trophy for the best lady driver in the series. They both found it took extreme concentration to control the car, which was still in road trim, when it was on the limit. It was the only privately entered RV8 to compete that year.

An even more hectic season followed in 1996, with John and Pauline driving both the MGB and the RV8, on occasions sharing both cars at one event. From twenty-three outings, John took twenty-one Class wins, which included six 'Fastest MG'; amongst those was the MGCC Banana Trophy at Goodwood, which the author has previously won on six occasions in his Fully Modified MG Midget. It is rare for a road-going car to take this award. Over the year, John and Pauline won a total of thirty-five awards; John took the MGCC Sprint Championship, the MGCC Hill Climb Championship, and was overall Moss Norwester Open Speed Champion. He held twenty-seven Class records and remained unbeaten in the MG/Rover V8 Class since its inception in 1994.

It was back to the MGB for 1997, in what was to be John's last season on the circuits and hills in that particular car. He started the year as the sole driver, but son Peter made his debut at Scammonden Dam Hill Climb in August and took a third in Class. He went on to secure Class seconds in the five final rounds of the season at Ty Croes (two), Wiscombe, Baitings Dam and Llys-Y Fran and finished the year third in Class, which John won along with the Moss Norwester Speed Championship once again.

In 1998, Peter took over the MGB, in which he established two new records and easily won his Class in the Championship, a feat which he repeated the following year as well. This was to be LPA 786D's final year as a sprint and hill-climb car as John was to return to his rallying routes in it and compete in European regularity rallies with Pauline as navigator. Peter moved on to race an MG Midget in the MGCC Cockshoot Cup Championship.

John now runs a silver MGF in the MGCC MGF Challenge. Driving the new car he was Abingdon Trophy Champion and Norwester Speed Champion in 1998, 1999 and 2000, also overall Norwester Speed Champion in 1998 and 2000. John's most closely contested speed event was against Jim Garvey's road-going special Midget at Scammonden Dam Hillclimb on 8 October 2000. This resulted in a dead heat and both drivers shared the Kimber Trophy.

Recently, John has built up another MGB, RFP 796B, to FIA spec for International Historic Racing. On 5 October 2001 he raced the red-and-black car for the first time in the 300km, Eifel Klassik at the Nürburgring where he finished twenty-eighth from 143 starters, second MGB home, behind the experienced Mark Ashworth. The Dignans prove that motor sport in MGs really is a family affair.

## David Franklin

Now better known for driving historic GT and single seaters on the hills, David Franklin usually tries to have at least two outings a year in his MGCC BCV8, 1981 Championship-winning MGB GTV8, 8000 DF. He still holds the class record at the Colerne sprint in the MG (84.08sec set on 30 August 1999) and is a regular at Porlock and Wiscombe. Deborah, his wife, has also done speed events, including the Weston Speed trials, in the car. Driving a Brazilian collector's Ferrari 712, seven litre, ex-Mario Andretti CanAm car, he set FTD at the Goodwood 2001 Festival of Speed going up the 1.16-mile (1.87km) hill in 48.26 seconds on 8 July.

In June 2001 he drove 8000 DF to Switzerland to take part in the Jo Siffert Memorial Race at St Ursanne des Rangiers, a 3.3-mile (5.3km) hill climb up a mountain road south of Basle. David had driven there before, which was just as well given that it was very wet and misty the whole weekend. With a time of 2min 40.41sec, he took FTD, beating two Formula 2 cars, one driven by Siffert's son Phil, and two racing Porsches to head the top five.

*David Franklin's V8 on its way to Fastest MG Award, MGCC Wiscombe 1981.*

# 4 Historics

Like many cars launched in the 1960s, the MGB has found its way into historic racing, where only period modifications are permitted.

## The British Army Historic Racing Team Sponsored by Stena Sealink

In 1985, three long-time MG racers, Lieutenant Colonel Bob Birrell, Major Fred Boothby and Lieutenant Colonel Peter Everingham, were all serving in Düsseldorf and decided it would make sense to race in Europe rather than crossing the Channel every time they wanted to compete. Birrell, a Movement Control Officer, was in regular touch with ferry companies and was able to secure sponsorship from Sealink. One of their MGBs was already BMC Iris Blue and, given that it was a bit of an unusual colour for the model, easily recognizable from the pits and very similar to Sealink's colours, it was adopted as the team livery. The cars were run out of the team members' allocated garages below the Officers' Mess and were largely self-prepared, though Fred recalls that Corporals Burn and Chadwick often came along to assist as mechanics on race days.

The three MGB Roadsters were all early pull-handle models, two 1962 – 9430 RU (Birrell) and 965 XKM (Boothby) – and one 1963 version – 6162 PG for Everingham. The drivers mainly raced in the FIA Historic GT rounds at circuits such as Nürburgring, Spa, Zandvoort and Zolder, but also did other events at smaller circuits such as Hockenheim, Montlhéry, Seigerland, and Wunstorf. They also ventured back to the UK to compete at Pembrey, Snetterton and the annual MGCC meeting at Silverstone. On a good day in the FIA series they could come home 1, 2, 3 in the pre-1964 up-to-two-litre class, particularly if the Elans fell off. In an average season they would have a presence at about twenty meetings.

At one stage the team acquired an old Cologne city bus that had previously been converted to a transporter by one of the German F3 teams. Two Bs fitted inside, but the hydro-pneumatic suspension had a slight leak. Once the single-decker's engine had been turned off on arrival in the paddock, they had eight minutes to unload, before one corner sunk to the ground trapping the ramps beneath the vehicle. They soon went back to trailering the racers behind motor homes.

## Brian and Barbara Lambert

An Old English White Roadster, JAC 582D, acquired on his twenty-first birthday, was too much of a temptation for Brian Lambert and he was soon racing the car in Marque Sports events during 1968 and 1969. He found it tough going against the Elans but enjoyed some good dices with other Bs and Midgets and took some Class places. He was slip-streaming Chris Smith's Midget at Silverstone when his rival slowed going through Woodcote. Asked in the paddock afterwards why he had pulled off, Smith expressed surprise that Brian had not seen the Midget's damper pulley, which had come off and sawn through his fibreglass bonnet, before sailing over the roof of the MGB.

Brian was to have another lucky escape at Silverstone when his single master cylinder failed and he completely destroyed the car after clouting the bank at Copse. The car was cut up and

*A family affair: Brian Lambert (46) takes the tight line, whilst his wife Barbara (64) tries to go round the outside.*

salvageable parts sold. In 1969, he bought 345 AMO from Rod Eade and Charles Dawkins, but this was severely damaged at Thruxton after just six races. He aquaplaned off in the wet, then rolled it up the bank backwards at the end of the main straight. Having come to his senses he realized something was wrong when he looked up and saw the sky, the hardtop had been ripped off in the accident. He then observed a marshal peer tentatively over the bank and ask if he was OK. The marshal helped Brian out of the car then ran with him to the medical centre, halfway round the circuit. Presenting his charge to the doctor who asked why he had brought him in, the diligent official explained that this driver had just had a rather nasty accident and perhaps needed a check-up. The doctor then pointed out that,

having run him halfway round the track, he could not be too badly injured!

A few outings in his subsequent road MGB and the 1972 season in a Ginetta G4 were followed by retirement until 1993, when Brian bought the former race and rally Roadster, BGJ 849B from Keith and Anna Gurrier. He played himself back in gently with four BCV8 rounds, but found that being obliged to run what was basically an FIA car in the Road Modified Class did not make him very competitive. He decided that either he would have to modify the car, or buy another one, so when Alan Mills put KYR 294K up for sale the matter was decided and he bought it.

In 1994 and 1995 Brian ran his new acquisition in both the BCV8 and the Thoroughbred

Championships and his wife, Barbara, took BGJ out in both series as well. The former Mills Roadster, originally blaze in colour was, for sentimental reasons, resprayed Old English White with a black hardtop, just like his original B. He found running two cars in two championships an expensive exercise but his efforts were well rewarded in 1996. He won the Flemmings Thoroughbred Championship by one point but missed out on BCV8 honours by half a point, just failing to emulate Roy McCarthy and win both in the same year. Barbara took the Thoroughbred Championship Ladies Award in 1995, 1999 and 2000.

Brian intended to defend his crown in 1997, but participation in one of Barry Sidery-Smith's Spa races, driving BGJ, diverted his attention to events abroad. Co-driving Rod Longton's MGB in the Spa Six Hour clinched it, and Brian started to concentrate on FIA events. Today he finds that as in the 1960s, the MGB's reliability tends to make it more competitive against other marques in long-distance events.

Brian competed in the 1999 German GTM Championship, a series of eight one-hour races which saw him race in all but one round, with Barbara co-driving at some races. He drove his own car, BGJ, at Zolder, where the engine blew, Hockenheim, Zandvoort, Spa, Nürburgring and Austria's A1-Ring; he also co-drove the Mugello round in Rod Longton's MGB. He finished the year third in Class. He finds the 176 bends on German Nordschleife circuit, which rises through 1,000ft (305m), both the most demanding and frightening and puts Spa a close second as his favourite track to race on.

The 2000 Six-Hour Race at the Nürburgring was an exciting race for Brian and his co-driver, son Mark. After five hours they were lying seventh overall and second in Class, when Brian hit what turned out to be suspension debris from an MGA. Unbeknown to him it tore a small hole in the sump, allowing oil to escape and vaporize in the exhaust slip-stream. When the oil pressure light started to flicker he pitted and Bob Luff spotted the problem, which he managed to repair by panel beating the tear closed again. The oil was topped up and Brian continued his race. They still finished fifteenth overall from sixty-five starters.

Brian modestly states that his successes are in no small way due to Luff's knack of getting power and reliability from both engine and car. Nowadays, gearbox parts are proving to be a bit of a weak link in long-distance events. Whilst the close-ratio straight-cut gears themselves are strong enough, the baulk rings have, on occasions, failed. For instance, in the 2001 Spa Six Hour, he experienced selection problems and limped round for the last one and a half hours in top and was never more glad to see the chequered flag.

The year 2001 also saw the building of another FIA MGB, MYH 381D, a black example with an ivory hardtop, based on the ex-Ian Dyer BCV8 car.

## Rae Davis

Long-time MG racer, Rae Davis of Moto-Build, has fond memories of his outright win in the 1988 Macau Classic Car race, held the same November weekend as the famous Formula 3 event. Having heard of the race from a friend who lived in Hong Kong, he prepared and shipped his pull-handle MGB, 7448 HJ, out for the race. Unfortunately, the sponsored sea crossing fell through and he had to make his own, last minute arrangements to send it east on an empty vessel that had brought imported Japanese cars to the UK. He drove the car to Harwich, immobilized the engine and told the dockers that, owing to the sintered clutch and Weber carburettor, it would be best if they towed it on and off.

Four weeks later he flew out with tools and spares for the race, only to discover the ship had not arrived having lost three days riding out a storm. When he eventually collected his car from the docks, Rae found he had missed the lighters that had been chartered to take foreign competing cars from Hong Kong to Macau and had to make his own arrangements. He arrived at 11pm, and a customs official, summoned from his bed, requested documentation. Rae produced his FIA papers and the official latched onto the fact that,

*Rae Davis in the paddock assembly area with 7448 HJ before winning the 1988 Macau Classic Car Race.*

owing to previous engine problems, the block carried no engine number; he was thus reluctant to let the car in. When it was suggested that the engine number was underneath, he relented, obviously not wishing to dirty his uniform, and stamped the entry papers.

The field was a mixture of saloons and sports cars including E Types, Morgans, Lotus and GT Cortinas, an MG TD and even a Morris Minor. Prior to practice, the faster cars were asked to take it easy in order that the smaller cars could qualify within 107 per cent of the fastest and get a race. Rae put his car on pole and won the race; his nearest rival, the Jaguar, suffered brake fade at the end of the long start-finish straight. The trophy was so enormous that Rae was photographed sitting on it. However, he was not allowed to take it off the Island. He owned 7448HJ until 1990 and had other historic BCV8 and MGOC outings in it, including a Class win at Zolder.

## Angus and Ruth Dent

In August 1988, Aston Martin Owners Club member Ruth Dent bought her orange MGB Roadster, 'Jaffa'. A week later, she and husband

Angus took it to the MGCC Egerton Weekend and entered the autotest. They had become involved in helping at the AMOC Wiscombe Hill Climb and soon had the urge to cross over and compete more seriously themselves. The husband and wife team shared the B in the 1990 MGCC Speed Championship, driving it to and from events. Ruth recalls coming back up the M3 from Castle Combe; the car was going like a train, then she looked at the oil-pressure gauge, which read 20lb! Soon after, they invested in an Oselli fast road-engine.

Angus started racing the orange B, LPA 813K, in the Road Going Modified Class 1991 BCV8 Championship, whilst Ruth did another year of sprints before going circuit racing in 1992. Again they shared the car; Angus stuck with BCV8 and Ruth entered the Thoroughbred Championship or all-comers races. The pair also co-drove in the MGCC two-driver events. Sitting on the back of the grid at Donington for his first ever race, Angus glanced down to check his instruments; when he looked up, the lights had already turned green and the rest of the field had gone.

Tony Barnard was commissioned to completely rebuild the car in 1995 and Ruth went to

*Ruth Dent's MGB (56) leads Peter Wardle RGS MG (11), Jonathan Kent MGB GT (26) and Mike Reason Triumph TR (22) at an AMOC Silverstone meeting June, 1997.*

*'Jaffa' the Dent MGB races in both the Thoroughbred and BCV8 Championships. Here Angus (56) corners at Mallory Park ahead of Graham Grove (45) in a BCV8 round.*

check progress on return from holiday. She stepped into the workshop and saw a stripped-out Roadster shell lying on its side and thought 'someone's having a lot of work done', then realized it was their car. Ruth tried BCV8 in 1995, taking the Sideways Ladies Trophy, whilst Angus swapped over to the Thoroughbreds. 1996 was their busiest year, they took the car to twenty events and it was double entered at most of them. Angus took his first win, from pole, lights to flag, at AMOC Brands on 6 May and finished the year second in BCV8 Class B.

Ruth took the Ladies Award in the 1996 and 1998 Goldsmith and Young Thoroughbred Championship, and shared it with Barbara Lambert in 1997. She won the Thornley Handicap race at MGCC Silverstone 2000, her last event before she took maternity leave from racing. The couple race on the basis that provided you have a dice with someone and enjoy yourself it has been a worthwhile day out.

Having enjoyed competing at Spa, they began to become interested in European Historic events, which would eventually lead to the acquisition of an Iris Blue Roadster DYB 756C; in 2001, this was being rebuilt to FIA spec.

# 5 The MG Car Club BCV8 Championship

As MGBs became increasingly uncompetitive against the new-generation fibre-glass-bodied sports cars in Modsports and Prodsports events, Barry Sidery-Smith and Victor Smith inaugurated the series in 1977. The Championship still remains as popular as ever, with rounds at all the MGCC meetings, augmented by races with other clubs and the now traditional visit to Spa. In the early years it comprised races, sprints and hill climbs, but in 1982 became solely a race series. The first ever round of the Championship was at MGCC Silverstone on Saturday 4 June 1997 and Malcolm Beer's V8 recorded the first win.

Cars race in four classes:

A. Standard MG Bs and Cs.
B. Road Modified MG Bs and Cs plus Standard GT V8s and RV8s.
C. Full Race MGB 4 cylinder and Cs, plus controlled 3.9 V8s.
D. Full Race MGB V8s.

In 2001 another class was added:

AB. Invitation Standard MGB FIA.

Over the years the series has been sponsored by Collectors Car, Dutton Forshaw, Moss Europe, the Wilkie Group and Ethyl Petroleum. Many

*Rod Longton's ex-Norman Conn 1963 MGB, 3373 MZ. Rod competed in over fifty races with the car in four-cylinder 1,950cc form, as raced here at Mallory Park in 1984. It then did another fifty after he had converted it to a V8.*

*Rod Longton's second MGB (66) also had an Irish racing heritage. At Donington Park in 1989 he is closely followed by Peter Hall (4) and Grahame Davis.*

drivers have competed in it during its history, but Rod Longton has raced in it every year since 1979.

## Dr Rod Longton

Getting restless following his two-year lay-off, Rod bought and sprinted a Lotus Elan Sprint from 1975. In 1977, a two-year-old MGB GTV8 became his tow car and he soon realized he could compete in both cars at the same event. For thirteen years the V8 was also used for his daily rounds as a GP. In 1978, the doctor went to watch one of the rounds of the BCV8 Championship. He recalls: 'I saw Terry Osborne, Bob Luff and Barry Sidery-Smith beating it up – it looked good fun, so I decided to have a go.' He bought an Archie Phillips-prepared ex-Norman Conn 1963 MGB, 3373 MZ, from Rod McDowell in Ireland, and the black-and-yellow car became well known, as Dr Longton regularly competed in it from 1979 to 1983.

In 1984, Rod thought that the V8s looked good, so he built a V8 engine and installed it in MZ, running the Roadster in the same livery from 1984 to 1988. When he converted the car he convinced himself that it would be the fastest MGB derivative ever racing. It eventually attained this status, but only after Bob Beadnell had bought the car and developed it further. He and Bob Berridge raced it until 1993, when Dave Tilley took it on. Towards the end of 1988 Rod wondered about reverting to four cylinders and possibly going Historic racing. Another phone call to Ireland established that McDowell had got another Archie Phillips MGB.

Having sold MZ to Beadnell, Dr Longton was now the proud owner of white MGB 6099 JZ, which had seen many previous victories in the hands of Joan Dobbs before being left to decay in the Irish countryside. Following restoration by Malcolm Beer, Rod campaigned this one in Historics and Class C of the BCV8s during 1989 and 1990. Rod explained that from then on his racing seemed to follow a pattern: when he was driving a B the V8s looked more exciting, but when in a V8 he longed to be driving a B again. Building or converting the cars kept him and his long-time mechanic, Jack Palmer, who assisted him from 1959 to 1999, busy.

At the end of 1990, a neighbour offered Rod a neglected GT, HDS 707N, which, for the £70

asked, looked ideal for the next V8 project. To power it, he bought an ex-works development TR8 engine from John White's Rallycross car. It was only 3.5 litres but produced 310bhp on the brake! The build was undertaken thinking it would be a cheap car, but Rod stopped counting when he got to £10,000. It was good to drive but, owing to work commitments, he only did about a dozen races in it during 1991 and 1992.

His most enjoyable race in an MGB derivative was in this particular car, which was British Racing Green. There was a full grid of modified Bs, Cs and V8s at Brands Hatch on 11 April 1990. Malcolm Beer, the man to beat, ended up in the gravel at Druids on lap one, leaving the race wide open. Rod, Bob Luff, Steve Williams and Bob

*Silverstone 1992, Rod Longton's ultimate BCV8 racer, HDS 707N, his only GT. The car was powered by a 310bhp ex-works development 3.5-litre TR8 engine.*

*BCV8 Championship gallery Zolder paddock 1982. Back, L to R: Barry Sidery-Smith, Colin Pearcy, Geoff Gear, Chip Ballenger, Francis Ridley, Peter Blackbourn, Freddy Yhapp, Joe Blackbourn, Pam Sidery-Smith, Rod Longton, Ron Gammons, John Brigden, unknown, Ian Miller, Colin Cork, Mike Hibbert, John Tadman. Kneeling: Grahame Davis, Terry Osborne, Terry Smith, Neville Mariner, Dave Jarvis, Paul Campling, Paul Campfield.*

Berridge had a ten-lap absolute ding-dong of a race, Luff beating Rod over the line by a whisker. This particular V8 also gave Rod a lap record and was fifth overall at Spa. Deciding an expensive engine rebuild would soon be due, Rod thought he would quit while he was ahead and sold the car to Derek Stuart. Derek competed in another twenty-five races, winning some, before taking the engine down!

In 1991, Jack Palmer's son, John, built another Historic MGB, based on a Californian import. This version, AJN 826A, was red. Rod mainly did Historic events whilst John drove it in BCV8 rounds, winning the T & L Trophy for the highest placed FIA spec car in 1992. AJN has been Mark Ashworth's Historic car since 1994.

Following the familiar pattern, an abandoned V8 racer project was acquired and completed in 1994. Initially raced with a Tony Price 1,950cc engine, AVU 900T was sprayed in the original yellow-and-black colours and became known as 'Déjà Vous'. For 1995, a V8 built to the new Class C regs was installed; John Palmer got quite attached to this car, bought a majority share in it and still competes in the Championship.

Rod's current MGB, another Historic of 1962 vintage, VFO 462, was built at John Palmer's Specialist Cars, Epping premises in 1994. At Donington, Rod had toothache and was not up to racing. He arranged a driver change and Barry Sidery-Smith took it out and had a good dice with the Porsche that eventually won the Championship that year. Rod suggested that Barry used the car for the 1995 FIA Historic Championship, in which he felt Barry stood a good chance of winning the class. 'Sideways' lived up to the Doctor's orders and duly took the crown.

The GTM German Historic Championship was tackled in 1999, Rod teaming up with Brian and Barbara Lambert with their car and fellow BCV8 stalwart Bob Luff, who went as team mechanic and Rod's co-driver. The series consisted of eight one-hour races for two drivers at Zolder, Hockenheim, Spa, Mugello, Zandvoort, 'A' Ring, Oschersleben and Nürburgring. Brian just beat Rod and Bob to third in class at the last round.

The year 2000 came to a premature end in September after Rod got punted, flat out into the Armco along the pit straight at Spa, the good doctor becoming a patient; but he was back in the cockpit in 2001. Since his return to racing in

1979, Rod has taken ten wins and about forty other top-three placings, to add to his tally of thirty-three wins and thirty-four second places from 150 races he competed in between 1960 and 1973. He has finished the year in the Class top five, eight times.

## Malcolm and Adrian Beer

The Beer family, proprietors of MG specialists Beer of Houghton, have been racing MGs since Syd started competing in an NE in the early 1960s, though he went on to be better known in his venerable K3. In 1976, Malcolm, who had previously excelled in Midgets, bought Bob Neville's V8 and became a regular BCV8 contender until 1997. He won the first ever BCV8

*Adrian Beer (31) hops the kerb on his way to another Class win in his first season of motor racing.*

*The Beer Dynasty* circa *1991. L to R: Malcolm, a young Adrian and Syd, pictured at Houghton Mill with a Jacobs Midget, R Type and Malcolm's V8.*

Championship qualifying race at MGCC Silverstone on 4 June 1977, where he also took victory in the Handicap Race, and since then has recorded over 400 wins. He took Class D end-of-year honours 1988 to 1993 inclusive and was overall BCV8 Champion in 1991.

After racing in the Metro Challenge from 1983 to 1985, Malcolm bought Terry Smith's V8 Roadster to campaign in the 1986 BCV8 series. He put the car on pole first time out but failed

to win. After three races, Malcolm rebuilt the car so the handling was to his own liking, going on to take the Class again, and he finished the year third overall in the Championship. He then sold the Roadster to Tim Ransom and wheeled out the GT once more.

One of Malcolm's finest races was at Silverstone on 27 May 1989. Having put the car on pole, it failed to fire up for the green flag lap and, after a push, he had to start from the back of the thirty-car grid. At the end of lap one, he was up to eighth place and hit the front when he blasted past Richard Horn's V8 along Club Straight on lap four. He won and also set the fastest lap, an average speed of 84.84mph (136.54km/hr).

One hectic weekend will never be forgotten. Malcolm had a big accident at Oulton Park on Saturday and trailered the V8 back to Houghton, where he worked overnight to straighten the chassis leg and fit a new steering rack, radiator and water pump. He says his mother has never forgiven him for using her oven to make the resin go off more quickly so he could complete the fibre-glass body repairs in time. After a couple of hours' sleep, he took the car to Donington for the Sunday round. As first reserve, he got a

race when another competitor withdrew, but despite setting the fastest practice time, he had to start from the back of the grid. He passed six cars going into Redgate the first time, was fourth at the end of lap one and went on to win the race.

Over the years, he enjoyed epic dices with fellow V8 men Bob Luff, Steve Williams and Paul Campfield. Malcolm has held the BCV8 lap record at every circuit and at the end of 2001, despite not having raced for four seasons, those at Donington Park National (1min 18.60sec) and Grand Prix (1min 48.27sec) circuits still stood. Through the business, Malcolm prepares several of the cars in the series, and during 1999 and 2000 groomed his son Adrian for his motor sport debut.

*Bill Nicholson (10) leads Terry Osborne (1) through Bridge during an early BCV8 Championship race at Silverstone in May 1981. Bill's car has a works-style long nose, as used at Le Mans.*

Adrian tried his hand at karting but, whilst he enjoyed the racing, found the atmosphere not to his liking. As an alternative grounding for circuit racing, he took his mother's Elan to various track days to learn the circuits. He joined BCV8s in the newly inaugurated Class AB, for FIA spec cars in 2001. Driving his Roadster, BNK 322A, he won first time out at Silverstone on 3 March and went on to take a total of eight wins and two third places from eleven outings, and established eight lap records. He was 2001 Class AB Champion and came second overall in the series. At the end of the season, he took the rebuilt car out in the Birkett Six-Hour Relay at Snetterton, where he drove for one and a half hours, whetting his appetite for long-distance events. However, the question that everyone is asking is, when will he race Malcolm's V8?

## Bob Luff

In 1965, engineer Bob Luff returned to England from America where he had been designing sewing machines. In 1967, he decided that he would buy a sports car and answered an advertisement for an MGB in *Exchange and Mart*. He found the Roadster, AWH 757B, in a scrap yard in Slough – it particularly caught his imagination because it had twin two-inch SU carburettors. Bob told Mr Rouse, the proprietor, that he would meet the £220 asking price provided he got it running . Two days later, Bob found himself behind the wheel 'popping and banging' his way towards the newly opened M4 Motorway. Once he put his foot down, the engine cleared and the car fairly flew. Subsequent investigation would reveal that the MGB had a full race engine and a close-ratio gearbox.

Bob rebuilt the MGB in the corner of a friend's commercial workshop in Wallingford, Oxon, using his engineering skills, and once it was on the road, began to think he might like to race it. He had only ever been to one motor race in his life, a wet meeting at Goodwood that had not exactly left a lasting impression, so he went to spectate at Brands and take a more objective view. He liked what he saw, though admits that

the speed some of the sports cars reached appeared somewhat intimidating.

A Silverstone test day seemed good value at £12, so Bob turned up and paid his money for what turned out to be an open session for all types of car. After a few laps, his confidence grew and he found himself executing two 360-degree spins at Woodcote. Having taken to the pit lane to contemplate, he decided that he would enter the corner as fast as possible and leave his braking to the last moment. Coming down the old back straight he got to the point where he felt he should have braked and went a bit further before hitting the middle pedal. At that moment, Jochen Mass and Hans Stuck changed up as they passed him in their single seaters.

Meanwhile, another local MGB owner had heard of Bob's exploits in Wallingford and asked him to repair his car. One thing led to another and soon Bob found he was spending more time working on customers' MGBs and less on the freelance design work that ostensibly earned him his living. He therefore set up BLC Engineering in four knocked-together, rented lock-up garages, again in Wallingford, during 1972. The business thrives to this day, from different premises in Wallingford, and Bob is proud of the fact that he has never had to advertise for work.

AWH was raced in Modsports until 1977, when Bob joined the BCV8s. In those early days he raced at Bentley Drivers Club and Peterborough Motor Club plus the annual MGCC race day at Silverstone. He often came up against the likes of Bill Nicholson and Barry Sidery-Smith. Bob recalls chasing Bill round Silverstone in 1975 and although he did not manage to beat him, they shared fastest lap which established a new record.

Bob, who ran the car in the BCV8 Modified Four-Cylinder Class, was classified second in the first year of the BCV8 Championship, having run neck and neck with eventual winner, Barry Sidery-Smith, for most of the season. He had a good day at Brands on 8 April 1978, when he forced erstwhile leader Bill Nicholson into a rare mistake and won the race. He also

*Bob Luff's V8 Roadster (96) leads the field at the MG Car Club Snetterton meeting in September 1997.*

recalls some good dices with Bernie Bowler and John Lodge.

Bob tested one of his early 1,860cc engines on the special tuning dyno at Abingdon, where it produced 136bhp, which the Abingdon engineers found most impressive for a non factory-built motor. By 1985, business was so good he had little time to rebuild his racer for the new season and, when he started to finish outside the top five, he retired and sold the car to Roger Osborn-King. Unbeknown to himself, Bob had started to build his new racer in 1986, when he started work on a damaged 1980 MGB that he had bought intending to repair and sell on. Accident damage apart, the shell needed a lot of work, the poor weld quality making Bob think that it was a 'Friday afternoon car'. Deciding to go the whole way, he bought the ex-works 3,500cc V8 engine from Rod Longton's car, took

it out to 3,900cc and installed it in the suitably strengthened shell of his project.

Bob had his first race with V8 power at the MGCC 1987 Snetterton meeting and has competed regularly with it ever since. However, in recent years, Luff has mainly raced four-cylinder MGBs in the FIA Historic Championship, for which he has built half a dozen cars for customers, which all carry discreet BLC Racing decals. He currently co-drives for Brian Lambert.

Bob says that, over the years, the BCV8 Championship drivers have become accustomed to measuring the severity of damage to their car following an accident, in 'kitchen's worth'. This apparently stems from one wife's comment suggesting that the money spent repairing the car could have bought her a new kitchen. Hence half a kitchen is a shunt but two kitchens represents a full re-shell!

## John Tadman

Given what happened to him during his first race, at MGCC Silverstone in 1983, it is surprising that John Tadman, whose involvement started with marshalling for the MGCC, was ever seen on a grid again. He drove his green V8, VPH 88M, to the circuit with two friends and a tent in the back. On lap seven of the first event of the day, he misjudged an overtaking manoeuvre at Woodcote, hit the railway-sleeper wall and ended up with a banana-shaped car. His friends opined that he would not be racing again, to which John replied that he had not really experienced enough to know if he liked it or not. Three weeks later the car was 'sort of straightened', he did his second race and decided that he did enjoy it.

Working on an agency basis for Unipart in Oxford, John was driving the same V8 to work, late in 1983, when he passed a Citron Yellow V8 displaying a 'For sale' notice. He memorized the number, rang the owner and later bought PCF 900M. Over the winter it became his competition car, which John raced in BCV8 Class B, MGOC and some Thoroughbred races from 1984 to 1997. Malcolm Beer built the engine with new Rover Vitesse components that John bought, via full time Unipart employees who were able to purchase parts at cost plus 5 per cent. It produced 192bhp at the wheels.

The first season with the new car saw John towing the racer behind his Green V8, which, despite two further attempts to straighten it – one by a jig manufacturer demonstrating their

*John Tadman's MGB GT V8 parked in front of his transporter, a converted 1955 Bedford Super Vega Coach.*

latest product to John's tame coachworks – 'still crabbed along'. It was later replaced. First outing in PCF was at Brands on 1 April 1984 exactly ten years after it was registered. The racer was developed and John moved up the Championship points, from seventh in Class at the end of 1984 to third in 1986.

Despite the outcome, John's most memorable race was undoubtedly Zolder in August 1991, when throughout practice and race he diced with the 'Unleaded' V8 of Robbie Shaerf. They were side by side coming into Jacky Ickxbocht on the last lap and neither would give way. John hit the high kerb on the outside, which launched his car into the air, and Robbie drove underneath him, before John finally rolled into retirement yards from the finish. Robbie had always intended Zolder to be his last race of the season, so sportingly offered John, black and blue with

bruises, the use of his car to consolidate his third position in the Championship.

John rested up for two days before driving his converted coach transporter to Zandvoort, whilst Robbie took John's crumpled car back to England on his truck. This well illustrates the great camaraderie amongst the BCV8 boys. John says that to him, 'weekends away racing were a great circus of people barbecuing and partying with the race itself an added bonus.'

## Steve Williams

Looking after Roger Osborn-King's road/race Lotus Esprit introduced Steve Williams to motor sport. The pair decided that a dedicated race car should prove more competitive and Roger knew that Bob Luff had a Class C MGB for sale. The idea was that Steve and Roger would share the

*Steve Williams (98) goes through Russell during the damp MGCC Snetterton meeting, August 2001.*

racer, but Steve was not convinced that MGBs could provide serious racing. However, a visit to watch the BCV8 boys performing at Mallory Park convinced him otherwise.

They shared the ex-Luff car from 1986 to 1991, allocating the races so that they both had an outing at each circuit. After the first season, they wanted more power and, over the winter, Steve converted to V8 specification and they raced in Class D from 1987. In 1989, Steve finished the year third in Class and Roger was eighth. After the 1990 Silverstone meeting, Keith Gurrier, who was looking to sell his ex-Colin Pearcy V8 and knowing Steve and Roger were still sharing a car, offered Steve a race in his V8, as he could not make the next round at Brands.

Having trailered both cars to the circuit, Steve put the Gurrier V8 on pole but retired with mechanical problems. He took both cars home, repaired Keith's and returned it to him. Steve would have two more outings in Keith's car, the second at Lydden where he enjoyed an exciting race with Malcolm Beer's V8. The pair were in close company for most of the race and on the last lap, Steve had two wheels on the grass as he tried to snatch victory on the finish line. He washed all the mud and Lydden chalk off and returned the V8 to Keith. When the race was reported in the following Thursday's *Motoring News*, Steve received a phone call from Mr Gurrier who was none too happy with his rallycross tactics! He was not offered the car again.

It had already become apparent to Steve that to stand any chance of winning the Championship (his best thus far had been a Class third in 1989) he would have to get his own car and do all the races. Malcolm Beer told him that the Terry Smith-built V8 Roadster that he had raced, before selling it to Tim Ransom, who had finished 1987 second overall and won Class D, was for sale. A deal was done and Malcolm delivered it on 30 July 1990, Steve's birthday.

Malcolm recommended that, as the car had stood, it should have a rebuild before Steve raced it. However, a problem with the original car meant that all it got was a change of oil and brake fluid before he took it out at Castle Combe. This Wiltshire circuit is Steve's favourite track, as there he first raced an MGB, led his first race and won his first race. He also secured his first outright Championship there in 1996.

His most enjoyable races have been against Malcolm Beer. They had a superb session at one MGCC Silverstone, swapping places three or four times a lap. Steve also recalls the time they took turns at passing each other round the outside of Gerrards at Mallory. Having finished second in Class D in 1991 and 1992, he was third in 1993, and won in 1994. In 1998, Steve founded Steve Williams Sports Cars and took a season out from racing to establish the business, which specializes in Lotus.

## Geoff Gear

Geoff Gear always thought he had it in him to race and, having been told that if you got an MG and joined the MG Car Club you could remove the hub caps and go out there, that's exactly what he did. In 1976, he bought a BRG Roadster, KAE 155E, and did a few meetings. The following year he was amongst the first drivers to sign up for the new BCV8 Championship. In 1978, he finished fourth in the Standard Class. He had an enjoyable race at Mallory on 6 June, when it started to rain as the competitors were called to the line. The cars on racing tyres scrabbled for grip, so along with Terry Osborne and John Carter, he found himself in a three-way battle for the overall lead and was delighted to finish third.

For 1979, he bought a brand-new rubber-bumper GT shell plus a rotten Roadster for running gear and set about building himself a fully modified V8. An electrical engineer, he worked for Phillips who had a well-equipped machine shop, and Geoff either mended the machinists' televisions in return for them fabricating him things, or used the lathes to make parts himself. He made solid suspension bushes and mountings for his special 1in anti-roll bar and turned bottom trunnions that could be used to adjust the camber angle.

*Three-wheeling through the Thruxton Chicane, Geoff Gear's V8 (96) is closely
followed by Paul Campfield's CV8.*

The rear suspension retained leaf springs with
anti-tramp bars on brackets to Geoff's design,
as were the turreted shockers. He built his own
adjustable pedal box, and utilized Franklin
front disc brakes with Rover Vitesse four-pot
callipers but made his own rear disc conversion.
A fabricated alloy adapter plate, bolted onto
the original axle holes, carried the Metro callipers, and Saab 99 rear discs were found that to
have the correct PCD. When he found the half
shafts bent under power, he had to put springs in
the callipers to prevent pad knock-back.

He bought a couple of Rover P6 engines
and assembled the first one himself after having
the parts professionally machined. This let go at
Thruxton as he changed down for Church,
Geoff joking that his V8 became a V12 in as many
seconds. The second engine was entrusted to
Swindon. Geoff initially stayed faithful to SU

carburettors, but after a couple of years he went
to a Holley 600 'Double Pumper' that required a
slightly milder cam. The main bearings wore
unevenly, which was put down to the block
twisting slightly, but provided they were changed
every season, it was no real problem. The red line
was set at 6,800rpm.

Geoff always told his helpers he found pit
signals superfluous, but at one wet Brands
meeting they could have won him the race. Cars
were coming off all over the place but Geoff kept
going, though his rear vision was nil because of
the spray. He knew that he was fairly well up and
decided that perhaps he could go a little faster
just in case there was somebody on his tail. He
spun to retirement in the Clearways catch
fencing on lap five, then discovered he had been
leading by almost half a lap.

One of his best outings was at Silverstone

where he qualified third, but in error was placed on the back of the grid, despite his protestations to the start line marshals. Really fired up, he made a demon start and went from last to third by the time he exited the first corner, Copse. He finished third behind Terry Smith and David Franklin. He ended 1982 third in Class. Geoff retired at the end of 1980 and the car is now raced by Roy McCarthy.

## Terry Smith

For many years, Bristolian Terry Smith, aka 'The Feltham Flier', had been hill climbing and sprinting all sorts of machinery, ultimately Repco Brabhams, but in 1980, David Franklin persuaded him to buy an MGB GT V8 and join the Championship. He entered the meticulously prepared car in Standard Roadgoing Class, winning every time out. He and David had taken their respective V8s to Aldon's rolling road and done back-to-back tests on six cam-shafts to find the one that gave the most power. There were mutterings that the car was not 'legal', which Terry fiercely denies but to prove a point, he

decided that he would build a full race V8 Roadster from scratch.

A pressed-steel MGB Roadster shell was purchased for £600 along with a £65 donor car for running gear. The racer utilized fibre-glass front wings and doors, a factory gearbox that reputedly came out of Tony Pond's rally TR8, and one of the first Quaife MGB LSDs. Initially, the car ran with a 3,900cc engine and always had a thick front anti-roll bar and lots of negative camber. To comply with regulations the leaf springs had to be retained, but anti-tramp bars and a Panhard Rod kept the back end in check. Despite trying telescopic shock absorbers, Terry raced with up-rated lever arms as he found they allowed the suspension to move through a more satisfactory plane. The car was always run in Terry's distinctive blue-and-silver livery.

Franklin, who owned the Huntsman Garage, had a customer in Switzerland who wanted a V8 engine which gave 290bhp, so they sold him Terry's and he used the money to buy and develop a 4,200cc powerplant for the racer. The Rover engine, originally built for a Formula 5000 car, was rebuilt using parts from Tom

*'The Feltham Flier'. Terry Smith driving his 1983 Championship-winning MGB Roadster V8 at Oulton Park in 1984.*

Walkinshaw racing, who were running the factory Rovers, and by using an enormous Holley carburettor it was developed to give phenomenal power. Based on a 1973 Rover 3500S block with a highly modified Rover Vitesse head, it had a compression ratio of 11:1 – of course five-star petrol was available in those days.

Terry competed in a total of thirty-six races with thirty-four wins and two retirements in the modified car – despite all the power, the V8 also proved to be quick in the wet. The oil pump broke at Thruxton and Walkinshaw recommended a Buick pump with a stronger, modified shaft and Motul oil. The other retirement was as the result of a broken drive-shaft on the start line at Donington, the shafts later being replaced with stronger, modified ones from a Ford Escort Atlas axle. Making a concerted effort to compete in every round of the 1984 championship, Terry won it outright. In 1983 and 1985, years when he also competed in other cars, he came second.

Colin Pearcy and John Lodge were his main rivals, Terry describing John as a good friend and someone you could confidently have a very close dice with. They only tangled once in what he describes as 'only a slight coming together' at the Cadwell Park Hairpin. He vividly recalls a race at Brands Hatch when, on entering Paddock Hill Bend, he heard a slight noise on his offside, he lifted momentarily and was amazed when the 1,460cc Modified MG Midget of local man Steve Everitt overtook him.

After a few outings in 1985, Terry sold the V8 to Malcolm Beer. Terry went on to compete in the International Supersports Cup, driving a Lola T70 and is now involved in the organizational side of the series.

## David Franklin

Having worked with cars all his life, David Franklin started competing in 1965 driving various Hillman Imp Sports belonging to his then employers Cathedral Garage, the Bristol Rootes Group dealers. In those days, you used the same car for hill climbs, sprints, PCTs, races and rallies. He left the firm in 1969, buying the Imp Sport, now a very modified example that had to be trailered to events. In 1970, David set up The Huntsman Garage in Westerleigh Road, Down End, Bristol, named after the adjacent Huntsman Inn. Over the years, using his Imp-honed knowledge of aluminium engines,

*David Franklin racing his 'wife's shopping trolley' at MGCC Brands Hatch 1976. The car was originally purchased for his wife to go shopping in and David still drives it on the road to all the events he competes in.*

*John Lodge's first MGB, RPP 914D, purchased as an MOT failure, avoids a 'moment' at Silverstone's Woodcote Corner in March 1979.*

he became an acknowledged expert on the Rover V8 power unit. Subsequently he looked after the racers of, amongst others, John Day, Chris O'Neill, Colin Pearcy and of course his good friend Terry Smith.

By now becoming a bit of a hill specialist, he sold the Imp and replaced it with a Vixen, Formula 4, again with Imp power, and in 1973 upgraded to a Formula 3 Ensign. In 1978, driving a March 772P, which he purchased direct from Robin Herd, David became the only driver in the history of the series to win both the RAC Sprint and RAC Hill Climb Championships in the same year.

In 1975 David bought his wife an MGB GT, one of the last chrome-bumper models, as a shopping car and put his own 8000 DF plate on it. In 1977, having been 'wound up to do so by Roy Ashford', David entered his first BCV8 race, at Brands on 4 December. Driving Deborah's absolutely standard GT, he won from pole position. This was a good day's sport, and he found the other competitors a nice bunch, recalling that Vic Smith, Vic Young and Ian Polley made him particularly welcome.

Seeing one of the last rubber-bumper V8s for sale at a good price in 1976, David, who always liked the Rover V8 engine, went into the showroom and bought it to replace the GT. The new car, which was blaze in colour, was again driven on the road by Deborah, whilst David used it for the odd race and a few speed events, when he was not competing in his other car. Having enjoyed his outings in the BCV8 series, he decided that he would seriously compete for the 1981 Championship. The engine was taken to Swindon, race-prepared and bored out to 3,600cc. Now a bit hairy for the supermarket car park, a Mini took its place as the shopping car.

Taking part in all rounds including sprints at Colerne and Curborough and Wiscombe Hill Climb, Franklin won every event outright, taking pole position in every race bar one, a wet Brands Hatch where he was just pipped by Rod Longton. Whilst his adversaries were using slicks, David, who drove his V8 to and from all events, had to use road-legal tyres. He ran on Kleiber V12 GTSs, later changed to tarmac-rally rubber from the same manufacturer. He took the crown and, on the way, broke seven lap records. The same year he was also doing well on the speed scene in his newly acquired McLaren CanAm car.

For 1982 it was back to the hills in the McLaren, but David still found time for two BCV8 wins and one second place. He still has the V8 and tries to give it at least one outing a year. Having moved from his Down End premises in 1998, David still runs Huntsman from a smaller workshop in the area.

## John Lodge

John Lodge, whose father used to work in the BMC Competitions Department, built a Class A car based on RPP 914 D, a rusty MGB Roadster. His first BCV8 outing was at Brands Hatch on 10 September 1978; he enjoyed it and over the 1978–79 winter upgraded the MGB to Road Modified and raced in that class for the 1979 and 1980 seasons, securing two class second and third places, finishing class fourth in the 1979 Championship. 1980 was not such a good year, a big off at Castle Combe wrecking the shell, and putting John in hospital with two broken ankles and a broken jaw, before the season had hardly started.

Having recovered, John bought another rusty wreck and decided to go for the Fully Modified Class. Keeping his hand in by doing a couple of sprints in his road MGB, he started building his new car. John was well on with the project when his friend Bernie Bowler, an engineer, asked John if he would like to buy his left-hand-drive yellow Class C car, on which he had been promised first refusal. John decided to pass on the offer but had a hand in selling it to his publican, Roy Clayden, who again promised John first refusal should he sell. Roy, who converted the car to RHD, only did one season, 1980, finding, as John suspected, that racing and running a pub were incompatible. John then took it on, while his original project found a new owner in Richard Walden.

Bernie had engineered the car well and John soon got to grips with it in the 1981 season. It was still running on 6½in by 14in Minilites with Dunlops. Having set pole by 1.8 seconds, he savoured his first outright win at Oulton Park

on 25 July, after a three-way tussle with Terry Smith and Bill Nicholson. Terry went off at Cascades on the penultimate lap, then John managed to get past Bill and by 'weaving a bit' stayed ahead to the flag, winning by one tenth of a second. Nicholson was not impressed with the way he had lost the race and was expressing his opinion as his adversary was being interviewed on the line. That year, John went on to take two more race wins, six seconds and two thirds. He was second in class in the Championship to the V8 of David Franklin and also took one hill-climb win as well.

The 1982 and 1983 seasons did not go so well: overheating, eventually traced to badly corroded waterways in the block, made the engine unreliable. Then John had a run-in with Barry Sidery-Smith at Cadwell, which unbeknown to the team, bent the Salisbury back axle. It was only after two broken half-shafts and a damaged diff that the axle was stripped off and the dented case spotted. The 1982 tally was one outright and two class wins, one third, two lap records and a pole. He was sixth in class and fifteenth overall in the Championship.

The following season produced two race and four class wins, one class third and four lap records in the Championship, plus two class wins in speed events and an outright win in an invitation race. John, an HGV driver, had worked a six and a half day week for seventeen years, driving car transporters delivering new cars all over the country. It was good money, but it gave him little time when things went wrong with the racer. For 1984, he decided to concentrate more on the racing and took a job within the same company working nights collecting cars from the factory and transporting them to the compound fifteen miles away.

The pay was not quite so good, but it gave him the days to work on the car; he was going for the Championship. Finding good 14in slicks had always been a problem for MGB racers, so John changed his wheels for 16in diameter 9½in wide Revolution split rims, which gave a wider tyre choice. Donna, his other half, just happened to be Tom Walkinshaw's secretary, and one of his

*The John Lodge full race MGB, in large rear-wing guise, on the way to a win in the MG Invitation Race at the 1984 Sun Free Race Day at Brands Hatch. Such appendages were subsequently banned from BCV8 Championship cars.*

companies, DART, had the tyre contract to supply the British Touring Car Championship. John tapped into this supply and was almost ready for his title challenge. Ongoing development, such as using a VW Golf alloy radiator, had pared the B's weight down to 15½cwt (790kg), and the 1,950cc engine was on full song; there just remained the question of down force.

Pooling ideas with Richard Walden, who had now completed and was successfully racing John's project car, they developed rear wings. Having made various types, they booked a test day at Silverstone. Each took turns in lapping the circuit with different wings, which had strips of tape stuck to them, whilst the other leant over the pit wall and photographed the tape in the airstream. Not exactly a wind tunnel, but it worked.

Both Lodge and Walden came out for the 1984 season with huge wings on the backs of

their cars. Whilst such devices were frowned upon and discouraged, the Championship regulations did not contain a specific ban on them. By now, the organizers had put the full race V8s in a separate class, so John took nine wins in the separate Class for Fully Modified Bs. He admits the opposition was not too strong, so he still pitted his own car against the V8 boys for outright victory, which he managed on three occasions. John won the 1984 Dutton Forshaw BCV8 Championship and, in addition, took one hill climb and one invitation race win.

After the final BCV8 round at Oulton Park, John and a number of other competitors, including Colin Pearcy and Doug Smith, booked in for an extra night at the Swan Inn at Tarporley to celebrate. The party went well, but it was the barman who ended up the worse for wear, thoughtfully hung by his collar from a hook on the door by the intrepid racers. The next morning, John came down to breakfast to find his MGB bonnet the centrepiece of the hastily re-arranged floral display at the foot of the staircase. It looked rather fetching with the blooms poking through the large radiator aperture. John took it in good humour and Hayden Sore (Smith's mechanic) and Andy Biswell (Pearcy's mechanic) commanded new respect for their flower-arranging skills.

The 1984 BCV8 round at Zolder was another notable outing, given that John, who had again secured pole, stalled at the start of the warm-up lap. Starting from the back of the grid for the twelve-lap race, he executed thirty-five overtaking manoeuvres, including lapping some drivers, to chase Terry Smith over the line for second place.

The best year ever was 1985: not only did John have sponsorship from Moto Build (the car now in their livery), he also retained his crown – but he really had to work for it, having some cracking races with Martin Dell, who had by now set up the ex-Mike Chalk White Tornado to his liking. Martin and John were battling at the front of the pack in virtually every race.

John's best race of all time was the BCV8 round at the GM Dealers Silverstone Race Meeting. Smith and Colin Pearcy disputed the overall lead in their V8s, but Lodge and Dell were neck and neck for third overall and the Class lead. For eight of the ten laps they swapped places twice a lap. On one tour they lapped a back marker at Copse, one passing him on either side – the unfortunate driver did not know what to do and spun off. From laps one to nine, John, who was ahead at the final bend, took a wide line through the original Woodcote Corner, which allowed Martin to take the tight line and get past again on the straight. At the end of lap ten, John went in tight, forcing Martin to go wide, and thus John was in front at the flag. The victory was slightly soured as both were called up before the Stewards for the lapping manoeuvre at Copse, though in fairness the back marker admitted neither car touched him and that he spun of his own accord. To complete the day, John took the lap record at 1min 1sec.

The tally that year was three outright race wins and nine Class wins, plus one hill climb class win and one invitation race win. Unhappy with the rule changes for 1986, which effectively banned rear wings overnight, John left the series, selling his car to restaurateur and sixties pop star Don Fardman. He continued racing a Royale RP6 Gp 6 Sports Car in the HSCC series and did half a season in the 1988 Honda CRX Challenge, finally hanging up his helmet in 1990. He now runs his own courier company and is still indirectly involved with racing, given that he does a great deal of contract work for Williams F1 and firms that service motor sport.

## Dr Mark Ashworth

Like fellow BCV8 racer Rod Longton, Mark Ashworth, often referred to by race commentators as 'The Flying Doctor', has to fit his racing around his life as a busy GP. He started competing in 1978 with an Oulton Park sprint on 29 July followed by a Baitings Dam Hill Climb on 1 October. The following year he was driving the same car, a bracken-coloured MGB, HRB 989N, in the Standard Class of the BCV8s. He put the car on pole the first time he raced at the MGCC Silverstone meeting, a totally wet day that one of the magazines reported as 'the Silverstone Regatta'. Mark finished third behind the Midget of John Vernon and Paul Richardson's MGB, to record a second in Class.

At the end of his first season, Mark finished second in Class to Richardson. To round off the year, he joined Richardson, Paul Campling, Peter Chowne, Peter Sullivan and Adam Wiseberg in an MGB team, which took part in the 750 Motor Club Six-Hour Relay Race at Donington Park. They finished thirteenth on scratch, sixth on handicap.

In 1980, HRB was re-sprayed metallic purple with a red stripe, to match the racing B of Mark's cousin John Hewitt, who prepared both cars. Despite Mark's chassis-bending off at Oulton Park, the team fared well, with Mark and John scoring equal points at the top of the Standard Class points table. On count-back of wins, Mark

*Mark Ashworth has a tyre-clouting moment at Donington. He kept the engine running and was able to continue the race with only minor body damage.*

took the Class and was second overall, whilst John came second in Class. He continued in the BCV8 Class A for the next two years.

'Ethel', the legendary John Hewitt MG 1100, saw action in Mark's hands in the 1983 MGOC series, which resulted in some places, but also a Brands roll that required a new body shell. The following year he raced in the same Championship and BCV8 series, driving John's former Modified MGB, 9521 MG. The arrival of children had caused Mark to consider retiring. This meant forgoing racing for a while and driving his white MGB GT V8, YBF 284M, in the Norwester Speed Championship. With its Franklin engine the car was quick and Mark won the Championship in 1985 and 1986, when he ended the season with a hat-trick of victories. He

also had five outings in his 'wife's shopping' Metro Turbo – after he broke the diff on the hill at Baitings Dam, he took it back to the dealers and claimed a new one under warranty!

Mark invited his new sponsor to watch him race at Castle Combe. Arriving after practice, he was most impressed to learn that his man had secured pole position. Imagine Mark's embarrassment when he put the car off in the ditch at Quarry, the first corner, on the first lap. The company boss must have seen the funny side of it though, because he continued to back the car for a couple more seasons.

Next, the recently inaugurated MGCC Cockshoot Championship caught Mark's attention; he liked the idea of racing the B with an aero screen. He competed in the series on and off between

1984 and 1992 and won it five times. During this period the B changed from purple to blue, to red with blue-and-white stripes, and windscreen and aero screen were interchanged, along with wheels and tyres, depending whether it was a BCV8 or Cockshoot round. In 1990 the car was converted to full race BCV8 (Class C), in which Mark won the Class in 1992.

The change in BCV8 regulations, which would allow V8s with limited modifications to race within the same Class as the full race four-cylinder cars, coincided with Mike Entwhisle asking Mark to share the drive in his MGA Twin Cam at the Eifel Klassik. They finished third in the GTP category and Mark was hooked on Historic racing. Rod Longton and Barry Sidery-Smith were also competing at the Eifel and experienced engine problems with Rod's car after a dented sump had knocked the pick-up strainer off and starved the bearings of oil. The

two doctors did a deal and Mark became the new owner of AJN 826A, purchased 'as seen'.

Mark got Graham Miller to rebuild the unit for AJN and embarked on a very successful period with it, racing in FIA events as well as having some outings in the BCV8 FIA Historic Class. The five-bearing engine, which came with the car, was later replaced by a more authentic three-bearing version, though it did take nearly two years to source all the competition parts. He won the Class in 1996 and took the 2001 HSCC Classic Sports Car Championship.

The Nürburgring 1,000 Kilometres Revival race in 1997 saw AJN out in the hands of Ashworth, Entwhisle and Paul Rodman. A hose clip gave out on the warm-up lap and Paul had to dash into the pits, steam pouring from the bonnet, for a new one to be fitted. This meant he started the race from the pit lane, the last car away. But other than routine fuel stops and one

*Mark Ashworth races his Roadster, in which he won Class C of the 1992 BCV8 Championship.*

*'The White Tornado' cornering on the limit in the hands of creator Mike Chalk. The rear wheel-arches were amongst the widest seen on a four-cylinder car.*

set of tyres, they did not have to put another spanner on the MGB throughout the eight hours. They won the Class and came home eighth overall; and Mark regards this as his most prestigious race finish ever.

Another interesting outing was the 2001 Spa Six Hours when Mark shared his car with Martin Richardson and Graham Jones. For them it turned out to be the Spa 5 hours 55 minutes! Two laps from home, the thread that retains the oil filter broke and the engine pumped its oil out just as Mark was braking at the end of the fastest straight on the circuit. Despite this, they still finished thirty-fourth from the eighty-eight starters. Mark has recently bought a TVR 1800S, which, after a rebuild by John Hewitt and a full development programme, will replace his MGB in Historic events.

## Mike Chalk and the White Tornado

A long-time MG competitor and larger-than-life character, Mike Chalk started his racing career in Midgets during 1975 and owned and raced several examples until 1998 when he won the modified Midget Championship. During the late 1970s he bought and raced Rob Haig's ultra-light MGA in Modsports. The car had previously been banned from the MGCC MGA series for being too radical. It had a very rapid three-bearing MGB engine, which had a very special cylinder head that had been 'stitched up' on more than one occasion following blow ups. A third 'write off' accident at Lydden Hill made Mike decide that the A could not be rebuilt again.

Having looked at the BCV8 technical regulations, Mike decided that, as he had the engine, gearbox and running gear from the Haig's MGA, he would build himself the ultimate four-cylinder, Fully Modified MGB. This was based on a £50 body shell, with a few bits on it, purchased from Canvey Island in 1981. Other than needing minor welding round the spring hangers, the body was fairly sound, but to reduce weight all the outer panels were chopped off. Mike made his own glass-fibre front end, doors, wings and boot lid, and what was to become known as the 'White Tornado' began to take shape.

The front suspension was an inboard rocker-arm set-up, and incorporated the ex-Haig shock absorbers and disc-brake assemblies, as did the rear. Mike fabricated radius rods and a Panhard Rod to locate the rear axle, and mounted the shockers as far back on the axle as he could. The engine and gearbox were dropped straight in.

The first race was the MGCC 1982 season opener at Brands Hatch on 25 April, so Mike was out testing the Wednesday before; but he blew a piston as the result of an inherent distributor-advance problem. Following a hasty rebuild, Mike duly practised on the Sunday and put the car on Class pole. He led the early stages of the race but had to retire when the engine again let go.

He won from pole next time out at Castle Combe, despite the seat mountings breaking loose, which Mike likened to driving whilst sitting in a rocking chair. He says at this stage he was getting the odd comments from the V8 drivers whom he beat and an undercurrent of suspicion resulted in the organizing committee requesting an eligibility check following Mike's next Castle Combe victory. The car was jacked right up in the air and Bill Nicholson crawled in, over and under it and pronounced it 100 per cent legal.

Mike was to have mixed fortunes at Snetterton later in the season. Whilst leading the race on 11 July, he picked up a puncture three laps from home that handed the race to Geoff Gear's Modified V8. Mike continued to the finish but also lost places to Terry Smith, Colin Pearcy and Barry Sidery-Smith. On 1 August everything went according to plan when he put the Tornado

on pole and won the race after beating Gear by 19.8 seconds. Both drivers broke the existing lap records for their respective classes, Mike at 1min 18.8sec, 87.58mph (140.95km/hr), whilst Geoff's V8 record was 1min 20.2sec, 86.05mph (138.48km/hr), a testament to just how competitive Chalk's four-cylinder car was.

More wins followed but not many dices. This, combined with disillusionment with the way the car had been received, led to Mike selling the Fully Modified B to Anthony Binnington before the end of the season. Despite not completing the year, Mike still won his Class in the Championship and finished third overall to brothers John and Bill Hewitt. The origin of the car's name is down to Glyn Swift at Swiftune. He used to call Mike 'Chalky White', and because he would always dash into their workshop on his way to somewhere else, they accused him of being a tornado. One day when Mike collected the car from them, it had 'The White Tornado' on the bonnet.

Anthony Binnington campaigned the Roadster in the BCV8s for the latter part of 1982 and the 1983 season, and in fact put it on pole during his first outing in the car at MGCC Autumn Brands on 12 September; but he had an off in the race whilst dicing with Terry Smith for the lead. Despite further engine problems, Anthony enjoyed success in the car before selling it to Martin Dell, who was extremely competitive in the car, from 1984 to 1987. He finished the year second in Class in 1985 and 1987. Subsequently raced by Neville Mariner and Warwick Banks, Perry Godrez now competes in it.

## Colin Pearcy

The subsequent owner of many of the 1960s ex-works MGBs and one GTS, Colin participated in the BCV8 series from 1982 to 1987 in his Damask Red V8 GT, 5402 MG. Starting out as Road Modified, the car ended up in the full race class with a Huntsman 3,600cc engine.

In 1982, he came first in Class 4 of the championship and was second in Class the following year. 1984 proved a mixed bag. Colin finished

*Colin Pearcy's V8 GT, 5402 MG, in full race form with the Huntsman 3,600cc, 320bhp engine at Brands Hatch in 1983.*

second at Silverstone after a good tussle with John Lodge, who had to settle for third. Pearcy had a big accident at Snetterton on 17 June whilst dicing for the lead with John Lodge and Terry Smith. On lap eight, he tried to get past Terry to head the field as they came into Russell and the pair collided. Colin's car was spun round, launched and flew into the clump of trees just beyond the pit lane where it came to rest. He had managed to steer it away from head-on contact with the end of the Armco and, as the result of this, walked away from the impact relatively unhurt. Terry and John continued, but next time round, Terry came to a halt at Coram with a deflated front tyre and the race was stopped. The result was declared as at the end of the lap prior

to the accident, so Terry was awarded the win, with Colin second and John third.

Colin enjoyed a good outing in the V8 on the Brands Hatch Grand Prix circuit on 23 July 1986. He put the car on pole and easily won the race from Tim Ransom's V8 Roadster. He certainly laid any Snetterton ghosts at the Norfolk circuit on 6 September, when he led the race from start to finish, with Ransom and Malcolm Beer coming home second and third.

In 1986, Colin sold his GT to Keith and Anna Gurrier and moved into the British Touring Car Championship driving an MG Metro Turbo for Austin Rover, winning his Class in 1987. He then transferred his affections to Historic racing. The Gurriers had various outings in the V8:

Keith finished 1988 third in BCV8 Class D and was fourth the next year. In 1991, MG Midget racer Graeme Adams bought and competed in the car. Anthony Binnington and Barry Sidery-Smith are set to race it in 2002.

## Paul Campfield

Paul Campfield raced PKX 194H, a Class B MGC GT, from 1980 to 1984. Looking for more power, he decided the large engine bay of an MGC Roadster shell he had would be ideal to install a V8 in. Furthermore, the extra room would allow the exhaust manifolds a gentler curve and thus not restrict the gas flow. Paul debuted his unique CV8, LCM 253G, in 1985. His best race was at Castle Combe in spring 1988. As first reserve he started from the back of the grid and made his getaway, half on the grass, to make up ten places before Quarry. He then worked his way through the field and took Malcolm Beer on the last lap, exiting Quarry to

win the race and driver of the day award – the first of four overall wins he would take in LCM.

However, his most memorable race has to be Kirkistown on 25 June 1988, when he had what is generally regarded in BCV8 circles as the most spectacular accident in the history of the series. Whilst leading the race Paul had a moment, hit the sleepers at 120mph (193km/hr), then barrel-rolled eight times. Dr Mark Ashworth, who was also racing, stopped to assist. Despite being in a bad way for three months, Paul recovered. Barry Sideways is convinced the Ridgard seat helped save him. LCM, not as damaged as expected, was rebuilt and Paul raced it again in 1990 and 1991. For 2002, Andy Young will race the car as a six-cylinder MGC once more.

## Robb Gravett

Having won the 1985 MGOC Championship in his Robbco 1,500cc Midget, Robb Gravett, a former National Motocross Champion, moved

*Robb Gravett waits for his race in the Silverstone assembly area during the 1986 MGCC meeting at the circuit.*

to a Road Modified MGB. He campaigned this in both clubs' championships in 1986, when he was crowned BCV8 Champion and took the MGOC Class. The B had been built by Michael Hibberd for the 1983 BCV8 series and he drove it to second in Class in 1984. Deciding the car should handle better, Michael asked Robb to test it for him and come up with some ideas, which he did. However, he decided he would much sooner buy the car and race it himself. Eventually Hibberd agreed, replacing the MGB with a V8.

Robb modified the suspension and won first time out in the BCV8 Mallory Park race on 30 March, beating Rae Davis and Barry Sidery-Smith. He had six further wins in the series, finding that his main opposition came from Sidery-Smith and, on the faster circuits, Hibberd. He enjoyed an early race tussle with Barry at Brands on 13 September, where Robb went on to win. The season also produced six MGOC wins. Robb took the car to Zolder and ran it on slicks in the Fully Modified Class where, despite no other tweaks and having to ballast the car by lashing a tool box to the boot floor, he was on the pace and placed in the race.

In 1987, having sold the MGB to Colin Pearcy, who converted it to an Historic car, Robb moved on to Production Saloons. Driving a Sierra Cosworth, he took the Monroe and Uniroyal Championships. The following year, he joined the British Touring Car Championship in a Rouse RS 500.

## Phil Thompson

Over the years of the BCV8 Championship, many drivers have come out, raced on a shoe string for fun and then retired. Phil Thompson is one such driver. He drove his Roadster, PKX 118H, in the series from 1982 to 1984, picking up the Albion Saunders award for the best newcomer at the end of his first year. During this period, cars were developing quickly, and Phil admits that most of the tuning parts on his car were other people's cast-offs.

He recalls driving over to Rod Longton's house with his wife to buy a straight-cut gear set. When he handed over the money, Rod looked at Phil's wife and asked her if it was the week's housekeeping. Entering into the spirit, she replied that it wasn't a week's but a month's. Phil later did some JDC long-distance races and his last outing was at the 1987 Oulton Park Four Hour relay, where he was a member of the winning team. Phil is now Championship Co-ordinator for the MGCC Anglia Phoenix Championship, for which MGBs are also eligible.

## Roy McCarthy

After racing his red road MGA during 1970, Roy McCarthy built the first of his yellow cars, 1817 PX. It was based on a £30 wreck he bought from a barn, complete with roosting chickens. He moved on to a Healey then a Chevron B8 before going back to his A, on cost grounds, in 1975. Roy won the MGA Championship six times between 1971 and 1982, when he sold the car to Martin Shaw. He had a noted off, in his new MGA, built from a chassis and a pile of bits, at Brands Hatch Paddock Bend in March 1985, breaking the top two vertebrae in his neck. Undeterred, he designed a new roll bar whilst he was in traction, and was out in the rebuilt car the next season.

In 1988, Roy moved into the BCV8s in MGB Roadster GAP 159C, which had been given to him as a festering project by his doctor. In 1989, he took Class B and was joint overall Champion with Peter Hall. He also won the MGA Championship. The following season he drove V8 RFD 200M ('Zoom') in Class B and, despite a difficult season, drove it to second in Class, taking the V8 Register Trophy. This gave him the taste for V8 power and he swapped 'Zoom' with Richard Horn for his damaged Class D example, which Roy rebuilt over the winter. It was not all plain sailing but Roy did manage a couple of wins during 1991 and 1992. However, the running costs of a full house V8 saw him back out again in GAP 159C.

In 1994, he did both the BCV8 and Goldsmith and Young Thoroughbred Championships, doing fairly well in both. In 1995, he won both series outright, a testament to his preparation and the resulting reliability. Roy savoured a Castle Combe victory when he won the Thoroughbred race from fourth on the grid, beating the three Aston Martins that had qualified in front of him. Having disposed of two, he passed David Haines at Old Tower to take his victory.

In 1996 Roy was back out in the V8 and he enjoyed some good races with Malcolm Beer and Steve Williams, finishing the year second in Class D to Steve. He was third in 1997, but the next year's endeavours were brought to a premature halt following a big off at Mallory Park. The MGA was quickly brought out of mothballs to resume its winning ways, until 2000.

Roy was back in Class B of BCV8 in 2001 and came fourth in Class behind his sons Spencer and Russell. That year he also took the Thoroughbred Championship once more, the series going down to the wire at the last round at Cadwell Park, where Roy had to beat Colin Jones' MGA Twin Cam to win. Starting from pole, Roy was surprised that he out-dragged the two Healeys behind him to lead into the first corner. Keen to stay ahead of them, he outbraked himself into Park and spun down to twelfth. With everything to play for, he drove like a man possessed and won the race with Colin second, and thus took the crown by the narrowest of margins. During his first twenty years of racing, Roy brought home almost 200 trophies.

*This close-up shot of Russell McCarthy's BCV8 Class A car (20) shows just how standard a Standard Class car appears. Behind, Brian Cakebread (9) looks for an opening.*

*Spencer McCarthy tries the inside line on Andy Holmes at Mallory's Hairpin.*

## Spencer and Russell McCarthy

Roy's sons followed him into BCV8s, Russell in 1995 and Spencer in 1996 when he shared his brother's blue Class A Roadster, which he raced in Thoroughbreds. Their mother, Pam, BCV8 Championship Secretary, suggests they have motor racing in their genes. Russell took 1996 third in Class, the youngest driver in the top ten and was third again in 1998. For 1999, Russell's blue car, LVF 302L, originally built in the McCarthy workshop from the shell that Geoff Pyke destroyed after colliding with an Aston, was converted to Class B. He won first time out in it, at Silverstone, and went on to take the Class B Championship in 2001.

Roy built Spencer's green Roadster, VTD 601L, from a former Peter Collis car and Spencer finished fifth in the 1997 Class A Championship. 1998 was his year: he won the first race of the season, with the fastest lap, and went on to repeat this ten times, to take maximum score and win the BCV8 Championship outright: a twenty-one-year old taking the series in its twenty-first year. The car was converted to Class B for 1999 when Spencer took the Class Championship, a feat he repeated the following year.

2001 was the first season Roy and the boys raced against each other in the same Class of the same Championship – Thoroughbreds. Close racing was the order of the day throughout the year. At the final round at Cadwell Park, the McCarthys scored a unique 1, 2, 3, Russell winning the race, followed home by Spencer and Roy – the first time a family had shared the podium.

*A trio of McCarthys. L to R: Spencer, Russell and Roy, at MGCC Rockingham July 2001.*

## Peter Hiley

After winning the MGCC Midget Champion-ship for the fourth time, in 1989, Peter Hiley was looking for a different challenge and decided that he would build and race a Road Modified (Class B) BCV8 car. As the basis of his new project he bought a written-off, 1978 rubber-bumper car that had stood in the corner of one of his cus-tomer's premises for ten years. The car was re-shelled and ultimately very little of the original vehicle was used. The back axle was changed for the Banjo version, the overdrive gearbox dis-carded and the front suspension changed for a chrome-bumper set-up, for easier lowering.

When overbored to 1,950cc, the original block revealed impurities, so Peter used an easier-to-get-hold-of Marina 1800 block second time around. Despite other drivers saying they were not so good, Peter has continued to use them. He has always built his own engines with the help of his brother, Andrew. The white car, FYG 11T,

*Peter Hiley in action at Oulton Park, April 1995.*

made its debut at the start of the 1990 season; but Peter found that he struggled throughout, and finished the year sixth in Class.

Hard work over the winter produced an engine with more power for the following season. After five second places, at Brands (two), Silverstone (two) and Donington, Peter took his first MGB win at Snetterton on 30 July 1991, after withstanding ten laps of pressure from Ray Armstrong, who nearly had him at Russell on the last lap. Peter would frequently come up against Ray in future races. Four more wins, including a hat-trick, netted Peter the Class B crown for 1991.

Garage owner Peter Hall, with whom Hiley had enjoyed many a dice, took the overall and class championship in 1992, beating him by fifteen points. Hiley, who ended the year second in Class B, joint fourth overall, still took the laurels at Donington Park, Oulton Park and Snetterton. He invariably finished second to Hall at the other races. He described the season as a constant game of 'catch-up': Hall would win three or four races, whilst the Hiley team strived to squeeze more power from their engine. As soon as they recorded a win, Hall would be even quicker next time out and take another series of victories, almost as if he had a tap on the block to turn up the power. This process continued throughout the season.

Hiley reigned supreme in 1993 and 1994, taking two successive Championship wins; highlights were 1993 victories at Cadwell Park and Snetterton. Peter continued to run his B, which won him a total of twenty-eight races, in the series, but in 1996, raced Doug Smith's MGC GT. Peter excelled in the wet but found the car heavy in the dry. He recorded one win, two seconds and six third places and won the David Cleverdon Trophy for the highest-placed MGC. He recalls a meeting at Brands where he was leading the Class when oil leaked from the rocker box onto the manifold, with the car trailing a great cloud of smoke every time he went round Druids. He looked out for the black flag, which he was eventually shown on lap eight. Questioned why he had not come in earlier, Peter suggested that he only had two laps to go and no one else in the Class looked like getting past him. To which the official responded that no one could see to overtake him!

## Geoff Mansell

Accountant Geoff Mansell was well known in his MGA, which he raced from 1982 until 1990, when he wrote it off. He won the Modified MGA Championship in 1984. In 1988, having formed Mansell McCarthy Motorsport with Roy McCarthy, he built a pink Road Modified

*Geoff Mansell's Roadster just lifts a wheel as it corners.*

MGB, HCH 604D, in which he finished fourth in the 1988 Class B Championship. The following year, it was converted to full race specification and Geoff was second in Class.

Roy suffered a slipping clutch at a weekend Silverstone meeting and, as he had the higher points score, it was agreed they would swap cars for the race. Having discovered there were no spare numbers, they decided to change boot lids, doors and bonnets, thus the respective cars would show the correct numbers. Geoff raced Roy's yellow car with pink boot bonnet and doors whilst Roy had a pink car with yellow panels. Roy and Barry Sidery-Smith both went off at Luffield Two, Barry got going again, only to be black flagged for a flapping wing. Geoff went on

to win – though in reality the object of the exercise had been for Roy to maximize his points.

Geoff's best race was at MGCC Silverstone on 26 May 1990, when he and Mark Ashworth went the whole race hardly a coat of paint apart, with Mansell taking victory. That year he ended up second in Class but was third overall and won his Class in 1991. For 1997 and 1998 the car was converted to full race V8 spec. The car is now raced by Piers Townsend.

## Warwick Banks and Suzie Hart-Banks

Having not raced since 1965, former BMC works driver Warwick Banks was surprised to be

*Warwick Banks (95) smiles as he looks in the mirror and sees he has a few feet advantage over the pursuing pack of other V8s.*

*Suzie Hart-Banks (85) keeps her father Warwick Banks (95) at bay. Pilgrims, Lydden Hill 1995, where she went on to win.*

asked to compete in a Caterham whilst visiting America in 1988. He was even more surprised to win, especially as it was his first race on slicks. Having returned to England, Colin Pearcy invited him to have a Snetterton outing in 8 DBL, which he owned at the time. Warwick could not wait to get back into motor racing and joined the BCV8 ranks in 1992.

He bought a California MGB, which his firm, Warwick Banks Handling, Land Rover suspension specialists, built up to an FIA spec car, AEW 610A. Warwick put this on pole at the 1996 Coys Festival. Warwick (Championship Chairman from 1992 to 1995) and his daughter, Suzie Hart-Banks, had several BCV8 outings in this car and would go on to compete in the series driving other examples of the marque until 1996.

In 1994, Gerry Richards, who had built a full race V8 for the series, went abroad to work and offered Warwick use of the car, which he gladly accepted. For the WBH Team V8s, 1995 was a good season; Warwick, in the 350bhp Richards car, and Suzie, driving a 250bhp Class C example, finished the year second in their respective Classes. Suzie only failed to win her category by one point. They competed in a combined total of forty-three races, chalking up fifty-three Class and overall places, neither car failing to complete a race, and took a number of lap records along the way.

Deciding to stay in America, Gerry shipped his V8 out there and later invited Warwick to drive it for him in the MG race at Watkins Glen, which he won. He was told by the local drivers that they run 15 to 1 compression ratio, though they do use 110 octane fuel to achieve this.

## Peter Collis

As a twelve-year-old schoolboy, Peter Collis drove a car for the first time. Sitting on his father's lap, he took the family 2.4 Jaguar round an old airfield whilst his unconcerned mother sat in the back knitting. Always interested in cars, owning a ZA Magnette endeared Peter to MGs and he vowed that one day he would race one. In 1990, after twenty years of playing county-level squash, he purchased HGC 515K, a Harvest Gold GT, from Frank Thomson, who had finished tenth in Class A in 1989.

Peter was keen to get the obligatory novice cross off the back of his car as soon as possible and during the 1990 season competed in thirty-four BCV8, Cockshoot and Phoenix Championship races. He met a fellow competitor in the Mallory Park paddock just before his first practice session, introduced himself as a new driver and fished for some advice. But the other driver told him he was new too, and walked away Peter later discovered he had spoken to the very experienced Roy McCarthy who was not giving anything away.

Despite starting from the back row of the grid, he enjoyed that first race even more than he expected, especially as he took one place and finished second to last. Like many, he was hooked. Part way through the race he sensed this rumbling vibration and thought he had a problem with his car, but he was then lapped at 140mph by Malcolm Beer's fearsome full race V8 and the noise was gone. That moment determined his resolve eventually to race a V8.

The following year, he concentrated on Phoenix and BCV8 rounds, removed some trim from the car and went to Peter Burgess for an engine. For Oulton Park he fitted a tailgate with a drastically pruned inner panel, and taped the windscreen surround to make it more aero-dynamic. Barry Sidery-Smith quietly told him he could race that day but must have a complete tailgate fitted next time. He had a close race with

Brian Halford's 'Grey Whale' MGC, got two wheels on the grass at Lodge and went backwards into the tyres.

He sat on the bank after the incident looking at the car and working out in his mind how he could effect temporary repairs in time for the next day's race at Cadwell. Just as he had worked it out, another car went off at the same spot and ended up on top of the bonnet of his GT. There was now no way he could repair the car overnight, but he was still determined not to miss the race.

Arriving home at 6.30pm, he rang Dave Parker at Mech Spec and asked if he could borrow his car for Cadwell. Dave agreed but added that they had driven it back from a Castle Combe race with no brake pads. Peter collected the car and fitted the new discs and pads which had been left in the boot, grabbed a few hours sleep and set off to compete at Cadwell. Meanwhile, Keith Williams repaired the GT, using fibreglass front wings and Peter looked forward to his next race, a two-day meeting at Donington Park. Having put the car on the front row, he stored his tools in the back, sheeted it up and went home.

The following morning, he arrived, uncovered the car and lined up in the assembly area for his race. Going into Redgate for the first time, he felt a slight tugging on his safety harness; it was even worse going through the Craner Curves, and there was also a graunching noise coming from the back of the car. When he reached the Old Hairpin, Peter managed to glance round and to his horror saw his petrol can, tool box and spare wheel sliding about in the back. He pulled into the pits and did not contradict the marshals who assumed he had mechanical problems. Later in the paddock, Keith agreed to be his mechanic at future events, a role he still fulfils.

From ninth in Class at the end of 1991, Peter was third in 1992 and the following year, his last with the GT, he finished second and also took the Cockshoot Entune Cup. HGC 515K went to David Parker, who won the BCV8 Class Championship with it in 1995. Andy Bentley now races this GT in the Cockshoot Cup.

For 1994, Peter bought a supposed racing Roadster from the classified columns of *Safety Fast*. He collected the red-and-white example VPT 606L from a pub car park in Buckinghamshire and took it straight to Malcolm Beer for a rebuild, and commissioned another Burgess engine. This car netted Peter the 1994 Phoenix Championship and Class plus second overall in the BCV8s, losing the outright Championship to Peter Hiley by just one point. In August he sold the GT to Tony MacIntyre who used it to become 1999 and 2000 Standard Class Hill Climb Champion.

Lew Bergonzi decided to move from BCV8 to Porsche racing in 1995 and offered Peter his road-going MGB, 7662 PF, which he immediately bought. Whilst his original Roadster was quick, Lew's flew and he won first time out in it, after a hectic dice with Grahame Davis at Snetterton. More wins followed and paddock talk suggested Collis was only winning because he had Bergonzi's old car. Peter brought out his own MGB again and found that the extra confidence gained in Lew's B now enabled him to

drive his better, and he won in that as well. He alternated cars for the rest of the season and ended the year Class third. Lew did not enjoy Porsches and persuaded Peter to sell him back his MGB at the end of the season.

In an effort to combat the reliability problems that drivers in the Fully Modified Class were having with their four-cylinder engines, Malcolm Beer had suggested a change in the regulations for 1996. In Class C cars, 3.9-litre V8 power units with restricted modification were to be allowed, and Peter was tempted to take this route to his long-term ambition of racing a V8. He bought Hugh Pelling's former GT after being impressed with the shell's deep-purple respray when he inspected it in Dave Price's workshop. Malcolm Beer completed the rebuild. Peter ended the year second in Class C.

For 1997, Collis decided that he would convert the car to Class D and race it as a fully modified V8. He altered the body and suspension to suit, and used the now fully developed engine from the Rover Vitesse, which he had also been racing in the Slick 50 Saloon series. He has

*First time out in SXG 909, Peter Collis in his V8 Roadster at Cadwell Park. These extremely powerful cars can be a real handful in the wet unless the throttle is treated with the utmost respect.*

*Brian Cakebread (6) comes under pressure at Silverstone; his son Andy (34) follows.*

not looked back. Peter took the outright Championship in 1999 and won Class D from 1999 to 2001.

As well as the purple GT, RPH 636L, he also races SXG 909, a barn-find Roadster. Keith Williams, who won the 2001 Standard Class Hill Climb Championship in an MGB, rebuilt SXG as a V8 Roadster and painted it in the same purple livery. Both cars are now equipped with John Eales 4.1-litre engines with cross-bolted block, Arrow forged rods, billet crank with 5½in flywheel and forged pistons. Producing 330bhp at the flywheel, the engine is driven through a Cosworth gearbox. Peter has recently acquired Rod Longton's former V8, 3373 MZ, from Dave Tilley. Following a rebuild and a 4.6-litre engine, he is set to race this abroad in 2002.

## Brian and Andy Cakebread

Garage proprietor Brian Cakebread started racing the ex-Richard Wilson Class A MGB, NVG 312L, in 1994. He came second in Class A in 1996 and 1997, the year he was one of the drivers who became known as the 'A Train'. Brian, Andy Holmes, Russell and Spencer McCarthy and Graham Willard were the front runners in Class A that year and after each race start, the five cars would invariably end up nose to tail an inch apart, hence the name. He took the Geoff Mabbs Trophy for the most heroic drive at Castle Combe.

His most satisfying race was at Mallory Park in 1998, after the amount of negative camber on his car had been queried and vilified. Brian

*This MGA Twin Cam was the works pre-production car later sold to Development Department employee John Sharp, who successfully raced it with an 1,840cc MGB engine during 1963. Here the 'MGA/B' is driven by Colin Pearcy, who restored and competed in it in recent years.*

*Don Bunce cornering well-known racing MGB, JYH 770D, at Snetterton in 1967.*

*Jean Denton sometimes raced her MGB open with a full-width aero screen. Here she runs it in this form at the 1969 Mugello Race.*

*The British Army/Stena Sealink Historic Racing Team: Bob Birrell (76), Peter Everingham (54) and Fred Boothby (177) at Castle Combe in 1987.*

*Alistair Crawford's highly modified hill-climb V8 Roadster at Gurston Down in 2000. The engine produces 400bhp, so the car needs its large rear spoiler to help keep the back on the tarmac.*

*An aerial view of Rod Longton's 'Deja Vous', the car built in 1994 and painted in the same livery as his original BCV8 car. It is now owned and raced by John Palmer.*

*This rare 1964 MGB Coupé Berlinette is even more unusual given it has a continuous racing history in France since the mid-1980s. Jean Michael Viestroffer competed in it, as shown, from 1995 to 2000.*

*Despite a top speed of around 160mph (260km/hr) on British circuits, the racing V8s in the MGCC BCV8 Championship can still circulate in close company. Malcolm Beer (97) leads Peter Collis (74) and Tom Stewart at Snetterton.*

[above] *John Tadman's MGCC BCV8 Championship Class B V8 (62) was well known for its unique Gulf Oils livery.*

*Roy McCarthy's Saturn Yellow MGB (70) fends off Peter Hiley's white car (53) at the Mallory Park Hairpin during one of the many BCV8 dices they had during the 1994 season. All Roy's racing cars have been this colour.*

[above] *One of the many Class D V8 battles between Peter Collis (84) and Tom Stewart (1). Peter keeps Tom behind as he rides the Snetterton kerbs.*

*Mike Breedon (66) drove his factory-built V8 to BCV8 Championship races for fourteen years and now uses it for continental rallies. Here he leads Dave Saunders and Barbara Lambert at Snetterton in June 1997.*

*The MG Owners Club series provides really close racing: Jim Baynham (3) closes the door on Alan Yeoman (32) at Thruxton in March 1996.*

*Huw Taylor (5) leads the MGOC pack at Croft in 1997.*

*Phil Walker's MGOC-spec MGB GT negotiates the Thruxton Chicane in 1994. Following a subsequent accident, the car was re-shelled as a Roadster.*

*Barry Sidery-Smith has owned and raced the ex-works 1965 Le Mans car, DRX 255C, since 1973.*

*Jerry Trace (63) Elva Courier and Max Cawthorn (21) MGB, racing at MGCC Silverstone June 2001.*

*Dr Paul Scott corners his Gilbern GT1800 at Wiscombe Park Hill Climb in 1982.*

The unique WSM MGB in the pit lane at Rockingham Motor Speedway July 2001, when Anthony Wilson-Spratt raced the car, designed and built by his father Douglas, for the first time.

[right] Two very different MGCs dice during an MGCC BCV8 race at Brands Hatch. Chris O'Neill (97) is in a Fully Modified (Class D) car whilst Ian Young (60) drives a Road Modified (Class B), road-legal example.

[below]A unique occasion: 1992 MGCC Silverstone, the only time all six examples of the GTS appeared together.

*V8s at play: Peter Blackbourn (95) and Keith Gurrier (100).*

*MG Car Club Silverstone meeting June 1980. Terry Osborne (10) fends off the barely visible Bob Luff, whilst the author's Midget (23) makes up a little ground in the Modified MGB and Midget race.*

| MG Car Club BCV8 Series Overall Champions | | |
|---|---|---|
| Year | Driver | Class |
| 1977 | Barry Sidery-Smith | 1 |
| 1978 | Peter Malimson | 2 |
| 1979 | Paul Richardson | 1 |
| 1980 | Neville Mariner | 3 |
| 1981 | David Franklin | 1 |
| 1982 | John Hewitt | 2 |
| 1983 | Terry Smith | 4 |
| 1984 | John Lodge | 3 |
| 1985 | John Lodge | C |
| 1986 | Robb Gravett | B |
| 1987 | Tony Price | A |
| 1988 | Tony Price | A |
| 1989 | Peter Hall and Roy McCarthy | A and B |
| 1990 | Nigel Petch | A |
| 1991 | Malcolm Beer | D |
| 1992 | Mark Ashworth | C |
| 1993 | Peter Hiley | B |
| 1994 | Peter Hiley | B |
| 1995 | Roy McCarthy | B |
| 1996 | Steve Williams | D |
| 1997 | Tom Stewart | C |
| 1998 | Spencer McCarthy | A |
| 1999 | Peter Collis | D |
| 2000 | Adrian Hall | D |
| 2001 | Andy Cakebread | A |

qualified fifth in Class, and during the race, got up to second, behind Lew Bergonzi. Coming up to the hairpin on the last lap, he managed to get up the inside, turned into the corner, momentarily closed his eyes as the gap was so tight and when he opened them, he had come out of the corner in front and managed to hold the place to the line to take a Class win. He was second overall and 1999 Class A Champion.

Brian bought DVX 298G from Barry Sidery-Smith at the end of 1999, and used this to move up to Class B, which has been a steeper learning curve than expected. Meanwhile his son Andy took on the Class A car and capitalized on both the years of development they had put into it, and his natural driving talent, by winning fourth time out in it, at Snetterton on 5 August 2000. He won his Class in ten out of his eleven races in 2001, taking the Championship outright.

*Another winner's garland for 1988 Championship winner Tony Price.*

# 6  The MG Owners Club/ BARC Championship

Peter Palmer and Dave Jarvis were two very early members of the MG Owners Club, which Roche Bentley founded in 1973. Towards the end of 1980, Peter was racing an MGA and Dave had done a couple of BCV8 races in his road MGB, 4955 MG. They got together and suggested to Roche that the club ought to have its own race championship and he agreed. It seemed unfair to them that the spectators paid money to come and watch drivers, who had themselves paid to take part in the races. One of the ideas was to arrange for the drivers to receive some start money.

## The Formation of the Championship

As the MGOC was not on the RAC MSA list of motor clubs, Peter Palmer approached Mark Poynton at the BARC, whom he knew, to ask if they would take the series on board and promote it. There was initial resistance, as there were already other championships catering for MGs, but Dave and Peter convinced them it could work. They also pointed out that there was a huge untapped source of spectators in the growing ranks of MG Owners Club members. The BARC finally agreed and a five-round series was put together for 1981. Roche said that the MGOC would fund the start money and race trophies for the first season.

The two founders were joined by Jim Baynham, another novice driver, and he recalls the three of them along with Roche sitting in a Hampstead pub during the winter of 1980 sorting out the regulations. It was decided that it would be a combined series for MGA, MGB, MGC, MGBGTV8 and Midgets/Sprites to race

in two classes: A, Standard and B, Modified. The main difference between their regulations and those of the MGCC BCV8 Championship was that slick tyres would not be allowed: all cars had to run on treaded road tyres. The series ran in this format until 1988 when the Modified Class and all V8s were dropped due to rising costs, the owners of some of those cars then defecting to the BCV8 Championship.

The first BARC/MGOC race was at the BARC Brands Hatch meeting on 7 June 1981; despite Dave and Peter's optimism just eight cars took part. Dr Spike Milligan won in his modified MGA, beating Charles Buchanan in his Modified MGB by 15.2 seconds. John Hewitt and Jim Baynham were third and fourth in their Standard MGBs, taking first and second in that Class. Still, all drivers received start money and nearly everyone got a trophy.

Since those early years, the series has gone from strength to strength. In 1987 the front-wheel-drive Metros, Maestros and Montegos were admitted, whilst in 1990 it was decided there was no longer a place for the MGC in the series, again on cost grounds. There were now two classes for 'Standard' cars: Class A, rear-wheel drive Midgets and MGBs and Class B, front-wheel-drive MG saloons. Certain MGAs would also be eligible. In 2000, MGFs were admitted to Class A, but from 2001, they had their own Class.

## Jim Baynham

Jim has regularly competed in an MG every year since that first race in 1981, though he did defect from MGB to Midget, then Maestro from 1983 to 1986. At the end of his first season, he won the novice class in both the BARC/MGOC and MGCC BCV8 championships. His BRG Roadster, KAE 155E, was originally raced by Geoff Gear, Neville Marriner and Julius Thurgood, then Moto Build ran it in the Willhire 24-Hour Race at Snetterton before it was sold to Jim. After two years, Jim decided to build a Midget, which he considered would be more competitive, and sold KAE to Ian Harwood.

Ian ran it in the series in 1983, coming fourth in the last round of the year at Oulton Park. New owner Les Smith competed during 1985 and part of 1986, after that it spent most of its time in his garage. Meanwhile, Jim destroyed his Midget at Mallory Park and, fancying a try in FWD, replaced it with a Maestro, which he also wrote off at Mallory. During this period, Les had

been along to spectate and whilst he intended to race Jim's old B again, never seemed to get round to it. Following his Maestro's demise, Jim rang Les and asked if the car was for sale. He was told that while it was not on the market as such, he would be prepared to sell it back to him, which he did in 1987. Jim has raced it every year since. Between 1981 and 1999 he competed in 155 BARC/MGOC races in his three different cars.

Still to win the Championship, Jim has driven the highest-placed MGB four times: 1994, 1995, 2000 and 2001. He came close to taking the crown in 2001 but an engine failure at Cadwell put paid to his chances. Although he has had lots of Class wins over the years, Jim remembers his best race as the one which gave him the first outright win. It was the final round of the 1994

*Is it a bird? Is it a plane? No, it's Jim Baynham. Despite literally flying through the chicane, Jim still won this race at Thruxton in October 2001.*

*Another competitor from the early days of the MGOC championship, Dave Jarvis raced his modified MGB until 1980.*

season, the SUNBAC meeting at Silverstone on 29 October, when he beat David Kimber's MGB by 1.25 seconds after seven hectic laps. Roy Clarkson and Alan Yeoman, both in Bs, were third and fourth. Jim set the fastest lap of the race at 1min 30.21sec. Following thirteen years of trying, it was a moment to savour. Unfortunately, as it was the last race of the day, on a cold autumn afternoon, there were not many spectators left in the grandstands to share his moment of glory.

## Dave Jarvis

A BCV8 round at Snetterton in 1980 marked the race debut of Dave Jarvis in his Mallard Green MGB, 4955 MG. Having got into his stride, he put the road car aside and built up a red, modified car with a green stripe, HWB 775J, which he campaigned in both the BCV8 and MGOC series. He was a competitor in the MGOC Championship from 1981, when he raced at the second round at Thruxton and finished fourth, until he retired from racing in 1985.

His other best outings were at Snetterton in 1983 where he claimed third place, and he was

fourth at Brands later that year. After his own race at Thruxton on 18 September 1983, when Dave finished fifth, he lent BCV8 competitor Rod Longton his prop shaft so he could compete in his race later in the programme. Throughout this period, Dave was organizing the calendar, liasing with the drivers at meetings and arranging the end-of-year dinner dance, as well as preparing and racing his own car.

He recalls a good dice with Jim Baynham at Snetterton; they were going through the Bomb Hole side by side when Jim had a spin. Realizing that he was about to hit his good friend's driver's door head on, Dave put his car sideways and they collided door to door, avoiding personal injury but not damage to the cars.

In a Norfolk hotel the night before a Snetterton race, Dave had retired early to get a good night's sleep, but his fellow competitors decided that he did not need one. He was aroused by a group of drivers literally bursting through his bedroom door and was concerned that the damage would get them a bad name, but the lads assured him it had all been taken care of. Down in the bar they had engaged the proprietor in conversation and asked him how much he thought one of his bedroom doors was worth. When he told them he did not know, they had pressed him for a figure and he had eventually suggested £50. Whereupon one of them shouted, 'We'll take number six please,' and slapped £50 down on the bar.

Phil Rule, a police officer, who would become involved on the organizational side of the championship in 1986, was also present, though not aware that the damage had been paid for in advance. He started to read the riot act till all was revealed. The rest of the weekend saw him endure the nickname of 'Inspector Damage'.

Having sold his modified car, Dave still has his road MGB, 4955 MG, and in addition owns four pre-war examples of the marque, including the late Geoff Coles' supercharged J4 spec J2, which itself had a distinguished racing history.

## Grahame Davis

During the first fifteen years of the Championship, Moto-Build, the company that Grahame ran with his brothers Rae and Darryl, was a pivotal part of the series and introduced over fifty competitors to it. Their uncle, Cliff Davis, raced Tojeiro MGs in the 1950s. Grahame has only ever worked on MGs since he left school and first started competing in ZA and ZB Magnettes,

which he drove in stock cars from 1968 to 1970, taking the Championship in 1969 and 1970. He admits his first ZB was a rust-free ex-Rhodesia car that was really too good to race. The start and prize money he made racing stock cars, usually three meetings a week, paid his mortgage.

Grahame's introduction to circuit racing was in 1980, when he and co-drivers Rae Davis, John Trevillian and Julius Thurgood brought MGB, KAE 155E, home third in Class in the first Willhire 24-Hour Race at Snetterton. He competed again the following year, this time in a V8, NEE 565M, but retired it as the result of an accident. Graham went on to race that car in the BCV8 and MGOC Championships until 1983. That was a season of close encounters with John Hewitt (one or other of them won every MGOC race that year). Grahame did nine rounds, recording four wins, four seconds and one retirement.

An Old English White MGC Roadster, UYO 762F, replaced the V8. It had been bought for £100 as a shell and boxes of bits, and, as ever, was only completed the night before its first race. Grahame used it in 1984 to win Class A and finish third overall in BCV8, whilst racing a Midget with the MGOC. The following season he modified the MGC, came second in BCV8 Class B and won seven out of the eight MGOC

*Grahame Davis bought this MGC Roadster (123) as a body shell and boxes of bits, and turned it into a competitive MGOC championship car. Here he leads one of the Midgets, which other drivers told him his C would never beat.*

races he entered. The car was driven to and from all meetings, usually in excess of 100mph and Grahame's wife, who accompanied him, claims that it was the only car she felt safe in whatever the speed.

Given the C's reputation, he drove it cautiously during his first wet practice session, wondering if he were mad to be out there. When the times were published he was second fastest; come the race, he made a good start and won. Grahame took the 1986 Owners Club Championship outright. He won nine of his ten races and finished second to Jeremy Lindley's Midget in the last round at Thruxton. He also won his Class in the BCV8s. Grahame raced a Group N Cosworth Sierra from 1987 to 1990, when he took the championship.

Darryl Davis had built up a multi-coloured MGB Roadster, MGC 303D, for the 1991 MGOC Championship. He did four races, his best finish being fourth at Cadwell Park, and then offered Grahame a drive to see if he could get on better with it. His first outing was at Snetterton, where all the Midget drivers told him that, since he had been away, it was their cars that won most of the races. They had to eat their words when he won, leading home the Midgets of Terry Farman and Andrew Storer. Grahame went on to take four more victories and one second place in his remaining outings that year. It was even better

*The Moto-build MGB GT V8 of Grahame Davis battles it out with Barry Sidery-Smith's similar example (15) at Silverstone.*

in 1992 when he chalked up nine wins from nine races! He continued in the series, on and off, until 1996 and still recorded wins.

Grahame suggests his closest MG race ever was one he had with Gerry Marshall at Snetterton, where, both in Bs, they did the final three laps of the race virtually side by side. They lapped Anna Gurrier, one either side, whilst going through the Bomb Hole. Grahame ran low on fuel so Gerry just beat him to the line.

## John and Bill Hewitt

Manchester MG specialist John Hewitt was another MGB competitor to race in the MGOC series during the early years, taking part from 1981, when he won all four races he entered and became the first Road Going Class Champion, until 1988. In 1984, he did just four of the ten rounds, which resulted in one win and three third places. John also sprinted and hill climbed in MGBs; he was MGCC Norwester Speed Champion in 1981 and 1982.

John and brother Bill had their best year in 1983 when, with a tally of six wins and three second places from nine outings, John won the Championship outright and took the Modified Class. Driving his standard car, Bill scored five

wins, three seconds and a third to come second overall and win his Class. On 28 April 1985, John had the honour of recording the greatest margin of victory in the history of the series, when he beat Mike Hibberd at Cadwell Park by 45.7 seconds.

The Hewitts continued to race Bs, Midgets and even a purple MG 1300 known as 'Ethel' in the Car Club BCV8 and Cockshoot Cup series; John has also done a number of FIA Historic races in an MGB.

Bill started his racing in 1981, driving an Austin A35 in Classic Saloons, on the basis that if you can drive one of those quickly you can race anything. Apparently, the way to get one to handle is to lower everything as far as it will go, then put 700lb (315kg) springs on the front. From 1982 to date, Bill has regularly competed in both the Car Club and Owners Club series. He turned up for the first MGOC round in 1982 and found that, because his name was Hewitt, people expected him to be good. He half lived up to expectation, putting it on pole, but got punted off at the first corner in the race and finished seventh.

Having got that over, he went on to finish first or second in the other eight rounds he competed in. During 1982, he did a total of thirty-two races

*The John Hewitt Team cars, which won their respective classes in the 1983 MGOC Championship. John's Modified car is on the left, and Bill's Standard version right.*

*John Hewitt's Standard Class MGC (40), as raced in 1987.*

in the MGOC, BCV8 and Classic Saloon Championship (driving the A35) and won twenty. He took his Class in both the MG Championships and came second in Class in the saloons, after missing some rounds that clashed in order to race the MG.

The first round of the 1983 season, at Donington, was excellent. It rained in the lunch break and, standing in the gents just before his race, as one does, Bill, slightly concerned about the track conditions, asked the Formula Ford driver beside him if he had raced yet and if so what the track was like. In a heavily accented voice, the other driver said that he had been out and the track was OK. Based on this Bill gave it his all, won the race and much impressed his new girlfriend, who was attending her first meeting with him. The name of the Formula Ford driver who gave him advice on the track conditions? Ayrton Senna! Afterwards in the bar, Gerry Marshall congratulated Bill on a good win, which impressed the lady even further.

Bill won the race featured in the 'Battle of the Bs' video that Tony Price made at Silverstone. Having had practice problems, Bill started thirteenth on the grid and was intent on making up places during the race. Price lost it on the second corner and the whole field scattered in avoidance. Out of the mêlée, Bill found himself in third place behind Gerry Marshall. He went on to win the race, but was disappointed that the tape showed very little of his car, with the person who did the commentary very casually mentioning that he had won.

## Richard Horn

After an initial year in the Standard Class in 1983, Richard Horn upgraded his car to run in the Modified Class, where he competed until 1987. During 1983, he blew up the engine and, after Oselli had 'stitched' the hole in the block, he kept it as the basis of his engine in future years. It has been suggested it was so quick because the fracture had relieved all the stresses in the block. In 1984, Richard had seven wins, one second and one third place from the ten Owners Club races he did and took the Championship outright. His main opposition came from Robert Nettleton's Midget. Richard found that, if he could get in front off the line, he could usually hold him at bay through the corners and pull away along the straights.

During 1986 and 1987, he raced in both the MGOC and MGCC championships but found twenty-six races a year a bit hectic. At one 1986 Mallory Park meeting he was competing in races for each Championship. In MGOC, you could run with an aero screen, but for MGCC, cars had to have full screen and hood, which meant swapping them over between the practice sessions and races. During the second event, he suddenly heard a creaking noise, then noticed the screen was moving; they had not done all the

bolts up. He finished the race but never admitted to anyone why he had to slow in the closing stages. In 1987, five wins and three seconds netted him highest-placed MGB in the Owners Club series.

Richard concentrated on Class C of the BCV8 Championship in 1988, when he won the Class and finished the year second overall. For 1991 he moved to Class D in a full race V8 that he built round a scrapped rubber-bumper GT bought from Richardsons of Staines. Richard finished the year fifth in Class but retired after a few races in 1992. Roy McCarthy now races the car.

## Nigel Petch

Spectating at Mallory Park and Snetterton with his father honed Nigel Petch's interest in motor racing and, having served his apprenticeship at

*1989 Champion Nigel Petch (27) on his way to winning the first-ever motor race at the newly opened Pembrey Circuit in his MGB Hive MGC.*

Vauxhall, he was set to make his career in the motor trade. Meanwhile, a £40 MGB had replaced Nigel's Rover 2000 as everyday transport and he was breaking the odd MGB for spares to keep his own going, selling off surplus parts to defray the running costs. Calling in to Sharpes of Wisbech, the local Austin Rover dealers, to enquire about an MG in the showroom, Nigel got talking to the manager and, as the result of this chance meeting, landed a job as salesman. The twelve months working there provided him with valuable experience in all aspects of running a garage business.

In 1982 Nigel and Sandra Petch founded 'The MGB Hive', initially selling cars, then looking after cars for customers. In 1986 the business had expanded to such an extent that they moved to their current premises at Marshalls Bank, Wisbech. In 1985 Chris Hatcher, one of the Hive's increasing band of customers, asked Nigel to build him a racing B, so Nigel decided to build two and have a go himself.

Nigel raced his Standard Class, red Roadster, UFL 988H, in the series from 1985 to 1987, finishing fourth in his third race, at Cadwell Park in 1986. He scored his first win in the final round of 1986 at Thruxton, having finished second there earlier in the season. In 1987 he did not finish outside the top five all season, taking one win, three seconds and three thirds. Used to setting fastest time in practice, he was perturbed to be pipped by the Maestro of Darryl Davis, so, encouraged by his wife Sandra, he built himself a Maestro for 1988 and won the Championship in it.

Still yearning to race a rear-wheel-drive MG, Nigel built up his well-known silver-and-red MGC Roadster, 654 DXE, for 1989. In this car he had many a dice with the Davis brothers, recalling a first corner tangle with Grahame at Oulton Park, where he went on to beat him. That year, he recorded two wins, four seconds and six thirds on the way to winning the championship for the second year running.

The MGOC declared MGCs ineligible to race from 1990, so Nigel, who regarded his example as a competitive car that he liked to drive, moved over to compete in the MGCC BCV8 series. He won his Class and the 1990 Championship outright. He raced in the Rover 216 series from 1991 to 1993. Nigel and Sandra still retain 654 DXE, which is now back in road trim.

## Mark Garner

A collector of MGs, Mark Garner did some karting, which he found expensive, then took his wire-wheeled GT along to an MGOC racing open day and decided this form of motor sport was for him. His father also attended and borrowed Roadster WDJ 978M from Nigel Petch to drive round the circuit. They bought this car and converted it into Mark's racer, which he campaigned in the series from 1987 to 1992.

Beer of Houghton modified the cylinder head and helped with the engine, whilst Mark, who had served an engineering apprenticeship, did the body and chassis. During the first two years, when he was really learning the ropes, Mark raced along with Nigel Petch and Chris Hatcher as the MGB Hive Team, and in 1990, his brother in-law's butchers, J.H. Bradshaw of Huntingdon, provided backing. 1989 was a bad year, with two consecutive non-finishes early in the season as the result of accidents. The second, at Oulton Park, saw Mark avoid a spinner, who then bounced back onto the track and T-boned his car. Side by side in the ambulance on the way to the medical centre, he recalls asking the other driver if he was injured. In response to the negative reply he expressed the opinion, in the heat of the moment, that it was a shame he wasn't.

It took the rest of the year to repair the car, so Mark only had one complete race that season. He bought a second-hand front for £20, drilled spot welds and cut the old front off, chalked out on the garage floor where the replacement should go, then welded it back together. It all worked out and in 1990 he enjoyed his best season, the highest-scoring MGB at the end of the year. By now he had learnt the little tweaks, like filing the camshaft woodruff key to advance the timing, and machining the front suspension

*Over the years, the Owners Club series catered for all models of MG. Mark Garner (30) shows that the rear-wheel-drive MGB often had the upper hand over the front-wheel-drive saloons.*

bushes to get a little negative camber. To combat the falling octane rates of pump fuel, he mixed it with a little aviation fuel. The overdrive, operated by the switch in a Triumph Dolomite gear knob, worked on second, third and top gears.

His best race was round ten at Snetterton, where the drivers performed in front of the Anglia Television cameras for their programme 'Wheels'. Mark was on the front row, just one hundredth of a second off pole position. Early in the race, he got nudged into a spin and fought his way back to fourth place on the final lap. Coming into the last corner, he managed to get alongside Andrew Storer's Midget and just headed him over the line to take third place. Chris Stocks, the race winner, and second-placed Richard Bennett were the men to beat that year.

A change of job saw Mark retire in 1992. He says that, as well as the racing, the MGOC series was a very social thing. Most drivers would arrive the evening before, set up their caravan or tent and then join in the barbeque, where everyone enjoyed themselves.

## Sean Valentine

A rolling shell and lots of cardboard boxes of bits purchased from a Birmingham lock-up garage in 1994 formed the basis of Sean Valentine's racing MGB GT. It took him a year to build up the car to what he believed to be racing spec and he had his first race at the Thruxton-hosted, second round of the 1995 Championship. This fast track is hardly ideal for a novice driver's first race; a dropped valve in practice and a spin into retirement during the race convinced Sean that he had a lot to learn, and that is exactly what he did. At the end of that first season the car was rebuilt to a higher spec based on the year's experiences.

Throughout his time in the series, Sean had many a dice with fellow MGB driver Huw Taylor, and the pair developed their driving skills and moved up the grids together. Following the rebuild, Sean's GT, originally white, was resprayed Java Green, which has now become the Valentine racing livery. He remembers the double-header round at Ireland's Mondello Park in 1996. He finished fifth in the first race of the weekend but second time out it was wet; he managed to come home fourth and savoured beating Jim Baynham for the first time.

1997 saw Sean's maiden pole position at Silverstone on 8 March, with a time of 1min 18.13sec, set on the last lap of practice. Next time out he had his first podium place after a good battle with the Midgets of Terry Farman and

*Sean Valentine corners his GT on the kerbs at Snetterton in 1999, the year he was highest placed MGB in the series.*

Mick Mercer at Castle Combe on 31 March. The three of them pulled away from the rest of the field and crossed the line within 0.91 seconds of each other.

On 22 August 1998, he notched up his first win at Oulton Park, beating his old sparring partner Huw Taylor. He and Huw were on the front row of the grid and Sean managed to get away first; three corners into the race, he looked in his mirror and saw no one – there were red flags at the fourth corner as there had been a pile up behind. Sean managed another copy-book start and, after ten hectic laps of side by side racing with Huw, he crossed the line to win by 0.98 seconds. This was followed by another victory next time out at Cadwell Park on 13 September, when he beat the Midgets of Julie Clark and David Rees.

Valentine had an excellent 1999 season, chalking up another win at Oulton where he again beat Taylor, this time by 0.194 seconds, seconds at Donington and Silverstone, thirds at Snetterton and Anglesey, and four fourth places. He ended the year second in the series and best-placed MGB. Wanting to get away from the Midgets and race in an all MGB environment, he has now modified his car to compete in Class B

of the BCV8 and Thoroughbred Championships, where he again scores top five places.

## Huw Taylor

In 1994, Neil Taylor rang Jim Baynham expressing an interest in the Championship and asked if he knew of any Midgets for sale. Learning that Neil was over six feet tall, Jim suggested that he would probably be better off in a B and pointed him in the direction of Mark Garner, whose car was up for sale. Within days, Neil was the new owner of MGB Roadster WDJ 978M. Assisted by his son Huw, he fettled the car, which had stood around for a year, before taking it out in three rounds of the 1994 Championship – twelfth at Mondello Park was his best placing. Toward the end of the following season, Huw had passed his driving test, completed his ARDS course to obtain his competition licence, and was keen to have a go himself.

Following in father's footsteps, Huw's first outing was at Mondello Park, where he came thirteenth in one race and matched Neil's 1994 twelfth place in the other. However, his lap times were quicker and it was decided that he would henceforth become the team's driver.

He competed in three more races that year; he did not finish in two and came home twelfth in the other. He and fellow novice driver Sean Valentine would become friends as well as on-track rivals, and as their experience grew, would crib each other's ideas for making their cars go faster.

Huw managed to get out for seven races during the 1996 season – seventh at Mondello Park proved to be his best outing. For 1997, the bodywork was rebuilt and strengthened by Ray Downes. Huw, now working for L. H. Owen, was building his own engines and, as a result, his name was moving higher up the results sheets. He had a good third at Silverstone, where he beat Phil Gladman, and finished the year with two fourths and a fifth place. A winter rebuild of both car and engine, and a few more tweaks, produced an air of optimism for the 1998 season.

The second race of the year, at Snetterton, saw Huw on the podium for the first time after he finished third behind the Midget of Peter St Barbe and Phil Walker's B. He also smiled when he saw that his friend and rival Sean Valentine had finished ninth. The first visit of the year to Mondello produced a fourth, but back there later in the season he again savoured a podium third. The one he really remembers was the final round of the season at Donington, when he beat Phil Walker to record his first win. It was a very close race between Huw, Phil and the Sprite of Ian Johnson; less than one second covered all three cars at the finish.

All the stops were pulled out for 1999, with the rebuild carried out in even greater detail. Other than one retirement – round eight at Thruxton after the car was launched on the Chicane kerbs and landed on Julie Clarke's Midget – he did not finish outside the top five all year. The season produced no wins as, in Huw's word's, 'when Terry Farman was out in his Midget, he was unbeatable'. However, he did take seconds at Angelsea and Oulton Park, where Sean slowed through Knicker Brook and forced Huw to go for the brakes, unsettling the car and allowing his rival to get away. Both laughed about it in the paddock afterwards. Whilst they often traded paint, they were always confident to race in close company because, as great off-track friends, they trusted each other implicitly.

The pair went to the final round at Donington Park on equal points. Farman was already the runaway winner of the Championship, but the two MGB drivers were to slug it out for second spot. After a hectic race, Huw came third, eight-tenths of a second behind his friend, so he ended the year third in the series.

The pair entered and won both the Moto-build 1000 two-driver one-hour races at Snetterton. They drove Huw's car one year and Sean's the other. In 1999, Huw was so confident of winning that he booked a holiday the week before the race, on the strength of his share of the prize money. Having been successful and the cash collected, the pair went off to divide it before joining their friends in the bar. In response to demands to buy a round, Huw had to get his dad to bail him out, as he had conveniently left the prize money in his tow car.

It was decided that, to win the Championship, he needed to be driving a Midget, so the MGB was put up for sale, finding a new owner in Tony Roberts. The search for a Midget proved unproductive, so Huw ended up buying a BMW 318 to race in the Kumho Tyres BMW Championship. After a learning year in 2000, Huw won the series in 2001 and is due to defend his crown in 2002, driving an M3 in Class A.

## Phil Walker

There have only been three years out of the last thirty when Phil Walker has not raced, and one of those, 1981, saw him try his hand on two wheels – trials riding. Starting in karts during 1972, he moved to MGs when he bought his trusty white MGB GT, HMH 394K, in 1982. Following a few sprints he had his first car race at the MGCC Silverstone meeting in 1983. Over the last twenty years, he has driven the GT in MGCC and MGOC series, run two V8s, one in the BCV8s the other in the Anglia Phoenix Championship, gone back to karts and had two seasons in Classic Formula Fords, where he claims he has some unfinished business.

Early on in his MG racing, when he was still driving the GT to circuits, Phil had a race at Oulton Park on Saturday and was due out again at Cadwell Park on Sunday. He had an off at Oulton that bent both front wings and broke the headlights. He followed his friend's camper van and trailer on the journey from one track to the other, tucking in really close to the trailer as it got dark. On arrival at Cadwell they turned in, then got up at dawn and woke the rest of the paddock whilst they attempted to hammer the front of the MG to something resembling its original shape. Thanks to tank tape, the broken headlights were repaired and stuck back in their holes. Phil got his race.

Phil's first appearance in the BARC/MGOC series was at the final round of 1986 at Thruxton, where he finished seventh. He did not appear on the MGOC grids again until 1994, when he did seven rounds and was a midfield runner in his self-prepared car. He was back in 1997 when in his words he 'decided to do it properly'. Tony Price of T & L Autos built him an engine and did some other tweaks on the car. Phil contested every round, came second at Snetterton and Brands, won the last race of the year at Donington and finished third in the Championship, the best-placed MGB.

His best ever racing moment also came in 1997, during round eight of the MGOC series at Thruxton. That year, the Midgets of Terry Farman, who would go on to take the Championship, and Mick Mercer were the cars to beat. Mick was leading the race, closely followed by Terry and Phil, who came barrelling through in hot pursuit. As he followed the Midgets into the Chicane, they both took a wide sweeping line and Phil thought 'thank you very much'. He straight lined his GT over the kerbs, passing Terry in the first part and taking Mick in the second to lead the race as they crossed the start/finish line.

Unfortunately, the pounding from the kerbs had put the GTs tracking out, which induced terrible understeer, and the two Midgets got back in front again, but Phil held on for third and his first ever visit to the podium. After the race, former MGB works driver Warwick Banks, who had been watching, congratulated Phil on his move in the Chicane, which just about made his day. He was seventh next time out at Silverstone but following that he had thirteen consecutive podium places over the 1997 and 1998 seasons.

While 1997 Thruxton marked the high spot, 1998 Oulton Park was surely the low spot of Phil's time with the GT. He was nudged into a spin at Old Hall, collected by Peter St Barbe and pushed toward the descending pack, with Julian Morris hitting the passenger door at about 70mph. Phil was left wedged between the two doors, almost like being in a single seater. Concerned he might be injured, the marshals told him not to move, but he managed to open the door and walked away without a scratch.

Tony Price re-shelled the car as a roadster using a Heritage body, most of the other parts from the original racer, except the roll cage which had taken a pounding, being bolted into the new car. Phil missed the next round at Cadwell but the car was finished the night before the following race at Lydden where it came sixth, having not turned a wheel before practice that morning. Phil sorted the Roadster before the final outing of the year at Donington, where he led the race for nine laps only to lose out to Huw Taylor the last time round.

His tally for the 1998 season – three wins, four seconds, two thirds, a fourth and a sixth – were not enough to secure the Championship, which went to Peter St Barbe's Midget by a margin of just three points. Phil came out and did the first three rounds in 1999, but his heart was not in it and he needed a new challenge. For some while he had been thinking in terms of another V8 and, knowing that Tony Price intended to retire in 2000, decided to get him to prepare one for him to race.

After selling HMH 394K to Steve Lewis, Phil bought a genuine Abingdon-built V8, XLL 326N, to replace it and Tony gave it the treatment. The purple car, which has a 3,500cc engine that the driver professes never to need to rev above 5,500rpm, has done consistently well in Class A of the MGCC Anglia Phoenix Championship, despite Phil opting to run the car on road tyres rather than the slicks that he is permitted to use. In 2001, he secured victory in Class A of the Championship after he won the last race of the season at Croft.

## Nigel Woolcott

Graphic designer Nigel Woolcott first raced in the series in 1987, driving his bright yellow Midget, and made an increasing number of appearances over subsequent seasons until 1992, when he competed in every round. Whilst he enjoyed driving the Midget, Nigel became pre-occupied with the fact that an MGB GT had never won a BARC/MGOC race, and plans to build a winning GT began to formulate in his

mind. He spoke to David Gathercole who convinced him that, with the right bits, it could be done. However, others were not so positive, one well-known outfit suggesting that if it had been practical they would already have built such a car and won in it!

Having decided to go ahead, Nigel purchased a £250 shell as a basis for the car, though with hindsight it would have been more economic to have used a new Heritage shell. His acquisition proved to have new panels welded over old rusty ones, and it took a lot of work to get right. It was originally intended to debut the GT at the start of the 1995 season but, as the time loomed ever nearer, it became obvious the new racer would not be ready. Nigel dusted off the Midget, went

*Nigel Woolcott (1), who won the MGB category in the 1996 BARC/MGOC Championship, leads a packed grid into the first corner at Silverstone.*

out and found that he could still win races in it. Six firsts, four seconds and two thirds secured him the outright 1995 Championship.

Meanwhile, work on the GT came to a halt, lack of funds meaning that it had to be put on hold till the end of the season; the primed completed shell, with glass-fibre front wings/bonnet and aluminium-skinned rear tailgate to reduce weight, were stored. The project was completed over the winter and was ready for testing prior to the start of the season. It had been built with a three-bearing engine to reduce friction, non-overdrive gearbox and lever-arm dampers in accordance with the regulations.

To compensate for the weight difference between Roadster and GT, the Championship regulations permitted modifications to the GT that were not allowed on the open car. Nigel's car duly incorporated these. A tubular exhaust manifold replaced the standard cast item and 175 tyres were fitted rather than 165s. It was also permitted to replace the side and rear windows in Perspex or polycarbonate material. The car was painted the same yellow as his Midget.

Initial testing revealed an inherent understeer problem, but this was dialled out by lowering the car by the maximum amount permitted. The opening round of the 1996 series was at Silverstone and the circuit was wet for practice. Used to the Midget's slight skittishness in the wet, Nigel found the GT handled well and, although he did not feel to be going that fast, found he was regularly overtaking other drivers. At one stage he wondered if he had failed to see some yellow flags. When the time sheets were published he was delighted to find he had put the car on pole position, over one second ahead of the second car on the grid.

Unfortunately for Nigel, it turned dry for the race but he still finished fourth in what was, after all, his very first race outing in the MGB GT.

After another fourth at Thruxton, second at Mallory and third at Snetterton, Nigel chalked up his first win in round six, at Oulton Park. He shared the front row with Terry Farman's Midget. Terry and Nigel pulled away together and went into Lodge Corner side by side, each looking at the other and thinking 'I am not going

---

**BARC/MGOC MG Championship Best Placed MGB/Winner**

| | |
|---|---|
| 1981 | John Hewitt (Standard) |
| 1982 | John Hewitt (Modified) |
| 1983 | John Hewitt (Modified) |
| 1984 | Richard Horn (Modified) |
| 1985 | Grahame Davis (GT V8),   Robb Gravett Champion (1500 Midget) |
| 1986 | Grahame Davis (MGC) |
| 1987 | Richard Horn (Modified),   Jeremy Lindley Champion (1275 Midget) |
| 1988 | Noel Wincote,   Darryl Davis Champion (Maestro) |
| 1989 | Nigel Petch (MGC) |
| 1990 | Mark Garner,   Rae Davis Champion (Maestro) |
| 1991 | Grahame Davis,   Terry Farman Champion (1275 Midget) |
| 1992 | Grahame Davis |
| 1993 | Grahame Davis,   Tony Moss Champion (Maestro) |
| 1994 | Jim Baynham,   Richard Hollebon Champion (Maestro |
| 1995 | Jim Baynham,   Nigel Woolcott Champion (1275 Midget) |
| 1996 | Nigel Woolcott,   Fergus Campbell Champion (Maestro) |
| 1997 | Phil Walker,   Terry Farman Champion (1275 Midget) |
| 1998 | Phil Walker,   Peter St Barbe Champion (1275 Midget) |
| 1999 | Sean Valentine,   Terry Farman Champion (1275 Midget) |
| 2000 | Jim Baynham,   Darryl Davis Champion (MG*F*) |
| 2001 | Jim Baynham,   Nick Evans Champion (Maestro) |

to brake first, you are!' In consequence they both went off onto the grass and resumed in seventh and eighth positions.

Duly hyped up, Nigel 'wrung the car's neck and it responded'. Having got clear of his rival, he discovered that the GT was heavy enough to allow him to overtake another car round the outside at Island, stay under it through the hairpin then pull away. He executed this man-oeuvre over the next five laps and was soon chasing race leader Alan Yeoman, who had won that first race at Thruxton. On the penultimate lap, Nigel was able to get past him at Island and go on to record the first ever MGB GT race win in the MGOC Championship. The GT had such grip that, unlike other competitors, Nigel found that he did not need a separate set of deeper-treaded tyres for the wet.

Further wins at Croft, Brands, Silverstone and Snetterton, plus Snetterton and Cadwell seconds with a third in girlfriend Julie Clarke's Midget at the Mondello Park double header, saw Nigel finish second in the Championship, just one point behind winner Fergus Campbell's MG Maestro. He considers that, had he taken his GT to Mondello, he may well have won the race and taken the Championship.

After a couple of outings in 1997, Nigel sold the car to novice driver Phil Emsley who did nine races during 1998, taking eighth place at Lydden Hill toward the end of the season. David Brand ran the car in 1999 – ironically he lives a quarter of a mile from Nigel. Kelly Isherwood, made her race debut driving the GT on 29 September 2001.

Nigel is still much involved in motor racing. Having run Julie's Midget for her, he now looks after her Formula Ford 2000. Ginettas also play a big part in his life. Having himself won the 1999 series, Nigel fronts Team Spirit Motorsport, running three G27s, for Anthony Rogers, Clive Steeper and Chris Pollard in the 2001 Pentel Ginetta Championship. Rogers took the Class B Championship.

# 7   Barry Sidery-Smith

Barry Sidery-Smith must surely have recorded the longest continuous racing history in MGBs, having competed in various examples of the marque for thirty-eight seasons at the time of writing. He has taken part in well over 500 events and brought home around 400 trophies for numerous wins and places in races, sprints and hill climbs.

Had he been successful in his trials with either Queen's Park Rangers or Fulham football clubs in the mid–1950s, Barry may have become a professional footballer and never have got involved with MGBs or motor racing. After two years' National Service, where he played football for the regiment, he concluded his time as a corporal in charge of motor transport. When he came out in 1956, Barry continued the motor connection, joining his father at Surbiton Car Hire, one of the early businesses hiring out cars in post-war Britain. The firm had a fleet of thirty vehicles and also sold and serviced cars. Barry soon established a sports car side and, to go with this, acquired an Austin Healey 100, LJY 614, as his daily transport.

Though, as a youngster, he had rides in various MG T types that his brother brought home from his job at Car Mart in London, it was not this, but taking on a paper round, which awakened Barry's interest in motor sport. Joss Foster, the newsagent, had a Parker/JAP 500 racing car and he soon graduated from watching Joss prepare the car, to working on it himself. Before long, Barry was helping out on race days at Brands Hatch and Goodwood and became hooked.

Barry entered his first motor race, at Goodwood in July 1959, driving his Austin Healey 100. Having qualified halfway down the grid for the Saturday race, Barry decided to use a little forward planning and his football-honed athletic prowess to capitalize on the Le Mans-style start. After he parked the car with the door slightly ajar and the ignition switched on, he crossed the track to await the drop of the flag, whereupon he sprinted to the Healey and was one of the first away. Approaching the Chicane, he glanced in the mirror and, seeing no one behind, lost concentration and promptly spun away his advantage.

Not content with that, he was due to race Foster's 500cc Parker at Brands Hatch the next day. However, after something broke during practice, Barry scratched from the race and obtained permission to drive his Healey in another event later that day. Over the next few years, he had occasional outings in the Healey and also raced a Triumph TR 2 and a TR 3. Barry's first appearance in an MGB was in 1964, when he raced Richard Worts' rebuilt and re-registered ex-works example, 94 HJJ, which had originally been one of the incarnations of 6 DBL, the one that had been rolled at Silverstone. The car was prepared by Barwell Motorsport at nearby Chessington, the tuning firm of the time.

Barry soon enjoyed his first major success in the car, coming third in an international race at Brands Hatch on August Bank Holiday Monday 1965. Graham Hill won the event in an E Type Jaguar. Barry and HJJ parted company in difficult circumstances, when the first Mrs Sidery-Smith departed with Richard, leaving Barry without a wife or a car to race – given the situation, Don Bunce got the drive.

Barry replaced the car with one of his own, MGB 665 FXF, Jenny Tudor-Owen's original

*Barry Sidery-Smith pits the Barwell-tuned, ex-Jenny Tudor-Owen B, 665 FXF, against Anthony Binnington in OMO 70, the first right-hand-drive MGB off the production line.*

Barwell-prepared car, that he purchased from George Konig's London mews house. He continued his racing in this and only sold the MGB to help finance the purchase of his Old Byfleet house in 1969. By now, he was regularly buying and selling various examples of the model and found, ironically, that ex-works cars were fetching less than standard ones! Since 1985, FXF has been owned and raced by Malcolm Young.

94 HJJ would pass through Barry's hands again, after Worts sold the car and replaced it with JYH 770D as Don Bunce's racer. A friend told Barry he had seen HJJ advertised in *Exchange and Mart* so he went to look at it. It was parked on the forecourt of a block of council flats and the owner, who used it as a road car, showed him the spare wheels and tyres, which were stored on his second floor balcony, along with the Hawks he kept. He bought and raced the car before selling it to Ken Dalziel, who drove it on the road for a year then sold to Gerry Marshall, who had some

excellent outings in the car before it ended up in the yard at Motobuild, after it had been in a fire. Colin Pearcy discovered the B there, traced its history and, when he realized what it was, reinstated it as the original 6 DBL. He restored and raced the car.

Sidery-Smith acquired his nickname, 'Sideways-Smith', following an accident at an MGCC Silverstone meeting. He went off on the exit of Woodcote and slowly rolled his B on its side, coming to rest on top of a *Daily Express* banner. He was pulled from the car by a young marshal, Brian Wright, who nowadays is Clerk of the Course at most of the MG Car Club race meetings. The pair still joke about the incident when they meet.

Barry has been happily married to Pam since 29 September 1969 and she has shared several of his subsequent racing MGBs. Daughter Heidi recalls being very frightened when, as a child, she sat on Pam's lap in their ex-works MGB, whilst

*Barry leaves the start line at the Brighton Speed Trials on Marine Parade. The double-decker bus accommodated the timekeepers and commentators.*

Paddy Hopkirk took it round Brands Hatch for some demonstration laps. She jokingly claims to have had a deprived childhood, saying that when all her friends went to the beach, she was at a race track. Whilst Heidi has driven at test days, she has shown no interest in taking up racing herself.

In 1971, Bob Shellard asked Barry to negotiate the purchase of the 1965 ex-works Le Mans car, DRX 255C, which he had seen advertised. Barry did the deal, and Bob then raced the aluminium-bodied car, before going abroad in 1972 and asking Barry to sell it for him – the asking price £795! The car's racing pedigree proved of little interest to the few prospective purchasers who answered the advertisement and Barry concluded that making a sale would not be easy.

By some quirk of fate, Pam decided to tidy up their collection of old race programmes and,

while glancing through them, realized that Bob's ex-works car was the one she and Barry had seen racing at Le Mans seven years before. Whilst they always knew it was a former factory car, they had not, until then, realized at which events it had been raced. Despite the shortage of funds, they somehow managed to buy DRX themselves in 1973 and still own it today.

What was probably Barry's worst race ever took place whilst he was dicing with Shellard, who was in DRX, at Oulton Park. Driving FXF, he followed Bob through Fosters, trying to pressurize him into making a mistake but it was Barry who got it wrong. He went wide onto the grass and came back onto the tarmac at high speed. The car rolled end over end into a ditch where it continued to roll to a halt. The fact that Barry walked away from the accident is

*Three eras of leading MGB racers. L to R: Bill Nicholson, Paddy Hopkirk and Barry Sidery-Smith. Barry's ex-Le Mans car is on the left; the other MGB belonged to former Daily Mail 'snapper' and BCV8 competitor Neville Marriner, who took the photograph.*

testament to the strength of an MGB. He threatened never to race again but was out within a month in the repaired car, which really only needed a new screen and surround, new hardtop and the dents knocked out of one wing. To add insult to injury, Oulton's management decided that the ditch was dangerous and filled it in before their next meeting.

In 1974, Barry bought Don Bunce's Nicholson-built racing MGB, JYH 770D, from an American air force officer who drove it round the base, on the road and did some races in the car. After a mechanical overhaul it became the next in the long line of Sidery-Smith racing Bs. He competed in it for ten years and then passed it to Ron Gammons as part of a deal to restore Barry and Pam's MG TC. Ron continued its competition history, mainly in rallies, and still owns the car today.

Barry was now racing both JYH and DRX, and Pam was also driving one or other in sprints and hill climbs, preferring the handling of the works car, but had never actually raced. In 1975 she drove it at a Silverstone test day to see how she would take to driving round circuits against other cars and decided she quite liked it. She had her first race at the 1975 MGCC Silverstone meeting; despite her initial misgivings – it was a wet practice session and a damp race – she

enjoyed it. As a result, she was a regular mid-field runner until 1977, when the cost of running two cars at a meeting meant she had to give up because, for business reasons, it was more important for Barry to race.

Pam found a new pastime showing Cavalier King Charles spaniels, though she still kept a racing connection her first two dogs, named Tappet and Weber have now been replaced by Axle, Bumper, Castrol and Dunlop – keeping to sequence, the latest addition is called Enzo. She caused some amusement at the obedience classes when she shouted the order 'Axle, stand'.

Though he enjoyed his racing, Barry still took part in sprints and hill climbs and was a regular contender at the Brighton Speed Trials, held every September at Madeira Drive, on the sea front. He took the award for fastest MG in 1971, 1973, 1974 and 1975. He also has his name on three prestigious MG Car Club awards: the Banana Trophy, the Hanks Trophy and the MG Challenge Trophy.

In 1976, encouraged by Gordon Cobban, later to become the hard-working general secretary of the MG Car Club, Barry and Victor Smith founded the very successful MGCC BCV8 Championship. Gordon first put forward the idea at a South Eastern Centre committee meeting held at London's Steering Wheel Club and it was discussed further at the MGCC 'natter' that Barry and Pam ran at the Bookham Grange Hotel. They formulated some basic regulations and set up a calendar of three races, four sprints and one hill climb for the 1977 season. This was the first co-ordinated Championship solely for MGBs. A regular contender, Barry was its inaugural Champion and is now Honorary President.

A redevelopment scheme in 1978 led to the business losing its High Street premises at Surbiton, so Barry relocated what had become his sports car garage to Westbury Garage, Westbury Road, New Malden. This was short lived because, within the year, a council road-widening scheme resulted in the new premises fronting a dual carriageway, and the fast-moving traffic effectively killed off the passing trade. Barry continued trading, keeping his vehicles in lock-up garages that he owned.

He formed an arrangement with Robin Lawton of Guildford Classic Sports Cars; Barry displayed a couple of his own vehicles in the showroom and ran the place when the owner was away. Today, Barry sells MGs and other historic vehicles to customers all over the world, thinking nothing of trailering one onto the ferry and delivering it anywhere in Europe. Amongst the more unusual vehicles that have passed through his hands are a rare Ferrari Dino 246 and the only original Mazda-powered Chevron B16. Barry sold this low-mileage example, which Julian Vernaeve retired at Le Mans, to a Swedish collector.

*JYH 770D rounds Brands Hatch Druid Hairpin with Barry at the wheel.*

In August 1980, Barry raced DRX 255C at Spa, his first outing abroad. Starting from ninth on the grid, he climbed through the field in the appalling wet conditions to win his Class and come home third overall, just six seconds behind the second-placed Aston Martin. A very special race, possibly his best ever, was made even more memorable when he was congratulated by none other than the great Fangio, who presented the awards and chatted with him whilst the rain continued unabated.

Barry regularly organized his pre-season test days at Goodwood during the 1980s, usually held in March. He hired the circuit and organized an ambulance, a doctor and a breakdown truck – an unwieldy six-wheeled Mark 10 Jaguar with a crane in the back. Friends from the MG Car Club were roped in as marshals to keep an eye on the four cars that Goodwood permitted on the track at any one time. Barry then had to hope that enough people turned up with their £40 to provide sufficient money to pay the bills for the day. If numbers looked down the week before, participants would receive an anxious call, asking if they had any friends who wanted to experience Goodwood first hand.

Fellow competitors were glad of a reasonably priced opportunity to shake down their cars at a weekend so they did not have to take time off work. Barry also offered tuition to those who had not driven on a circuit before, and these events whetted the appetites of many drivers who then found their way into motor sport. Later, Barry was instrumental in arranging for British MG owners to have the opportunity to race at Spa, and he also organized the DAF Trucks-sponsored MGB races at Zolder in the early 1980s.

Barry was joint second in Class, sixth overall, in the 1980 BCV8 Championship. Other well-known Sidery-Smith competition cars included his white V8, WUD 300M, which as well as race outings was invariably brought out at his Goodwood test days. In 1983, he purchased the ex-John Carter Road Modified Class, BCV8 car from Colin Cork, who finished the year second in Class B with it in 1982. Barry raced this 1969 white Roadster DVX 298G with fibreglass front wings, sponsored by Brown and Gammons, from 1983 to 1987. With a Gerry Brown-built engine under the bonnet and Barry in the cockpit, it was always a front runner in the Championship. He

*Pam and Barry Sidery-Smith pose with an International Trophy that Barry won, and two of his cars, MGB Roadster JYH 770D and MGB GT V8 WUD 300M.*

*Barry Sidery-Smith leading the pack in his MG Car Club
BCV8 Championship Class B car.*

won the Class in 1983 and 1984, when he was
also joint second overall, and was Class second in
1986 and 1987. Barry considers that, as it was not
an ex-works car or one that was eligible for FIA
events, perhaps he drove it a little harder than his
others. The car was later backed by Oselli.
Driving DVX, Barry was one of the MG racers
to parade the Formula 1 drivers round Brands
Hatch circuit prior to the 1983 European Grand
Prix. Jonathan Palmer was his passenger.

Barry's very last race in DVX, at Brands in
1999, was a memorable outing. He put the car
on pole, which his daughter claimed was a bad
sign as she reckoned that he always made bad
starts from pole. On this occasion, she was to be
proved wrong as her father made a copy-book
getaway to head the field into Paddock then pull
out a lead. However, the red flags came out on

lap two to enable the marshals to extricate the
driver from a car that had rolled into the gravel
trap at Paddock. Barry had it all to do again and,
to make matters worse, he had to keep the car
running on the start line as it had needed a push
start before the race.

He sat there watching the temperature gauge
slowly climbing! Fortunately the incident was
soon cleared and the engine cooled down on the
green-flag lap. This time he did not make such a
good start but went on to win the race. It had
been the intention to sell the car at the end of
the season, to help fund repairs to the house.
Barry did a deal in the paddock immediately
after the race and delivered the car to its new
owner, Brian Cakebread, the following week.

Since 1990, Barry has taken part in a large
number of historic races, both in Britain and

Europe. Driving Rod Longton's B, VFO 422, he won the GT 11 category in the 1995 FIA Historic Championship, the first MGB to take the title. Another event he vividly remembers was his race for the lead with Colin Pearcy during the Abingdon Trophy Race at the Silverstone Coys Festival in August 1996 on the GP Circuit. After eight very hectic laps, he crossed the line in second place, just 1.2 seconds behind Colin, though Barry did set the fastest lap at an average speed of 79.83mph (128.47km/hr).

One of Barry's recent racing highlights was being invited back to Goodwood, where he had his first race, to drive the ex-Le Mans car in the RAC TT Celebration Race, a one-hour event, at the Goodwood Revival Meeting in September 2000. He shared the car with *Motor Sport* editor Andrew Frankel and they qualified well up the field during the Friday practice session. Come the race on Sunday, it was wet and one of the propshaft UJs broke after three laps, forcing retirement.

Despite notching up his milestone sixty-fifth birthday in January 2001, Barry continues to race examples of MG and other classic marques and still receives regular requests from other owners for him to race their cars. Despite owning and racing many examples of Road Modified MGBs, he says that his most enjoyable drives have been in other people's Fully Modified cars. Racing on road tyres means that you are near the limit all the time but the slicks on Modsports cars make it so easy. He is still an avid armchair football fan and friends wishing to contact him avoid telephoning when there is an international match on the television.

# 8 Sports and Grand Touring Cars with MGB Power

The 1960s saw the emergence of many small manufacturers, most utilizing glass-fibre bodies to make what, in most cases, were excellent sports cars. Whilst many of the companies were equipped to make the tubular chassis and their own bodywork, few produced their own engine and so looked to the mainstream manufacturers to supply them. Many went to Ford, but BMC did deals with some, and four companies, Elva, Gilbern, Ginetta and TVR, all built models with an MGB engine under the bonnet. Examples of these marques inevitably found their way into motor sport, particularly as their power-to-weight ratio was better than the MGB.

## Elva Courier

Founded in a building behind the Swan Inn at Bexhill, East Sussex, by Frank Nichols, 'Elva', an abbreviation of *elle va*, French for 'she goes', produced sports racing and Courier sports cars from 1955 to 1968. The early Couriers had MGA engines, but the Courier Mk III and IV, which were built under licence by Trojan at Purley Way, Croydon, Surrey, came with either Ford or MGB power units. Later, they produced the Elva Sebring Courier, a purpose-built racing model with lightweight body, magnesium wheels and a limited slip differential.

They also made a few examples designated 'Lightweight', though it seems there was minimal difference between these and Sebrings. Some Mk IIs had their MGA units upgraded to MGB engines. Evergreen Tony Lanfranchi raced Elva Sports Racing Cars and also ran a 130bhp MGA-engined Courier during the 1961 season. Many Couriers were sold in America for racing, and to commemorate this after Nichols' death, his ashes were scattered at Helkhart Lake Track in Wisconsin, on 14 May 1998.

## Courier at Le Mans

Dick Osteen and Ron Lutz, two American racers based in France, bought a pair of MGB-engined Couriers in 1963. They enjoyed moderate club racing success with the engines bored to two litres and endeavoured to try and get an entry for the 1964 Le Mans 24-Hour Race. Osteen secured a reserve place and negotiated with Trojan and the BMC Competition Department to supply a car and engine. A Mark IV with lightweight body along with gearbox, differential, two engine blocks and various Special Tuning parts, was delivered in January 1964. If the car failed to participate in the race everything was to be returned or paid for.

The car was built up with the help of other American ex-pats, and they even managed to persuade a local technical college to balance all the engine components as part of a project. Much to Trojan's chagrin, the pair modified the nose to make it more aerodynamic. The Courier was tested at Montlhéry in March, where it reached speeds of 126mph (203km/hr). Funds for development were raised by selling subscriptions to a supporters club.

The car ran well during trials, the only problem being the lightweight body panels distorting at high speed, which also caused the diff to overheat. Bracing the bonnet and fitting oil pump, cooler and ducting for the diff, solved these issues. During qualifying, Osteen managed to get the blue-striped white machine round the circuit in 4min 56.0sec, just under the mandatory

*Equipe Elva London on the Silverstone grid at the 1964 International Trophy Meeting. L to R: Alan Hutcheson (24), mechanic, Ernie Unger (team manager), Derek Spencer (chief mechanic), Ken Baker (25). Baker raced with the hood up to see if it made the car quicker, but the roof was so heavy that it cancelled out any aerodynamic gain.*

five-minute lap to qualify. However, no other entrants scratched and the Courier failed to get a race.

As consolation, they entered the Coupes de Paris at Montlhéry in September and, by dint of a tossed coin, Dick drove and won the race from pole position. It also finished tenth in the larger-capacity race later in the day. In accordance with the agreement, the car was returned to Trojan who sold it to a new owner in England. It later appeared in 1965 events at Castle Combe, Brands Hatch and the Martini race at Silverstone. It is probably now in America.

### Equipe Elva London

For the 1964 season, Elva supplied to Ernie Unger, free of charge, two dark-green Trojan-built Sebring Couriers for him to run on their behalf, along with two Mk VII Sports Racing Cars. The Couriers were to be driven by Alan Hutcheson, who apparently brought Barwell engines into the deal, and former E Type Jaguar racer Ken Baker. Based at Derek Spencer's workshop in Maida Vale, London, the team had a four-figure budget that Unger had negotiated with Esso. Regulations at the time meant that sponsors' names were only allowed to appear on the transporter, not the cars themselves. Unfortunately, things started badly at the first outing and did not really get much better.

Unger recalls that at Goodwood on 30 March the scrutineers ran a magnet over the engine parts and discovered that, contrary to regulations, the racer had been supplied with an aluminium

*Pushing through the corner, one of the Equipe Elva London Couriers at Silverstone.*

back-plate. Alan Hutcheson was permitted to do three practice laps to qualify whilst the mechanics scoured the local garages for a steel back-plate that they managed to obtain and fit prior to the race, which the car had to start from the back of the grid. All this was to no avail, as Hutcheson retired early on lap four with engine problems.

A single entry for Baker at Goodwood on 18 May fared slightly better: he came twentieth from twenty-nine starters. There were two further outings at Silverstone, then Oulton Park on 11 April where, at an average speed of 78.71mph (126.67km/hr), Hutcheson secured a Class win. He beat the MGBs of Bill Nicholson and John Sharp, who set the fastest lap at 80.16mph (129.01km/hr). Despite this, dissatisfied with the Couriers' competitiveness, the team returned them to Trojan shortly afterwards.

**Moto Baldet Racing Team**

Trojan subsequently supplied two Sebring Couriers (probably the ex-Equipe Elva cars) to Andre Baldet, to run as part of the 'Moto Baldet Racing Team' in selected sports car races. MGB specialist Bill Nicholson prepared the cars and he and Trevor Fowler drove them. The team competed in about five events, trailering the cars to meetings except for Silverstone, where they were driven the few miles from their base on trade plates.

Their best showing was at the SMRC Snetterton August Bank Holiday meeting, when the cars ran first and second, with Fowler going on to secure overall victory, but only after the leading Aston and E Type both retired. Baldet recalls that they also took a couple of Class wins. The cars were sold off, the former Hutcheson car being advertised for £950. Nothing more is known of their history, though Jenny Dell's Sebring may have been an ex-Baldet car.

**Jeremy and John Trace**

Brothers Jerry and John Trace have enjoyed a long and successful association with Elva Couriers since 1964, when Jerry purchased his 1961 example, JHC 292, from his friend Danny Gladwyn. Jerry has raced the 1,622cc MGA-engined car with its HRG Derrington head nearly every year since. It was the last car to go up the hill at Firle, in East Sussex, before the storm clouds of authority began to gather over crowd safety concerns: the competitor who went up after him crashed and climbed the spectator banking, and subsequently, the hill lost its licence. During a race at Silverstone, Jerry's car got terribly out of shape under braking for Woodcote and was then overtaken by its own rear wheel, which hit the bank and bounced over the main grandstand. He believes he is still the only driver to get a wheel to clear the grandstand.

Things improved, reduced wheel offsets re-solved the handling maladies, and in 1977 Jerry won his Class in five races out of eight in the new BARC Thoroughbred Sports Car series. After a year-long battle with John Chatham's Healey 100/6 and the TR3 of Reg Woodcock, Jerry became the first-ever Champion. He also took the 1977 AMOC Thoroughbred Championship. He currently competes in the MGCC Moss Thoroughbred Sports Car Championship with MGB power.

John raced his red example 5268 JH between 1976 and 1984, when he laid it up until he sold it in 2001. He finished fourth in Class in the 1977 AMOC Thoroughbred Championship. New owner Alex McQueen Quattlebaum in-tends to continue racing it.

## Danny Gladwin

Courier enthusiast Danny Gladwin had built up three or four cars from kit form. A kit delivered on Thursday morning would usually be driven down to the pub by Sunday lunchtime, despite the rather vague two-page assembly instruc-tions. He used to pass the Trojan works on his way from Eastbourne to work in London. In October 1964, he collected a Trojan Trobike, a self-assembly mini motorcycle, which he had ordered. Whilst paying, he spotted a dark-green Sebring Courier under a sheet in the corner of the workshop and asked if it was for sale. He bought the unregistered car with about 700 miles on the clock for £700. Factory records showed this car, chassis number 1139, as 'Lightweight stock' and it seems it had been used as a demon-strator. It had a Barwell transfer on the rocker box cover and was extremely cammy.

Danny registered the car AHC 584B and supercharged the engine with a kit based on a Marshall Nordec cabin blower. The blower was geared up, so when the engine was on maximum revs at 7,500, it was running at around 10,000 rpm. Whilst the supercharger gave no problems, its oil supply from the engine reduced the pressure by 10psi and Danny found that he had to change the big-end bearings every 1,000 miles.

He used the Lightweight Courier for com-muting and, like his previous example, regularly hill climbed it at Firle, his local hill. Depending on the class structure, he would often win his Class. The gearing was ideal for Firle and he only had to use two, screaming over the finish line at 80mph (129km/hr) in second. The car's nimble-ness meant he could beat blown eight-litre Bentleys, but he admits he could not match Malcolm Knight's Aston Martin DB 1. By 1968, when his family had arrived, the Sebring Courier was sold and replaced with a Lotus Elan +2.

## John Haynes

John Haynes ran 1959-built Courier 27 ALO throughout the 1964 season. He had bought the car from Pat Ferguson, who had raced it with a 1,498cc B-series engine. John rebuilt the Elva over the winter of 1963/64 and fitted a 1,798cc MGB unit, with Special Tuning parts purchased direct from Abingdon. The Courier, which John sprayed Brilliant Gold, was also fitted with a Perks and Dolman hardtop. Driven to and from meetings, the engine often oiled plugs as the result of its racing tolerances. A dozen spares were always carried and changed regularly en route.

The bonnet was held by four fasteners, one in each corner, and on the way home from one meeting, he failed to secure it. The panel flew off at 80mph and landed upside down, halfway up a tree, with the matt black inner surface facing down. It took over an hour to find and retrieve it.

He finished fifth the first time out at Good-wood on 14 March. At the same circuit on 25 April, John had a terrific dice with Brian Kendall's Morgan Plus Four during the Marque Cars race. John led off the line but was passed by the Morgan at Woodcote on lap one. John got ahead again down Lavant on lap three and pulled away to take his first-ever outright victory, at an average speed of 79.50mph (128km/hr). How-ever, Kendall's manoeuvre at Woodcote saw him driving on the grass. At the time, the BARC, in a bid to discourage what they regarded as reck-less driving, penalized competitors who either

*Mike Bird in 27 ALO (39), the Elva Courier which John Haynes used to race, leads Jerry Trace's version (41) at Silverstone's Copse Corner, May 1970.*

spun or drove on the grass. Kendall's sixty-second penalty meant he was not even placed and White's Morgan came second 2.8 seconds behind Haynes. The penalty system was finally withdrawn towards the end of the season! John enjoyed further success with the Courier.

## Maurice Gates, Mike Bird and Norman Cochrane

Serving at the time at RAF South Cerney, where sprints are held today, John Haynes was posted to Aden at the end of 1964 and sold his Elva to Maurice Gates. He raced, sprinted and hill climbed the car, driving it to the venue wearing a jacket and tie, usually with a friend following in another car laden with tools and spares.

Norman Cochrane and Mike Bird, who purchased the car in 1968, replaced the pressed-steel wheels with Minilites and competed in it until 1974. Norman did hill climbs and sprints, including events at Greenham Common, before the USAF took it over as a missile base. A sprint

track was set out on the runway with straw bales, which were also used to make chicanes. Norman recalls that you usually tried too hard on the second run and clipped a chicane – no harm done, one simply picked the straw out of the engine bay.

Mike raced in club events and often found himself up against Reg Woodcock's rapid Triumph TR2, which he admits usually beat him owing to the TR's better cornering ability. A Silverstone off, around the same time as Mike moved house in 1974, saw the car locked away to await available funds to effect a repair. When the Elva was eventually mended, Cochrane and Bird had gone back to their motoring roots and acquired Singers again and the Courier still did not see the light of day. Over twenty years after John Haynes had raced the Courier, his wife Annette traced it and arranged to buy it back, to give to John as a surprise Christmas present. It is now displayed in the Haynes Motor Museum at Sparkford.

## Carl Ripley

Following two years of racing a friend's Marcos Ford 1600, garage owner Carl Ripley bought a Courier from a lock-up for £400 and raced it between 1970 and 1972. It took a season to get it sorted; a baffled fuel tank, racing radiator and a five-bearing engine with a Ryder big valve head his major items of expenditure. He received technical help from Bill Nicholson. He recalls the first time he beat Nicholson's MGB at Silverstone on 3 October 1971; Bill packed up to go home but his wife made him go back to congratulate Carl. Despite fluffing the start, Carl took a class win at the 1971 Silverstone season closer on 10 October, beating the Lotus Elan of Max Payne, and set a new class GP circuit lap record at 1min 48.6sec. That made all the work worthwhile.

1972 started with another Class win at the BARC Silverstone Easter meeting, and Carl continued to race the Elva successfully until he left the garage business at the end of the season. The 1964 blue Courier with a yellow stripe across the bonnet was left at the premises, and he later heard it had been wrecked when a scrap car was dropped on it.

## John Playfoot, Tony Barnard and Alan Miles

Engineer John Playfoot, who ran the machine shop in the Elva works at Rye, acquired several Couriers and built up the original Elva production model, chassis number 2, for racing in 1987. Initially, the car ran a full race 1,650cc MGA engine, with a Leyland Sherpa block and Norton Commando pistons. Local driver Tony Barnard, who had worked for Nerus and Elva, piloted the car in 1988. The engine detonated during practice for the first race of the season at Mallory Park.

Barnard then built up a moderately tuned MGB engine with 1.75in SUs. The Courier was prone to spinning and took a bit of sorting, but this achieved, Tony had some enjoyable races in it, winning the Class in the 1988 MG Car Club Pre-66 Classic Car Challenge. The following year, they changed the carburation to a single Weber and again won the class.

*The Lotus Elan (221) locks a wheel as it tries to catch Carl Ripley's Elva Courier (219), at Woodcote Silverstone, September 1972.*

*Alan Miles races the John Playfoot Elva Courier, VGN 111, in a Chapman Warren round. Alan won the championship outright in 1991.*

Alan Miles took over in the cockpit for 1990 and 1991, winning the Championship (then sponsored by Chapman Warren) outright the second year, after taking the Class in 1990. During this period, the car often ran with the original MGA lump, which would require a rebuild after four events, falling back on the MGB engine when it was not ready. Alan's main rivals were Roy McCarthy in his MGA and Steve Clare's Triumph TR6.

The Championship was derived from the original MG Car Club MGA series, which allowed the MGAs to run on slicks. It was a bone of contention with the drivers of the invited marques, such as Elva, that they could only use treaded tyres, which under most weather conditions put them at a disadvantage. Alan recalls a super dice with Neil Cawthorn's MGA at Pembrey on 15 September 1991. The pair of them were side by side constantly changing places, with ten out of the twelve laps below McCarthy's lap record. On this occasion, Alan was second, but only by half a car's length, and set a new lap record at 1min 09.48sec.

**Other Couriers**

D. E. J. Lomas won the Marque Cars event at the Aintree Circuit Club's tenth anniversary meeting on 2 May 1964. Mike Campbell won the Marque race at Goodwood on 3 April 1965, driving his Trojan-built Sebring Courier, chassis number 1140. Jenny Dell also raced an 1,800cc Sebring Courier; despite losing it at the Elbow on the first lap, she took a class third at the TEAC Lydden Hill meeting on 28 July 1968.

Hove resident Peter Garratt used his car for sprints and hill climbs between 1967 and 1973. He also invited BRDC President Mary Wheeler to drive it after she had sold her Grantura. Ken Baker competed in a few sprints driving the Trojan prototype SE, VV 8184, which is now owned by Stuart Tallack. In 1988, Nevill Young purchased a Ken Sheppard-built Mk IV Courier, EFU 419C, for restoration. It came with adjustable Konis on the front and 10in-wide rear wheels, leading him to believe that it may have had a previous racing history.

**Gilbern GT 1800**

The designation, created by combining the names of the two founders *Gil*es Smith and *Bern*ard Friese, Gilbern has the honour of being the most successful car to be made in Wales. The company was founded during 1959 at Llantwit Fadre near Pontypridd and its first model, the GT Mk 1, had the option of Coventry Climax, BMC 'A' Series or the MGA 1,558cc power units, the latter proving the most popular. After upgrading to the 1,622cc from the later MGA, it was natural progression to install the MGB's 1,798cc engine in 1963, the car then becoming known as the Gilbern GT1800. At one time, Gilberns became so successful on the hills that people referred to them as 'Gilbeams', after Pilbeam, the purpose-built sprint and hill single-seater.

### Peter Cottrell

Whilst Friese and Smith conceived the car, much of the Gilbern tuning work was carried out by the third director of Gilbern Sports Cars Ltd, Peter Cottrell, from Cottrell's garage in Mercer Road, Pontypridd. A great hill-climb exponent, Peter competed in the first production GT Mk 1 ever built, which ran all three engine variations. This car was replaced with a maroon GT1800, CTX 862B, as soon as they came out. Peter again tuned this to become a very competitive car, campaigning it between 1964 and 1966. In Stage 6 tune, he tried both a single Weber and twin 1¾in SU carburettors, but deferred to the SUs, for better low-down torque.

Peter, who had outings at Castle Combe, was a regular at Prescott and Shelsley Walsh. He also

*Peter Cottrell, the third director of Gilbern, leaves the line at Prescott Hill Climb in the GT1800, which he still owns.*

took part in sprints and a few races at Llandow, where he recalls some good dices with Millburn's Lotus. He won the Class at the first Pembrey sprint of the 1963 season, with a time of 16.56 seconds, beating Barry Jones' 3.8 litre Jaguar-powered Triumph TR3 by 0.07 seconds. Now in his eighties, Peter still owns his Gilbern and takes it for an occasional drive.

### Dr Paul Scott

Cambridge lecturer Paul Scott was a notable hill-climb exponent in a GT1800 between 1970 and 1990, though he was most active in the 1970s. Paul acquired his GT, AMJ 630C, in kit form from Ace Motor Company of 20–23 Radley Mews, Kensington, the London Gilbern dealer run by Emil Rosner. Having built the car and started to compete, a programme of modifications was instigated over a number of years. The rear trailing arms were adjusted by about 2in to make them more parallel; this slightly reduced the roll stiffness and increased the life of the bushes. The front anti-roll bar was up-rated to the MGB ⅝in version, and the wheels changed for 7in with 205 by 14 tyres. The otherwise standard engine ran on 1¾ rather than 1½ SUs, and a ZF limited slip differential proved its worth when tackling hill-climb hairpins.

Devon's Wiscombe Park and the former hill at Valence near Westerham in Kent were two of Paul's regular events. He managed to win the Gilbern Owner's Club Handicap on his first visit to Wiscombe with a time of 55.52 seconds, winning again in the rain in 1975 with 63.12 seconds. The following year he got hold of some old Dunlop CR 82 racing tyres and set his best time for the hill at 53.88 seconds. Valence successes included a class win in 1973, beating a TR4 and Morgan +4, and a second the previous year when he beat an Elva Courier and a Daimler Dart.

Paul found that the GT's Panhard rod layout, with the bar above, rather than below the back axle, promoted oversteer, especially when the LSD was fitted. This meant it was very easy to hang the tail out, a characteristic he enjoyed during a race at Lydden Hill, where he managed to hang the back right out coming onto the top straight. He also had a spectacular spin during Modsports practice at the MGCC Brands Hatch August meeting in 1978, when he went off at Paddock, narrowly missing the Armco. He found the Gilbern's weight advantage over the MGB to be quite useful and it also provided entertaining handling.

### Bev Fawkes and Dr Terry Parker

Having hung up his helmet in 1990, Paul sold his GT to champion hill climber Bev Fawkes in 1994. Bev was perhaps better known for setting fast times in his Reliant Scimitar fitted with a twenty-four-valve three-litre Ford Scorpio engine. Cambridge Motorsport rebuilt the Gilbern's MGB engine to full race spec with a scatter cam, big valve head and roller rockers. He campaigned the car from 1994 to 1996, sharing it with both his partner Delyth and Nigel Ellis, another Gilbern owner. Bev describes the GT as a very forgiving car to drive. Bev and Delyth both competed at Curborough on 19 September 1996, Bev recording a time of 37.96 seconds whilst Delyth did a 40.15. In 1999, the GT failed its MOT and, with too many other car projects, Bev decided to sell.

Long-term Gilbern enthusiast Dr Terry Parker bought AMJ 630C in 2000. Gilbern guru Chris Smith repaired the chassis, as the car had predominately been used for competition. With Paul Scott having strengthened the chassis in the usual weak points, it did not require as much work as many other cars of its era. Chris only had to replace the outriggers. To date, Terry has only competed in one event, the 2001 AMOC Sprint at Curborough, an injury keeping him out of action until the end of the year.

### Bernard Gray and Peter Sharp

G. S. Cars, of 35 Tower Road South, Warmley, Bristol, were the area Gilbern agents and proprietor Bernard Gray was a great motor sport enthusiast. In 1965 he asked the factory to build him a lightweight GT1800; the white car was registered FAD 694C. The body was so thin that you could almost see through it, the dash had minimum instrumentation and the interior had no rear seats, the platform simply carpeted over. The car originally had a three-bearing MGB engine that was used in various forms of tune, with kits from Abingdon.

When tuning over-reached reliability, Bernard changed to a five-bearing unit, which was built by workshop foreman, Vic Hornsby, utilizing MGA con rods, machined down to fit the crankshaft journals. It was such a close fit that the pinch bolts would occasionally touch the cam shaft. However, it was a generally noisy engine so they put up with it because it produced the power. To further reduce reciprocating weight, Peter Sharp came up with a set of hollow Volkswagen push rods. The new engine had an HRG cross-flow head and a pair of Lotus Cortina Webers.

A banana exhaust system was fabricated. This exited the car under the passenger door but later had to be modified after the pipe was ripped off on the cattle grid en route to the start at Dyrham Park Hill Climb. The original wire wheels were replaced with wide steel rims that had been cut in half and had a steel band welded in the middle. They ran it on second-hand 8in-wide intermediate tyres purchased from Vince Woodman.

Bernard rarely competed in events on Sundays, as he was usually playing his cornet in the Easton Salvation Army band, so his friend Peter Sharp would drive. Peter's first outing in the Gilbern was at the Yeovilton sprint where he set a poor time, having to steer with one hand and hold the passenger door shut with the other, but the catch was soon adjusted. GT door hinges are mounted directly on to the box section chassis and part of Bernard's showroom routine was to swing on the doors to demonstrate their strength to prospective purchasers.

The other problem that Peter recalls was the fact that the engine liked to devour the Weber 'O' Rings. On one occasion, the petrol caught light and he ruined a good jacket smothering the flames. They always fared well at their local circuit, Castle Combe. Bernard won the class at the speed trials there on 2 July 1966, with a best

*Bernard Gray and Peter Sharp shared this lightweight Gilbern GT1800, FAD 694C. Here the much modified version rounds Quarry at Castle Combe.*

time of 2min 50.0sec, Peter was second, lapping in 2min 56.2sec. They regularly competed at the Weston-super-Mare Speed Trials, sharing the car in the sea-front event organized by the Burnham-on-Sea Motor Club. On 1 October 1966, Bernard took a class win with a time of 24.93 seconds, whilst Peter's 25.19 secured third place. The GT was also raced, predominantly at Castle Combe.

In the course of his job as area sales manager for Duckhams Oils, Peter met many motor trade people who raced or just liked to drive fast cars. Occasionally he would contact Kitty Thomas, who owned 'The Combe' and hire the circuit for a Thursday afternoon. Having paid for the track and given St Johns Ambulance a donation to attend, he would charge drivers £5 for their afternoon's entertainment. Today they are called 'track days' and cost considerably more. As Bernard and Peter always went round for free, they knew every bump on the circuit.

One of Peter's Thursday afternoon regulars persuaded Bernard to let him have a go in the Gilbern, but put a rod through the side of the block. It was replaced with an MGB unit, which had been overbored to 2,060cc and again had an HRG head. The walls of the bores were so thin that Peter was concerned about reliability and had little more to do with the car. Bernard gave up competing in 1969 and the 1800GT then stood in the showroom. G. S. Cars salesman Mike

Chandler, who usually competed in his own Gilbern V6, asked if he could drive FAD at Wiscombe. Unfortunately, standing caused the brakes to stick, they pulled to one side and the car hit the post at The Gate.

The car was repaired and returned to the showroom. Ray Wilkinson, who was based at RAF Lyneham, had a GT1800 as everyday transport and was a regular visitor to G. S. Cars. On each occasion, he asked if the white racer was for sale but the answer was always no. However, when he enquired in March 1982, he was offered a test drive and, despite the traumatic experience, which resulted in him nudging another vehicle, he purchased it.

Ray, who describes the GT as a 'real wroughty snorty car', stiffened the front chassis, intending to use it for sprints and hill climbs. However, the nature of his work meant that he could not find time to compete and it spent the majority of his three years' ownership in a lock-up garage. He did trailer it to one National Gilbern Day but was disappointed that those attending seemed more interested in the concours examples, rather than his car with its racing pedigree. In 1985, he sold to David Evans, who dismantled the GT for restoration but never completed the project, selling it to Chris Smith in 1994. FAD is now being rebuilt for historic racing in Germany.

### John Classey

A successful campaigner of the marque for over twenty years, John Classey turned to Gilberns after failing to get his supercharged Triumph Heralds to handle! He first competed in a blue GT 1800, CKJ 849C, in 1968. In August that year, John bought Emil Rosner's own silver-grey GT, BYF 663B, from Emil's garage, Ace Motor Company. This particular example had been used as a press car and was road tested by *Motor Sport* when they reviewed the model in their January 1965 issue. With a modified bottom end and an Aquaplane cross-flow cylinder head, John found the engine amazingly free revving. It is believed that well-known racing driver of the era, Rivers Fletcher, competed in the car at Prescott during 1964.

Classey regularly drove his Gilbern at AMOC events on the hills and won the Wiscombe Cup in 1974, 1976 and 1977 – his fastest time ever was 57.84 seconds set in 1974. BYF was his only mode of transport and he claimed that it let him down only once. John's modifications were to fit a 4.2 diff and a close-ratio gearbox and increase the compression ratio to 10.8:1. As well as Wiscombe he was a regular at Curborough, where his best time was 48.21 seconds in 1975, and at Valance (39.64 in 1970).

In 1979, John was unfortunate enough to have a minor collision with a parked car, which damaged the near-side front corner of his Gilbern, and he decided that, rather than carry out repairs, it would be simpler to re-shell it. In so doing, he ended up with virtually a new car. Coincidentally, Emil Rosner had salted away in a basement one of the last GTs to come out of the factory. It was the same silver-grey colour as BYF, albeit a year later than the original. Over the years, a few parts had been robbed from the Gilbern, to keep customers cars going. The engine and gearbox were missing, but it is believed that Emil may have bought the GT from Gilbern without them.

This GT was sold to John and the mechanics at Ace swapped over his engine, gearbox and the other missing parts onto the 'new car'. As it had never been registered it was given John's original chassis plate and registration. John carried on campaigning his GT and when he died it went to Michael Jones, who enjoyed driving it on the road as part of his small collection. Whilst in his ownership, the car was the subject of an article in the August 1994 issue of *Classic and Sportscar*. In 1999, it was sold to Howard Wadsworth.

The original damaged Classey chassis/body was stored in a Kent barn and some years later sold to Chris Smith, who modified it to take a V8 engine. In 2000, deciding he would not find time to complete the project, he sold it to Dr Terry Parker, who intends to restore the car to its original specification.

## Martin Ingall

Founder of the Gilbern Owners Club, which he set up in the winter of 1969, Martin Ingall is more recently known for competing in Austin Healey Sprites. Having previously owned a 1964 example, he bought his second Gilbern, a 1967 GT1800, JAA 999E, from Major Stewart in 1968, when it was eighteen months old. Martin used this Connaught Green car as his everyday transport and for hill climbs and sprints, before selling it to his brother John to use as a road car in 1972. Martin's first event was his local hill climb at Valence, in July 1969.

Martin was also a regular at Wiscombe, setting a time of 58.76 seconds at the AMOC members day in 1971. He recorded a time of 58.21 at the Shell/RAC Championship round at Wiscombe

*Martin Ingall flat through the Esses at Wiscombe Park Hill Climb, Devon, in April 1970.*

during May 1971, an outstanding time for a Gilbern GT. He sprinted his example at Brands Hatch and Crystal Palace, also taking in his other local hill at Bodiam.

In 1972, he was third in the Gilbern OC Wiscombe Cup, the awards being presented by Jon Pertwee (Dr Who), as the actor was staying the weekend with Major Chichester, who owned the hill. Competing in the Gilbern, Martin often found himself up against Paul Scott for marque honours. John and Martin Ingall later moved on to compete in a Cooper T 65 Formula Junior.

In 1982, Martin bought the GT back from his brother and stored it in the same barn where the Classey's damaged GT had lain. JAA is now in the final stages of a body-off rebuild and, when complete, will return to competition use, this time in historic road rallies.

### Other GT 1800s

Alan Smith competed in his example, as did Ace Motor Company workshop manager Mike Sutton, who hill-climbed his version, CKJ 942C. Mike Chandler was another Wiscombe regular; he drove a special lightweight GT which had two litres under the bonnet and wide tyres. His 1972 time for the Devon hill was 54.7 seconds.

### Gilbern V8 GT

In 1965, Bridgend driver Ken Wilson, who competed in speed events in a diverse range of machinery, asked Peter Cottrell, whose Gilbern GT1800 had just beaten his Alfa in a sprint, what he could come up with to beat him. The pair discussed various options and eventually settled on a V8-powered Gilbern GT. Peter was reluctant to ruin a chassis on the off chance the project would work, so Ken agreed to buy one to experiment with.

Wilson obtained a 4.7 litre Chevrolet engine from one of Doc Merrifield's legendary racing projects and it was put on the workshop floor next to a brand-new chassis. Peter attacked this with an angle grinder until the power unit fitted, then fabricated new mounting brackets. They mated the engine with a Jaguar gearbox and back axle, put a body on and gradually the unique vehicle took shape. ETX 450C was bright red, with a white bonnet stripe, and an extremely quick car, if a bit of a handful to drive. Ken competed in the car for about a year and won the class for Touring Cars and Improved Touring Cars over 2,000cc at the Weston Speed Trials on 1 October 1966, with a run of 24.80 seconds for the standing half-kilometre.

Ken then asked Cottrell to take over the

*Ken Wilson about to get into his Gilbern GT V8 by the Pier at the 1966 Weston Speed Trials on the sea front at Weston-super-Mare.*

driving, which he did for about eighteen months, during which time he enjoyed some good outings and worked on the car's overheating problems. He recalls taking it to one meeting and getting it up to 170mph (274km/hr) on the old A50 trunk road. Wilson then decided to sell the vehicle, having first got his mechanic to remove the V8, which was required for another project.

It was advertised by the Ace Motor Company, who displayed it in their showroom, minus engine, for some long while, before storing it at a farm near Basingstoke. By 1980, Ace were well established as Saab dealers so they advertised a grand Gilbern clearance in the *Exchange and Mart*. Marque enthusiast, David Ellison, who had inspected ETX in the showroom, viewed it again at the farm, where it was now back on standard axle and wheels. He bought the former V8 GT, without an engine and also a standard GT1800, for his brother.

He intended to install an MGB engine with overdrive gearbox, which he already had, but the overdrive unit fouled the chassis. In the car's boot he found some engine mountings which happened to fit a Ford Twin Cam engine with twin 40s, which also stood in his workshop. So for no better reason than the engine virtually dropping straight in, the Gilbern GTV8 became a GT twin cam. David's wife, Catherine Ellison, drove it in the 1990 Manx Classic and David competed at Wiscombe in May 1991. In the same ownership, the car has not competed since.

## Ginetta G11

Agricultural and constructional engineers Bob, Douglas, Ivor and Trevers Walklett set up Ginetta Cars at Woodbridge, Suffolk in 1958. In origin the name 'Ginetta' was based on the genetta, an elegant cat-like animal found predominantly in Africa and Europe. The G2, the first production model from the four brothers, who were all motor-racing buffs, was launched in 1958. Whilst most of their sports models utilized Ford power, the G11, of which seven in total were made, had an MGB engine under its glass-fibre bonnet.

Of the seven cars, two or three were assembled privately by enthusiast Russell Madden, who persuaded Ginetta to make chassis and bodies for him, which he then built up into complete cars and sold.

In appearance, the G11 was very similar to the MGB and actually utilized the latter's doors. It has been suggested that, unhappy with the similarity, BMC cut off the supply of doors, hence the very limited run. A G11 Coupé appeared on Ginetta's stand at the 1967 Racing Car Show, along with its race-proven best seller, the G4. Tom Kenny's Madden-built example, ROC 180M, is the only Ginetta G11 that has any competition history.

## Tom Kenny

Tom, a mechanical engineer, purchased the car on 22 May 1991 with the sole intent of campaigning it in the Scottish Hill Climb Championship, but it would take him four years to prepare the car. Purchased as a rolling shell, with separate MGB engine and overdrive gearbox, which would not fit into the car, he had to buy the correct engine and box and fortunately ended up with a mildly tuned example. He had it bored to 1,950cc and retimed the existing cam to slightly increase the power band.

The Triumph Vitesse disc brakes were upgraded to Capri vented discs with Austin Princess four-pot callipers. The top wishbone was rose-jointed to allow camber adjustment, whilst the rear had an 'A' frame added. Having completed these modifications plus the standard safety requirements such as roll cage, Tom Kenny was ready to take to the hills.

A successful inaugural season saw him take the Thoroughbred Class of the 1996 Scottish Hill Climb Championship and he was also presented with the Best Newcomer Award. He won his Class at Fintray on 25 August and Forrestburn two weeks later (setting a new Class record). He also took one second at Durris, four thirds, a fourth and a sixth.

Looking for more power, Tom installed a 4,700cc small-block Ford V8 engine and gearbox along with a Jaguar axle; thus the only

*It looks like an MGB, but closer inspection reveals it is, in fact, Tom Kenny's Ginetta G11.*

competition G11 effectively became a G10. In this guise the Ginetta produced nine Class wins, which included six records, three of which still stand. He still owns the car but now competes in a Jim Sword-built JASAG V single seater, which has claimed nine FTDs.

## TVR Grantura Mark III & 1800S

The longest-established manufacturer featured in this chapter, TVR dates from 1949; it takes its name from Trevor Wilkinson, the company's founder, and despite many changes of ownership, it is still making sports cars today. Following the now familiar pattern, Ford powered a good number of models but the Grantura progressed from Coventry Climax and MGA, to MGB engines. Works entries with MGA power in 1962 produced few worthwhile results, and it was predominantly left to private entrants, some with works backing, to uphold TVR honours in subsequent years.

### Ex-works cars with Tommy Wood, Gill Baker and Ian Massey-Crosse

Following their ill-fated outing at the 1962 Le Mans 24-Hour Race on 23/24 June, when both cars failed to finish due to overheating, TVR entered the works Granturas in two other

events. Two cars were out at Brands Hatch on 4/5 August: Peter Bolton failed to start following a practice off in YFR 751, and Ninian Sanderson was a finisher in YFR 752. At the Goodwood Tourist Trophy Race on 18 August 1962, Rob Slotemaker failed to start, Peter Bolton retired with engine maladies, but Keith Ballisat finished eleventh overall having completed eighty-seven laps of the 100-lap race, the team's best showing.

The three competition Grantura Mk IIIs, YFR 751 (driven at Le Mans by Peter Bolton and Ninian Sanderson), YFR 752 (the reserve car driven by Ted Lund and Rob Slotemaker) and YFR 753 (the spare car) were then advertised in *Autosport* in August 1962 and sold for racing, without their registration numbers. YFR 752 subsequently appeared on another Grantura, road-tested in the 13 December 1963 issue of *Autosport*.

Haulage contractor Tommy Wood, from Hall Lane, Bradford, bought what was YFR 751 and used it in about ten sprints and hill climbs between September 1962 and July 1963. He was third in Class in the inaugural Harewood Hill Climb on 15 September 1962, and the following weekend he took a Class second in the RAF Church Fenton Drag Sprint. His last outing was at Church Fenton on 14 July 1963.

*Ken Booth races one of the ex-factory Le Mans Granturas at the street circuit in Hamilton, Ontario, whilst visiting the owner, Gill Baker, in Canada, circa 1980.*

In 1964, wishing to sell the car, Tommy had it re-registered and was allocated 7955 KW, a Bradford number. Advertised for £1,100, it found a new home with local solicitor Derek Scott, who intended to use it on the hills, though no record of this has been found. The ex-Le Mans Grantura then went through a succession of owners until purchased in 1978 by dealer Ken Booth, who collected it from an address in Warrington. After one race, at Oulton Park, he exported it to a friend in Canada.

Gil Baker enjoyed five years of fun in the TVR, driving it on the road as well as taking in some competitive events. He raced at Mosport and, during a transatlantic visit, Booth competed in a race on the street circuit at Hamilton, Ontario, where he scraped the paintwork against the Armco during practice. In 1983, the car went to another Canadian, Ivan Schneider. In 1985, he sold it to Kansas enthusiast Tom Newcomer, who raced it in SCCA events. The car remained in his ownership until he died in 1995.

English TVR enthusiast Ian Massey-Crosse drove his white road Grantura, 3833 UN, in the pre-race cavalcade at Le Mans in 1999, which got him thinking as to the whereabouts of the original Le Mans Granturas. Convinced that they had gone to America, he contacted fellow enthusiast Guy Dirkin, who now lives there, who

traced the original YFR 751. Ian purchased it from Newcomer's executors and returned the car to the UK, the container arriving at Felixstowe in August 2000. It is currently undergoing restoration to Le Mans spec before use in Historic racing, and Ian hopes to reunite the car with its original registration number.

### Tommy Entwhistle

In 1964, Grantura engineering built three lightweight 1,800cc TVR Granturas, which went to Tommy Entwhistle, Paddy Gaston and Alistair McHardy. Following demob from the RAF in 1948, former Spitfire pilot Tommy Entwhistle founded The Golden Glow Nut Food Company, which marketed packet peanuts and snacks in post-war Britain. His love of cars led him to buy an MGA, which he raced in the early 1960s. He found it uncompetitive owing to its weight.

However, the locally manufactured and lighter TVR caught his eye, and following a factory visit in 1962, he bought the first of three racing Granturas he would own, in which he installed a 1,622cc MGA engine. This combination soon started to produce results and would lead to four very successful years, during which he won the prestigious Freddie Dixon Championship three times: 1963, 1965 and 1966. His TVR, now with a 1,798cc MGB engine, had an HRG cross-flow alloy head with twin Webers. Each winter the engine was sent back to Stuart Proctor's team at HRG to be fettled and run up on their dyno, where it produced 150bhp at the flywheel. Entwhistle also established a good relationship with Abingdon, who supplied him with parts and information.

The Entwhistle car was the ultimate lightweight: as well as thinner body mouldings, the chassis was fabricated with thinner-gauge tubes. TVR design and development engineer David Hives spent a great many hours lightening components. He recalls turning and drilling the brake back-plates, drums, and drive-shaft flanges. Paul Richardson, son of Ken who ran TVR's short-lived Competition Department, also worked in Development and made a set of lightweight door locks for it. The MGB engine had been radically modified with a 100-ton steel crank, alloy front and back plates, Healey 3000 cam followers and aluminium push rods.

Tommy's racing was not all plain sailing, as along with the victories he wrote off two cars. His worst accident was at Oulton Park in 1964 where, having smote the banking on the last lap, he rolled the car, which then travelled along the track upside down. Tommy claims the lack of seat belts enabled him to crouch down in the cockpit, reducing the injuries to just his hands, badly grazed as he clung to the steering wheel. On each occasion the car was re-bodied, had the same green-and-gold livery and always ran as TE 2.

In 1960, keen to have a personal registration number, Tommy had approached Lancashire County Council Vehicle Registration Office to enquire about the availability of TE 1, to be advised that it was about to be allocated elsewhere. He was given the name and address of the owner of the pre-war car that had been registered TE 2 and was told that, in keeping with procedure, if he could provide proof that the car no longer existed, he could have the number. The first letter, to the owner's address at Barrow in Furness, was returned but he traced the man to his new home and the resulting telegram, confirming the car no longer existed, enabled Tommy to claim the number. The total transfer fee was around ten pounds, including the number!

Entwhistle's main rivals drove ACs, Healeys or Morgans and he recalls that John Sharp was also quick in his MGB. Determined to beat Tommy, Donald Healey entered two of his works Le

*Tommy Entwhistle in his TVR Grantura TE 2. Tommy still has this personal registration plate on his present TVR.*

Mans Healeys against him at Mallory Park, but Tommy managed to hold them off. During the Marque Cars event at the Goodwood members' meeting on 22 June 1963, Tommy had a great tussle with the Alan Dence Morgan Plus Four, which just beat him after five hectic laps. Earlier on they were up against each other in the GT race, where Dence took Entwhistle for third place on lap four. Tommy also took the Grantura to Europe for three or four events and was placed in two.

Tommy enjoyed a good victory at the Goodwood season closer on 12 September 1964, winning after five laps of close racing with Campbell's Elva and Unett's Sunbeam Tiger. It was Unett who took the 1964 Freddie Dixon title after Tommy was forced to retire with a broken magnesium wheel at Crystal Palace. Hives, who usually crack tested them before each race, was away in America helping Gerry Sagerman set up the first American TVR dealership, so the test was overlooked. After the meeting, Tommy called in at Paddy Gaston's premises at nearby Kingston and borrowed a set of wheels so he could race at Brands the next day. The TVR Team, Tommy Entwhistle (1800S), Peter Simpson (V8 Griffith) and Arthur Mallock (in John Wingfield's 1800S), came third in the 1965 Silverstone Six-Hour Relay Race.

In 1967, Tommy was looking for a new challenge so he ordered yet another TVR to replace his existing one. Bernard Williams' team made him a prototype TVR Gem, a really lightweight moulding. The new incarnation of TE 2 was to have Ford V6 power. The three-litre engine, which replaced the original two-and-a-half-litre unit was disappointing, so he hung up his helmet. It is not the end of the story though, as, having rebuilt the car yet again, Tommy now races the same Ford-powered TVR in the Flemmings Anglo American Challenge.

**Bernard Williams**
Through racing the marque, Tommy got to know TVR director Bernard Williams, also the chairman of Grantura Plastics, who made the glass-fibre bodies for the cars. Grantura Plastics used to prepare Entwhistle's car before each meeting. Tommy took some shares in Grantura Plastics, became a board member and eventually took over as chairman on Williams' retirement in 1972. The company diversified into making speedboats, and also made the Yak, a glass-fibre-bodied Mini Moke-style vehicle.

Fibreglass expert Williams had something of a competition background himself, having been a leading Speedway rider in the 1920s. He used to race at Bradford's Greenfield Track, which also had a greyhound track round the outside of the Speedway circuit. He recalls that, in 1928, someone came up with the idea of a race between a greyhound and a bike. He was the rider chosen. The hare came round, released the dog from the trap, and the starter flagged him away on his Scott motorcycle. The dog had half a length of the straight on him, before his tyre bit and he got away. However, he made it up and beat the greyhound, called Black Spec, by about a foot.

**Gerry Sagerman**
American driver Gerry Sagerman, who raced from 1959 to 1974, spent most of his career driving MG-engined vehicles. Starting with an Elva Courier, he moved to a TVR Grantura MK III in 1963. Having been appointed TVR's U.S. agent in 1966, he purchased an ex-Tommy Entwhistle TVR 1800 rolling shell, built up his own MGB engine and close-ratio gearbox, and ran it in SCCA events.

The year 1968 saw the purchase of an ex-works TVR Vixen, which had been built to race on the Isle of Man. Fitted with the engine and box from the MK III, this car saw Gerry have many wins in SCCA races, and set new lap records for Production Class D at Lime Rock, Thompson and Bridgehampton circuits.

**Paddy Gaston**
Invalided out of the cockpit with TB, Squadron Leader John Howard (Paddy) Gaston rejected the replacement desk job the RAF offered him instead, so took his lump sum and set himself up in the garage business. His mechanical bent came

from his father, a Presbyterian Church of Ireland Minister, who designed and built motor cycles in his spare time. Paddy was soon racing an Austin A35 and went on to become somewhat of a legend in his supercharged Austin Healey Sprite RAM 35, in which he won the one-litre class and finished second overall in the 1960 Autosport Championship.

During a race at Oulton Park during 1962, Paddy had a bad shunt in an Elva that resulted in his back being set in plaster and he had to be driven everywhere by his stepson Christopher. He soon tired of the role of invalid and one day handed a pair of tin snips to one of his mechanics, ordering him to cut off the plaster so he could get back behind the wheel and race the next weekend! Hailing from Ireland, Paddy was typically a great storyteller, singer and reciter of his national poetry.

In 1963, he bought a new lightweight racing Grantura Mark III from the factory. The body was built using two-ounce rather than three-ounce mat, and the whole car weighed 12.5cwt (635kg). Paddy competed with the blue car, which had a stage-six MGB engine and carried the notional number plate PG 1, during the 1963 and 1964 seasons. He found things much tougher with the TVR than the Sprite, the Lotus Elans in the Class proving to be stiff opposition.

Paddy's garage and tuning shop were at Albany Park Service Station, 215 Richmond Road, Kingston upon Thames, Surrey. Whilst he ran his racers from there, the bread-and-butter work comprised fitting modified cylinder heads and Weber carburettors to BMC Minis and 1100s. In 1964 he took on a TVR agency that traded from Kingston premises as 'The New TVR Centre'. Amongst his employees was a very young John McDonald, who went on to form RAM Racing and is still involved in the Formula One world.

During his racing career, Paddy became great friends with Alec Hounslow from the MG Development Department at Abingdon. 'The powers that be' at BMC required all competitors to deal with Abingdon via the Competition Department but, owing to his friendship with Alec, Paddy was one of the select band of racers who obtained parts from Development, occasionally getting his hands on items that were still being assessed by the factory.

Whilst outings in 1963 were confined to the UK, in 1964 he took in some European events. He won the GT Handicap Race on 10 May, during the first meeting organized by the BARC at Brands Hatch. Abroad, Paddy with co-drivers Adrian Dence and Keith Aitchison, was forty-eighth from 100 starters in the Nürburgring 1000 Kilometre race on 31 May. He had not fared so well two weeks previously at the Ring, when he failed to finish the 500km race on 17 May.

Gaston was one of three Grantura drivers who competed in the Goodwood TT on 29 August, the others being driven by Tommy Entwhistle and Alistair McHardy. The cars gave a good showing, with Tommy and Paddy enjoying a dice for fifth, which went to Gaston after Entwhistle retired. He had lost it at Woodcote as the result of a huge effort to pass his adversary, tearing off his exhaust system in the process. Goodwood was effectively Paddy's home track.

As well as 'PG 1', it seems that Paddy also raced two other Granturas: APH 223B and 678 EFR. Both these cars were demonstrators and Gerry Marshall suggests that, as well as being raced, their identities may, on occasions, have been transferred to PG 1 for continental events, where registration documents were required for temporary export. APH was subsequently owned, and possibly raced, by Peter Simpson and both cars now appear in historic events.

When he sold the garage at the end of 1966, Paddy got involved in charity work and later volunteered to fly children out of Biafra and Nigeria to the island of St Tome. Afterwards, he holidayed in Portugal, liked it and bought a plot of land there to build a house. In March 1972, Paddy moved to his new home in Burgau, severing most motor trade connections. However, Alec Hounslow was still a regular visitor to the Gastons' home, where they also provided accommodation for the occasional holiday maker.

Along with other ex-pats, Gaston was in danger of breaking the Portuguese legislation that

forbade any English-registered car remaining in the country for longer than three months. He soon found a friendly garage proprietor over the border in Spain who would 'look after' their cars for a period, before the vehicles were 're-imported'.

Paddy retired to the Isle of Man in 1989, where he died in 1997. His son Mike followed his father's footsteps into motor sport, participating in both racing and rallying. He navigated Kerron Humphries' class-winning Ford Escort, which finished fourth overall in the 1986 Irish National Tarmac Championship. The pair also won the 1995 Irish Forest Championship in a Ford Escort.

### John Wingfield

Paddy sold PG 1 to John Wingfield at the end of 1964 and he ran it in 1965 and 1966, changing the 'number plate' to XPG 1. John would go on to race all manner of cars, and he forged a business partnership with Gerry Marshall, who was also well known for success in TVRs. A ood driver, John had little time for his appearance and his unusual trademark was the fact that, owing to his large feet, he always raced in socks without shoes, because this gave him better pedal control. His first outing in the TVR was at

Goodwood's season opener in March, when he came third in the GT race. He was just second to Mike Campbell's Elva Sebring Courier at Goodwood on 3 April, though John did set the fastest lap at 86.92mph (139.88km/hr).

Wingfield was second to Mike Campbell's Elva Sebring-MG in the five-lap Marque race at Silverstone on 3 April 1965. But for a spin at Woodcote on the last lap, he might have won. Arthur Mallock raced XPG 1 at Lydden and he also drove it as part of the TVR team in the Silverstone Six-Hour Relay.

John drove a Grantura in the Spa 500km race on 16 May 1965. To comply with the regulations, John Aley, who was racing his Mini in the Saloon event, was nominated as co-driver but Wingfield actually drove the whole distance himself, with Aley in the pits just in case he was needed. Following problems in qualifying, he started from the back of the grid and completed twenty-nine laps of the thirty-six-lap race to finish seventeenth from twenty-seven starters, the last driver classified. However, his placing of third in the Class for GT Cars from 1,601 to 2,000cc, behind a brace of Porsche GTSs, meant that he scored one World Championship point. This was the only such point scored by a TVR of that era.

## Dr Rod Longton

Rod Longton was the next to race XPG 1, acquiring the car in 1967 and running it for three years in the Brands Hatch-based Amasco Championship. His main adversaries were Don Bunce driving the Nicholson-prepared MGB JYH 770D, also Midget drivers Roger Enever, John Britten and Gabriel Konig. The Amasco was a very closely contested series with lots of wheel-to-wheel driving. At Brands on 29 September 1968, he was involved in a three-way scrap for Class lead with Bunce's B and the Sprite of Barry Wood, the TVR beating the B by the narrowest of margins, whilst the Sprite eventually succumbed and fell off. Rod finished the season equal second with Enever, John Gott taking the crown in his Austin Healey 3000.

For 1969, Rod decided to challenge Gott directly for the outright Championship and he bought a supercharger from Jean Denton for the TVR. The regulations state that supercharged cars must multiply the actual cubic capacity by 130 per cent to calculate the Class in which they run. So, with a calculated capacity of 2,337cc, Rod was in the same class as Gott. He only did one race before he was told that it was not acceptable to supercharge last year's car to change classes. It has been suggested that Gott, a member of the relevant committee, may just have had something to do with this.

Rod was determined to win the Championship, so for 1970 he bought a V6 TVR Tuscan, winning the crown that year and continuing to race it until his first retirement from racing in 1973. Asked how he managed to fit his racing in with his life as a busy GP, Rod replied that he had some very good partners, adding that he was unable to race abroad, as it was a bit much to expect them to cover for him for more than one day at a time.

## Paul Howard

Having parked his road-going Grantura in the Lydden paddock after practice for his final race of the 1968 season, Paul Howard got talking to John Wingfield. John commented that the road car looked too good to race and when Paul agreed he was told that Rod Longton was looking to sell his lightweight racing version. As a result of this chance remark, Paul Howard became the next owner of XPG 1. His road car had originally been raced with an MGA engine,

*Rod Longton (174) shows the way round Brands Hatch Druids Hairpin, in his ex-Paddy Gaston/John Wingfield TVR Grantura.*

*Lydden Hill paddock. Paul Howard tows Grantura XPG 1, which he raced in both Modsports and Historic guises, behind his everyday Grantura, in which he first started to compete.*

*Paul Howard leads a pack of Historics in his TVR Grantura.*

but a broken con rod on the way home from a meeting persuaded him to upgrade to a five-bearing MGB unit.

XPG came as a rolling shell, so over the winter, Paul built up an MGB-based engine with an HRG cross-flow head, the road car being retained as the tow barge. It was quite a sight to see the white TVR come into the paddock towing another white TVR on the trailer. Between 1969 and 1974, Paul competed in about

ten Modsports races a year, taking an outright win at Lydden, his favourite and local circuit.

In 1975 Paul converted the car to HSCC regulations, reverting to standard rim width and reducing the wheel arches. The car had always run fairly standard suspension with different spring rates and adjustable shock absorbers. From 1976 to 1979 he raced in the HSCC Classic Sports and GT series, latterly finding the TVR gradually being eclipsed as Divas and Elans were allowed in, exactly as Rod Longton had found in Modsports ten years before. During the twelve years he campaigned the car, Paul had an excellent finishing record and took thirty-six top-three Class places.

### John Belsey and Phil Hooper

In 1983, Paul Howard sold to John Belsey, who raced the Grantura at Brands Hatch and Donington Park in June 1984. Following an accident at Oulton Park's Old Hall Corner later that year, the TVR was out of circulation for about twelve months for repair, before being sold, via Straight 6, to a competitor in France. Paris garage owner Gerard Giardini ran the car, which was raced for him by other drivers. All that is known of this interim history is that it was raced as part of 'Écurie Bleu' in a *Le Figaro* magazine-sponsored race, probably at Montlhéry Autodrome. When Gerard retired to the South, he laid the Grantura up before selling to another French enthusiast, who mistakenly believed it to be one of the Le Mans cars.

In 2001, the car re-emerged from obscurity, after Englishman Phil Hooper, who now lives in France, purchased it after spotting the car sticking out of a French barn. As the result of research for this book, the author is delighted to have been able to put Phil in touch with Paul Howard, who has authenticated his car as the former, long

lost, Paddy Gaston lightweight Grantura, known as PG 1. The car is undergoing restoration and will hopefully appear in competitive events once more, this time in historic road rallies.

### Alistair McHardy

When he came out of the forces in 1962, Alistair McHardy knew that he wanted to race and, as his girlfriend of the time had a Coventry Climax-powered TVR, decided that he would consider buying one. He went to the 1963 Racing Car Show and ordered a BMC-engined Grantura with a lightweight body. This was delivered, in kit form, on 1 July 1963 at a total cost of £960 14/3d (£960.71). The white car was assembled in Alistair's newly acquired mews garage business in Brunswick Street East, Brighton by his mechanic Arthur Bonwick and, on 3 July 1963, registered 3545 AP. Later, an engine was bored-out plus 60 and race prepared by HRG Engineering in Kingston upon Thames.

Alistair's first race was at Aintree in March 1964 and, like all events, the car was driven to and from the circuit, usually with his wife Jan in the passenger seat. Although he occasionally suffered a mechanical problem, McHardy never had an accident at any circuit. At Brands Hatch on 10 May 1964 he enjoyed a good dice with the R. Buchanan-Michaelson-driven Simca Abarth,

*Lightweight Grantura 'PG 1' has recently surfaced in France, where it had been raced by Gerard Giardini. This photograph is believed to have been taken at Montlhéry. Paddy Gaston, John Wingfield, Rod Longton and Paul Howard all successfully raced the car.*

beating him to take fourth place in the Redex GT Race. He won at Aintree on 28 June and again at Brands on 13 August, beating Tommy Entwhistle (TVR) and Bernard Unett (Sunbeam Alpine) – top drivers of the day. Alistair also recorded fastest lap of the race at 60.03sec.

He enjoyed a hectic race at Oulton Park on 17 September 1964, when he hounded Entwhistle for all ten laps of the Freddie Dixon Race, but had to settle for second place, Tommy winning by two seconds. 3545 AP was also entered in the local hill climb at Firle near Brighton, Alistair breaking the hill record for Sports cars between 1,300cc and 2,500cc in May 1964 with a time of 26.36 seconds.

Alistair carried on racing till the money ran out, then put the car up for sale – the London TVR Centre advertising it for £1,100 at the end of the 1965 season. Michael Warrard purchased and used it for hill climbs and races, the car proving exceptionally quick in his hands on the local Firle hill. Subsequent owner, Duckhams oil-tanker driver Derek Alison, also raced 3545 AP. When Alistair went to work for Adcocks, the Rootes dealers in Chichester, knowing his background they built up a Special Saloon Hillman Imp for him to race. He won the first-ever Special Saloon race at the newly opened Thruxton Circuit on 17 March 1968, beating a Bevan Imp into second place.

## James Boothby

Proprietor of the London TVR centre in Reece Mews, James Boothby was a great motor sport character during the early 1960s. While better known for his outings on the hills behind the wheel of his D Type Jaguar, he also had competitive outings in Grantura 678 EFR. This was one of the earliest Mk IIIs to have an MGB engine and was built with both a lightweight body and chassis. Suggestions are that this example had one of the two experimental five-speed gearboxes that BMC were testing at the time. It was first registered to the TVR Car Company on 16 September 1963, with ownership then passing to Boothby, who used it as a demonstrator and for competition.

The first time he ever raced the TVR, at Goodwood, he wore his business suit, not his customary race overalls. He considered smart attire better suited his appearance in a grand touring car, particularly as his friends had made comments about the fact he was not out in his usual open-topped Jag, but lording it in one with a roof. He also hill climbed 678 EFR and was a regular at Firle, near his Sussex home.

James, a noted raconteur, was much in demand to speak on racing at the local motor clubs and always attended with his Alsatian, Flash. The chairmen knew that he needed to have his glass regularly topped up but he always requested a separate pint of beer as well. From time to time he would decant some of this into an ashtray on the floor, where it was eagerly lapped up by Flash, who at the end of the evening happily walked to the car.

## Mary Wheeler MBE: The Racing Grandmother

Founder member of the British Women Racing Drivers' Club (BWDC), Mary Wheeler and her husband, a former Rolls Royce employee, ran Wheelers Service Station on the A23 near Bolney in West Sussex. She started racing a TR2 at Goodwood following persuasion from her youngest son William, who was at school with Richard Sykes, son of BARC official Geoff Sykes. Les Allard taught her to do racing starts on the London to Brighton road.

Later, she bought a Grantura Mk I in kit form and remembers it came with some components missing and a surplus of others. She continued racing in this dark-green Mk I, 1223 CD, which she and mechanic Arthur Bonwick had built up. In 1962, Mary founded the BWDC, initially to campaign for better facilities for the increasing number of women drivers at race circuits, but it went on to become a much respected club in its own right. Arthur convinced her she needed still more power and, having had no luck in persuading Coventry Climax to assist in getting greater bhp out of their engine in the green car, she sold it and bought one of the first-built MGB-powered 1800S models.

*Mary Wheeler's Grantura Mk1, built from a kit and raced.*

This red Grantura, GVB 822D, proved to be a good car, with Mary taking many places in it at various race circuits, sprints and hill climbs, including local events at Firle Hill Climb and the Brighton Speed Trials. She recalls a win at Goodwood. It was traditional for the winner to appear on the club house balcony after the race to receive the crowd's accolade. As she approached the stairs for her moment of glory, the Clerk of the Course took her aside saying he thought it would be inappropriate as another driver, who had crashed in her race, had died from his injuries.

By now a widow, Mary was working for a local printing firm, using the TVR to drive to and from work. Bernie Garwood, who had a garage at Sayers Common, looked after the car for her. When he died, she sold it but continued to compete in friend Peter Garrett's Elva Courier. Peter Tatton, GVB's next owner, competed in Modsports events from 1972 to 1982, enlarging the rear wheel arches to take 10in steel wheels. Much of the interior was removed in an attempt to reduce the weight of the vehicle and additional telescopic shock absorbers were added at the front. This example is currently being restored by Jonathan Thomson, who purchased it in 1994.

In recent years, the organizers of the Brighton Speed Trials asked Mary if she would like to open the event by driving down the course in a current TVR. The idea was that the TVR and a Ferrari would go down together but, unfortunately, the Ferrari ended up in the barrier. Awarded the MBE for her children's charity work, Mary Wheeler is still President of the BWDC who, in December 2000, organized a surprise party for this amazing lady's ninetieth birthday.

### The Barnett Motor Company

Following financial problems, TVR was taken over in November 1965 by Arthur Lilley and his son Martin, who ran TVR dealers The Barnett Motor Co. From 1965 to early 1967, Gerry Marshall was sales manager at Barnett, so it came as no surprise that he would be seen racing a TVR. The car, LHV 41D, belonged to Martin Lilley and was the first 1800S built at the factory under the Lilley regime. Originally the demonstrator, with an immaculate finish after seventeen coats of paint, it was turned into a full race car.

### Gerry Marshall

Gerry had his first TVR outing at Brands Hatch in 1965. Driving John Wingfield's car, XPG 1, he came third in the Redex GT Championship event. This was Gerry's first non-Mini race and was also the first time a TVR had set a sub-sixty-second lap of the Brands Club circuit. He would go on to drive TVRs in many races, the V8-engined models particularly suiting his exuberant driving style. He enjoyed a superb battle with the Liège-winning Healey 3000 of Lionel Mayman at the 1966 BRSCC Whit Monday Snetterton meeting. Driving the BarMoCo 1800S, LHV 41D, Gerry slipstreamed the weaving Mayman down the pit straight, eventually getting past round the outside at Sear. The pair changed places twice more before Gerry pulled away to win the class.

Tony Lanfranchi co-drove the BarMoCo 1800S with Gerry in the Six-Hour race at Brands Hatch, on 8 May 1966. In the early stages of the extremely wet race Gerry was running seventh and working his way through the field. During the third hour the car, now with Tony at the wheel, was up to third, despite having clutch problems. Later, the TVR pitted to have a

*As well as racing TVRs in the 1960s, Gerry Marshall competed in the MGCC BCV8 Championship during the 1980s. Here he presents Rob Gill with an award at the 1980 BCV8 dinner.*

throttle cable changed. In the final half hour, Gerry got back up to eighth but rear hub failure, not an uncommon problem, resulted in a lost rear wheel at Druids and retirement. However, Gerry did record a number of wins in the car before it was sold to Peter Clark.

Gerry, Tommy Entwhistle, Dudley Hardwicke and Peter Simpson were members of the TVR team for the August 1966 Silverstone Six-Hour Relay. Whilst leading from pole in his V8 Griffith, on lap twenty Gerry was overtaken by his own rear wheel, the car eventually spinning to a halt. He ran back to the pits with the sash and another car took over whilst he readied his 1800S. Later in the race, he lost another wheel, the only time in his whole career that he lost wheels off two cars in the same day! Tommy Entwhistle drove the remaining four hours in his Grantura, the only one left, to come home twelfth.

Martin Lilley obtained Tommy's car for Gerry to race at the 1966 Mallory Park Boxing Day meeting. Despite having never driven it before, he went out and won the Modsports event. Gerry, probably best known for his time behind the wheel of his famous Vauxhall saloons Big Bertha and Baby Bertha, chalked up his 606th career win in 2001.

## Charles Blyth

Charles Blyth was an entertaining driver in his white Beta Cars' 1800S, BAC 666B, during 1967 and 1968. Charles bought it from Weatherleys Garage, Ivor, in August 1966. The car had originally been owned by Peter Simpson, who sold it to Godfrey Binks in 1965. Peter dealt in TVRs and raced a Griffith. BAC was not ready for Blyth's first race of the new season at Mallory Park, so Robbie Gordon lent him his London TVR Centre demonstrator for the day. Charles finished second to Roger Enever's rapid MG Midget.

Beta Cars was a tuning shop set up on 1 February 1966 by former Jaguar engine test-shop colleagues Graham Burrows and Les Ryder. Graham conceived a logo of a gold Greek 'B' on a blue triangle. They rented a brand new 1,500 square foot workshop, Pandex Works, Fosse Way, in Princethorpe, near Coventry, from the Blyth family business, which built steel-framed factory units and used the other half of the building to weld up their frames and roof trusses. Part of the deal was that Beta would prepare Charles's racing cars. Les modified cylinder heads for many of the top tuners of the day including Broadspeed and Bill Nicholson. When Burrows left after eighteen months, Charles stepped in to finance and manage the set-up. Ryder, an expert with BMC 'A' and 'B' series engines, built a very special power unit for his TVR.

Just outside Princethorpe was a length of road known locally as 'the straight mile' and the Beta engineers used it to set up and test customers' cars. The local traffic police would often park their Ford Zephyr out of sight at the back of the workshop and come in for a cup of tea. If a road test was due at the time of their visit, they would position the Zephyr across the only junction on the 'straight mile' to prevent other cars joining the road. Undoubtedly, they enjoyed watching the various cars being driven at speed with Les usually in the passenger seat, stop watch in hand.

As well as being straight, the road was also completely level. Simon Saye, who worked at the nearby Triumph factory, recalls using it for aerodynamic tests. They would drive the car up to a given speed, decelerate, then use a stop watch to measure how long the vehicle took to slow to the control speed: in effect, measuring the decay of speed. It was all basic stuff in those days and general use of a wind tunnel was a thing of the future. Les Ryder moved on from Beta in early 1968, setting up Hartshill Engine Development Services (HEDS for short) in Hatherstone Road, Hartshill, Nuneaton.

Charles Blyth had a real battle with Peter Cox's Triumph Spitfire and Gabriel Konig's MG Midget at Brands Hatch on 29 May, managing to split the pair for fourth overall after ten hectic laps. At the Castle Combe round of the Freddie Dixon Championship on August Bank Holiday Monday, he lost it at Quarry whilst lying third and was clouted into retirement by the closely following Porsche of Dickie Stoops. In order to reduce the centre of gravity the TVR had 13in by 7in Minilite wheels, instead of standard 15in rims – the revised size also gave a wider tyre choice.

Successful Mini racer Roger Edwards also worked at Beta Cars. He recalls working late one night and discovering that the company's Mini pick-up, which he used to get home to Kenilworth, would not start. Blyth's racer was the only running car in the workshop and, having phoned for permission, he duly drove it home. Returning to work the next morning, he went to pass a stationary bread van, which pulled out as he got alongside. Roger swerved onto the grass, the limited-slip diff bit and the TVR ended up embedded in a telegraph pole; the driver suffered a split lip and lost a front tooth. Summoned by the hospitalized driver, Les trailered the racer back to the workshop and told Charles he had better order a new body shell. He set to and helped the lads with the re-shell into a later 1800S body and the car was back on the track in three weeks.

Roger is convinced he was fated to write the car off one way or another. Blyth had entered a Marque Sports race at Castle Combe and, as Roger was taking the car down to the circuit, it was suggested he might like to drive it in the GT race. Blyth put the car on pole during his dry practice session, Edwards went out to qualify in

the wet and despite lack of grip and visibility, managed to put it on the front row for his race. Charles went out and beat Bill Nicholson to win his Class, then returned to the assembly area for Roger to take it out. Having not enjoyed his practice session, Roger declined to race and loaded the car back onto the trailer – whereupon he noticed all the wheel nuts were loose. Had he gone out he is sure the car would not have made it.

During 1971 and 1972, Charles Blyth competed in a Blydenstein HB Viva, including an endurance race at Nürburgring in 1972, where he co-drove with his brother-in-law David Wansbrough. Blyth was tragically killed whilst driving a Lancia Fulvia back to his Sicily hotel after practice for the 1973 Targa Florio.

## Tony Claydon

Designer Tony Claydon got the taste for motor sport having visited the Racing Car Show with friends during the early 1960s. Sports cars were his interest; his everyday car was one of the ex-works Le Mans Granturas that he had purchased from Ron Hills, who had raced it at Brands. Tony spent most Saturdays at the Barnett Motor Company where he got to know Gerry Marshall. Once, Gerry asked if he would like to go and collect his racing V8 Griffith from a nearby machine shop, which had worked the heads. Armed with the trade plates and Gerry's assurance that the car had been fitted with road silencers, he set off. Gerry had told him to drive carefully and not look conspicuous.

When he arrived at the workshop, Tony could not believe his eyes. Where the race tail pipes came out from under the rear of the car, each had a tube with a 120-degree bend sleeved over the pipes, which then went up the back of the car, through a 90-degree bend and joined a forward facing silencer above the roof. Everything was held together with self-tapping screws. He could not possibly see how he could drive that car through Barnett High Street on a Saturday morning and *not* look conspicuous!

When racing was discussed, Gerry had told him the only way he would find out if he had

*Gerry Marshall told Tony Claydon he would not go wrong by buying Charles Blyth's TVR. Tony races the car at Brands Hatch in 1970.*

the makings of a good driver was to buy a car with a known history and have a go. In 1970, Charles Blyth advertised BAC 666B for sale and Gerry agreed that it was too good an opportunity to miss. Tony paid £775 for the car with a spare three-bearing engine and trailer.

The car had stood for two years, so Tony checked it over but, apart from needing a new set of treaded Dunlop tyres, everything was fine, although he changed the rear rims from 7in to 8½in, preferring wider rubber on the back. His first race was at Brands Hatch on 26 April 1970. A large number of friends heard about his maiden outing and turned up to watch. Unfortunately, Tony had problems with the trailer on the way, arrived late and had to practice out of session. This meant that he would start from the back of the grid with a ten-second penalty, much to the amusement of the assembled supporters. Tony says that the ten seconds between the rest of the grid leaving the line and the flag being dropped a second time for him 'seemed for ever', but he was determined to make the best of it. He climbed through the field and finished eighth.

Tony had re-painted the TVR blue and, at Martin Lilley's suggestion, badged and raced as a Vixen, the company's new model. He took an

outright win at his fourth Modsports race, at the Brands Hatch Mini Seven Club meeting on 14 June 1970, at an average speed of 73.74mph (118.67km/hr). He shared the front row with Anthony Binnington's MGB and Irvine Laidlaw's Morgan 4/4. Tony and Irvine pulled away a little and then had a really enjoyable dice, with the Grantura leading the Morgan over the line by half a bonnet's length (0.2 seconds). Having read the *Autosport* race report, Charles Blyth rang to congratulate Tony, delighted that his old car could still win races.

Following a bank-clouting accident at Brands Hatch, Tony trailered the car up to the TVR factory at Blackpool overnight and slept in the tow car till the factory opened. He was awoken by Martin tapping on the window asking what he wanted – he realized what when Tony showed him the racer. The chassis man looked at it and assured him the car would be repaired in time for his next outing. Then Martin filled him up with coffee and sent him on his way back south.

Along with Mike Aitken, Paul Howard and Howard Reader (who briefly worked for the Barnett Motor Co.), Tony was in the TVR team that won the team prize at the 1970 AC Owner's Club Lydden Sprint. The same year, Mike and Tony started the TVR Club magazine *Sprint*, which still thrives to this day. A photograph of his car appeared on the front cover of the first issue. Despite a spin at Paddock Bend, Tony recovered to take third in the BRSCC Modsports race at Brands on 25 October.

Claydon continued to have success with BAC until 1974, when he changed the engine to an 1,820cc pushrod Ford, which he found lacked the MGB engine's torque. In 1975, he sold the car to TVR dealers Queensbury Garage and, despite recent enquiries, has never heard of it since. Following a brief flirtation with Pipers, which he could not get to handle to his liking, Tony returned to his winning ways in Modsports driving the ex-Bob Eccles Elan.

## Other TVRs

Arnold Burton, of Montague Burton the tailors, also a director of TVR, ran a Grantura with a 'B' series engine. Whilst his motor sport predominantly involved rallies, notably the 1961 Tulip Rally, he did compete in several sprints driving his car. Peter Clark and Ted Worswick entered Peter's example in the 1967 Nürburgring 1,000km but retired after three laps with transmission problems. It was an all-TVR battle at Croft on 20 May 1968, when Jimmy Goddard in his 1,800cc Northern Sportscars Vixen fought it out with Blyth's 1800S over twenty-five laps. Other notable TVR racers of the era included Michael Collins, who ran a 1,798cc car in 1967. In Holland, an 1800S registered EM-83-65, one of three LHD examples exported there in 1965, finished second in class at Zandvoort that year.

## Granturas in Historic Events

Like the early MGBs, TVRs are now eligible for FIA historic racing. Rob Grant, who started racing in a Sprite during 1962 and, amongst other vehicles, also competed in a Tom Boyce-tuned, pull-handle MGB, has owned his lightweight Grantura, 191 WNK, since 1987. This car, which had been entered at Le Mans in the 1960s, was restored by Arnie Johnson, with an 1,840cc MGB engine with Weber 45 and producing 120bhp.

## Rob Grant

Rob's first outing was the 1988 Coppa d'Italia, but a piston cried 'Enough!' on the third day while he was racing round the Mugello circuit. The repaired car then finished the season with some HSCC races and appeared at Prescott and Loton Park hill climbs.

The Grantura then entered its rally phase, with Rob competing in the 1989 to 1991 Pirelli Marathons, gaining two Alpine Cups. Following club racing during 1991 and 1992, Rob did the 1993, 1994 and 1996 Spa 6-Hour Races with Robert Baker-Carr as co-driver. Robert co-drove the Grantura with Nick Lees at the Silverstone Coys Historic Meeting, where they finished a creditable nineteenth overall, against much exotic machinery. The pair also drove in the Essen round of the 1996 European Historic GT series. The car was tenth overall, second in class in the 1996 Nürburgring 500km Marathon.

More endurance racing followed in 1997 and 1998. Rob suffered a broken throttle cable three corners from the finish of the 1998 12-Hour race at Magny-Cours. He tried to wedge the throttle open with his balaclava and crawl over the line but the marshals deemed the car to be in a dangerous position to be worked on and forbade him to continue. Nonetheless, he was still classified twelfth. Rob's highlight with the Grantura was having his entry for the 2001 Le Mans Legends race accepted.

It took place on the Saturday morning of the 24-Hour Race, the drivers sprinting across the track to their cars in a traditional Le Mans style start, for the warm-up lap. This was to ensure that everyone fastened their safety harnesses for the race proper. Competing in Class 7 for cars up to 2,000cc built from 1961 to 1964, Rob qualified forty-fourth and finished the race twenty-eighth from sixty-one starters.

## Nick Lees, Norman Nicoll and Rod Begbie

Navigating for Rob Grant on the Marathons kindled Nick Lees' interest in TVRs and, having raced for many years (his first outing in an Invicta), he was soon driving 191 WNK in a few events. In 1999, he decided to acquire his own Grantura and in partnership with Norman Nicoll bought 9299 VC, a former road car which had been converted to race spec for Roger Monk, who briefly competed during 1989. Rod changed the colour from orange to dark blue, also re-plumbed and re-wired the car, and competed twice in 1999.

By 2000, Norman had his licence and competed in five club races in quick succession to get the required signatures, his sixth race being a long-distance event at the Nordschleife in 2000. The idea always being to compete in European endurance events, the pair raced at Donington, Pau and Spa. Outings during 2001 took in Nordschleife on 11 August, the Eifel Klassik, and a two-hour race at Zandvoort in October.

Rod Begbie, Norman's nephew, had become involved in the racing of 9299 VC, and looked to acquire his own car to race. In April 2001, he purchased 678 EFR, another lightweight Grantura that had a contemporary racing history, before it appeared in historic events in 1990.

David Fenemore, who had obtained FIA papers, restored the car to racing specification, lowered it and replaced the transmission tunnel,

rear floor pan and bulkhead in aluminium. Having installed a Quaife gearbox, he ran it in the MGCC Chapman Warren Series. Stan Leithead, the next owner, bonded back the original fibreglass interior sections, increased the ride height back to almost standard and re-plumbed the exhaust, before he had a couple of outings in the 750 Motor Club Road Sports series. Finding it difficult to run his racing Elan as well as the TVR, he decided to sell.

New owner Rod raced at Cadwell (HSCC), Snetterton (AMOC), Brands Hatch and Croft (AMOC) to obtain sufficient signatures on his licence to upgrade it to international. He particularly enjoyed his race-long battle with Anson Howe's MGB at Snetterton, despite losing the place on his last lap. Just like his uncle, Rod's first international race was at the Nordschleife.

678 EFR was one of four Granturas to compete in the marathon race at Nordschleife on 11 August 2001. Rod Begbie's co-driver was Simon Armer, the others in the 'team' were Nick Lees/Norman Nicoll (9299 VC), Rob Grant/Anthony Binnington (191 WNK) and Joe Ward/Bernd Schmitt. Unfortunately Ward's car was badly damaged and, whilst the others fared a little

*This TVR Grantura saw competitive use in the 1960s. Joe Ward now races the car in European Historic events.*

better, none made the chequered flag for one reason or another. However, they were not too disheartened. In Rod's words, 'It is a terrific event and the privilege of racing at the Nordschleife is not to be missed.'

### Karl Schlagenhauf and Joe Ward

In 1998, German businessman Karl Schlagenhauf acquired, from Robert Baker-Carr, Grantura EFV 52D. Paul Barker had sprinted this car in 1966 and James Boothby's nephew, Fred, owned it in the 1990s. After a comprehensive rebuild by Cambridge Motorsport, including a 168bhp MGB engine, Karl entered it in the European historic series. German saloon car driver Bernd Schmitt and Joe Ward shared the driving. Amongst their successes was sixth overall in their first event, the 1998 Nürburgring Six-Hours.

Joe Ward now owns and competes in this Grantura and has been very well placed in many European Historic events.

### Roy Stephenson

In 1998, Steve Reid sold Roy Stephenson APH 223B, a former Gaston car, last owned by Michael Walker. The car was restored from its sad state to FIA spec in order to compete in European long-distance races. As a result of Roy's other racing commitments, the car's main outings were in 1999 at Spa and the Eifel Klassik, where he finished the three-hour race, which he drove throughout, sixty-fifth from 180 starters. The car, which has since been seen at a few club events, is due to have a more intensive season of European endurance races in 2002.

## The WSM MGB

Garage proprietor and former caravan manufacturer Douglas Wilson-Spratt was well versed in designing aluminium sports-car bodies and, in the 1960s, noted for his WSM (Wilson-Spratt Motors) Spridgets, which competed in all manner of motor sport events. Six members of the family were amongst those who drove WSMs, of which Douglas's son-in-law, Mike Lewis, was the most prolific competitor.

In 1966, Mike purchased the damaged rolling shell of the ex-Robbie Gordon racing MGB, 113 DJB, and handed it over to Douglas for his treatment. Robbie allowed Mike to borrow his race engine with its twin-choke Weber for as long as he competed in the car. As with all Wilson-Spratt's cars, a roll bar was an important part of the body frame and around this he built a very sleek aluminium body, lowering the windscreen line considerably from the original MGB height and incorporating a Kamm tail. In conversation, Douglas' cars were sometimes referred to as 'Wuzzums', which is what his wife Lorette called them. This last original example of a WSM was completed in April 1967, at a total cost of £800 minus engine. It still carried the registration 113 DJB.

### Mike Lewis

Mike Lewis used the car for work every day and at weekends drove it to the circuit, unbolted the silencer and went racing. He recalls after one Silverstone race he was too tired to fit the exhaust system, threw it in the back and drove to the paddock gate. He was stopped by John Gott, the racing Chief Constable of Northamptonshire, who warned Mike he was bound to be 'nicked by one of his officers'. Mike continued his journey and got away with it. He found himself racing against the established drivers in the up-to-two-litre sports car class and had many a dice with Bill Nicholson's immaculate MGB, the car to beat at the time. It was accepted that Nicholson's engine gave 20bhp more than that of Lewis, who relied on the WSM's weight advantage and more aerodynamic shape to even things up.

He debuted the car at the MG Car Club Silverstone meeting on 27 May 1967 where, during one of the five races he took part in that day, he was to have his first contest with Nicholson. The pair disputed the lead of the five-lap Abingdon Trophy Race which *Safety Fast*, the MG Car Club magazine, would later describe as the MGB race of the year. Nicholson just came out the winner. Mike's tally from the car's first meeting was one win, two seconds, plus fastest lap in every race. Lewis was equally at home in sprints and hill climbs and, during 1967, he had class wins in every event at Woburn Hill Climb and Chipping Norton Sprint, also taking the class records.

Race results continued, with class wins at Silverstone NSCC, at the AMOC meetings in May, NSCC in June, Llandow in September, and finishing the year with one at the Peterborough MC meeting at Silverstone on 9 September.

## Ben Grub and Robin Pinkerton

At the end of the 1967 season, Mike decided to forego racing, and to sell the car, bought the engine from Robbie. He then decided the car was so light that it would probably go almost as well with a standard MGB power unit, so he bought one and installed it. He advertised the race engine for sale and, the day the advert came out, a man from Scotland telephoned to say he would have it and would drive down overnight to pick it up. At 7am the next morning Mike drew the curtains to see the buyer in his car on the drive waiting for signs of life.

The WSM MGB found a new owner in Ben Grub. He bought it for road use and recalls the nitrided crankshaft breaking at 70mph. It was replaced by a balanced standard one and after that it ran without problem. Ben got married in 1969 and, needing a saloon, part exchanged the WSM back to Mike Lewis, coming away with a BMW 2002TI.

Mike then sold the WSM minus engine but with the straight-cut close-ratio gearbox, to Robin Pinkerton, who had recently taken over as sales manager at Douglas Wilson-Spratt's Delta Garage in Hockcliffe Street, Leighton Buzzard. Robin, who basically wanted the WSM as a fast touring car, decided the straight-cut gearbox would be too noisy, sold it and bought a standard engine and box. The block was bored out to 1,950cc and everything was meticulously balanced at Delta. Unable to get an overdrive gearbox, he changed the back axle ratio for a higher one, which was ideal for cruising. At this stage, the car, hitherto a racer with a stripped-out cockpit, was trimmed and had more comfortable seats fitted.

Soon after the new power unit was installed, Robin took the car on holiday to Spain, recording an average of 40mpg (6 litres/100km) on the trip, a testament to Douglas's aerodynamic design. As a member of the Sporting Owner Drivers Club, Pinkerton competed in a few sprints and hill climbs and remembers having good drives at Long Marson and Woburn. In 1972 he sold the WSM and an ex-Pat Moss Healey 3000 that he also owned, in order to finance his own business – Pine Tree Garage at Edelsborough.

## Barry and Pam Sidery-Smith

Barry Sidery-Smith owned the WSM from 1976 to 1980. Barry and his wife Pam double-entered it for the 1976 Brighton Speed Trials, Pam being elected to drive it from their home in Surrey to Brighton in the pouring rain. Apparently none of the windows would open and they all got misted up. During the event Pam recorded a time of 30.90 for the standing kilometre, whilst Barry went down in 29.50, Pam commenting that he invariably beat her by something like a second. The WSM was going exceptionally well that day as, following problems with its own engine, Barry had installed the power unit borrowed from his ex-works Le Mans car, which ran exceedingly quietly.

The Sidery-Smiths used the unusual Coupé as an occasional road car, doing the rounds of the MGCC 'natters'. Long-time friend Denis Whistlecroft shared the car with Barry, driving at the Silverstone Sprint in November 1976. It was wet, which resulted in a body-creasing excursion into the Armco.

## Tony Bianchi

In 1977, Barry sold the WSM to Tony Bianchi, who resprayed the car red and changed the registration to 270 RBM.

He describes the WSM as a fast, reliable road car in which he did a lot of miles. Tony enjoyed moderate success in a number of sprints and races he entered, which included events at Curborough, Silverstone, Snetterton and the Brighton Speed Trials. He also has recollections of taking it abroad for a hill climb. Top speed was about 130mph (210km/hr) and the car handled well, Tony finding it was even more 'chuckable' once he put on a set of Dunlop CR 65 tyres. The car proved to be extremely reliable and was driven to and from all events.

## Josie Tolhurst and Amanda Langton

Josie Tolhurst's husband Rodney bought her the car in April 1981 and, having got used to the WSM on the road, she raced at MGCC Brands on 12 September, at BRSCC Brands on 26 September, and she also recalls doing an HSCC event at Silverstone. Still racing single seaters, the lack of time to develop the WSM made the Tolhursts decide to part with it.

Amanda Langton comes from a family very involved in historic racing cars; whilst her contemporaries read the likes of *Woman*, Amanda's favourite magazine was *Autosport*. One day she noticed an advertisement for a Ford Escort race series at Brands Hatch, where for £800 you turned up and drove. She started saving and applied for her licence. Seeing his daughter's determination to follow him onto the track, her father, Soames, persuaded her it would be better to race the kind of vehicle they knew about and he acquired the WSM from the Tolhursts at the end of 1982.

The car was run in the HSCC Classic Sports Car and GT series during 1983 and 1984. In her first year, Amanda won the HSCC Best Newcomer Award and also the British Women Racing Drivers' Club trophy for the best newcomer. She enjoyed racing in the wet, which was a great leveller and enabled her to fare much better against more powerful machinery. Her 1984 outings included JODC Silverstone 7 April, JODC Oulton Park 28 April, AMOC Brands Hatch 20 May and BHRC Brands Hatch 10 June.

In 1985 Amanda moved to Formula Junior in a Lotus 22 and the WSM was sold to the Autotron Museum in Holland, where it was displayed for the next ten years. The Langtons then brought it back to England in 1996 and advertised it.

## Tony Wilson-Spratt

Having journeyed from his home on the Isle of Man 'just to see it again for old times' sake', Douglas' son, Tony Wilson-Spratt, returned to the island with the car. So, thirty years after he bought the damaged Robbie Gordon MGB, Mike Lewis prepared his father-in-law's creation for its Manx Vehicle Test. Tony has since done further work and raced in the MGCC British Sports Car Festival at Rockingham on 21/22 July 2001 and the JCC Snetterton meeting the following weekend. It is now registered NMN 97, 97 having been the traditional family number for many years.

*Amanda Langton races the WSM MGB in a Historic event during 1983.*

# 9  The MGC GTS Project

Unlike the B, which had its circuit debut some months after the car was first announced, it could be argued that the MGC was being groomed for racing by the factory even before the first production road car had been seen by the public. In 1966, Stuart Turner, the Competitions Department manager, instructed Pressed Steel Fisher of Swindon to make him some very special sets of MGC GT body panels, to be pressed in aluminium.

Five shells would eventually be built by bonding and riveting the aluminium front and rear wings and roof onto standard floor pans, which also had unclad steel A and B posts along with roof frame and supports. MGCs have aluminium bonnets, but the five GTSs also had alloy tail gates. MG folklore has it that six special shells were eventually manufactured, but Richard Hurl, who now owns a GTS, has checked the ADO register at Gaydon, which confirms that it was five.

Pressed Steel used Eric Fisher of Abbey Panels, in a nearby village, to hand-make wide wheel arches, which were riveted onto the wings to cover 7in Minilite wheels. The shells were stored above the offices at Abingdon until after the C had been launched. They had been sprayed red and came with black-and-grey thin needle-cord-covered trim panels, the fabric used in the works rally cars. The bodies would later be re-painted British Racing Green. It was intended that the cars would race in the Prototype Class.

## The Works Cars: MBL 546E and RMO 699F

The Competition Department got to work and built up two vehicles, which used the basic MGC

*MBL 546E on the 1968 Marathon de la Route at the Nürburgring. The car was driven to sixth place overall by Tony Fall, Andrew Hedges and Julian Vernaeve.*

suspension configuration, though, along with the brakes, components were upgraded for racing use. The cars had Perspex windows except for the laminated glass windscreen.

May 1967 marked the first appearance of what was to become known as a GTS, when MBL 546E was entered in the Targa Florio where, despite some long pit stops, drivers Paddy Hopkirk and Timo Makinen brought it home ninth overall, third in the over-2,000cc Prototype Class. However, the car appeared in the entry list as an MGB GTS Prototype and was powered by a 2,004cc, overbored MGB engine under an MGB bonnet. The first appearance in C guise was at the Sebring 12-Hour race in March 1968 – some say Sebring accounts for the 'S' designation. MBL 546E and RMO 699F, the sister car, had outings at Sebring and the Marathon de la Route.

As had previously happened with other 'works cars', the two original examples of the GTS remained in America following their last outing at Sebring in March 1969, entered by British Leyland America after Lord Stokes pulled the plug on works entries by the parent company.

MBL 546E apparently 'sat around' at Leyland's premises in Leonia New Jersey for about eighteen months before being sold to Bruce McWilliams of Pond Ridge, New York. He was a vice president of Leyland America and kept the car as a showpiece until it was advertised for sale by his wife, Gertrude, in October 1972. The asking price $4,500.

## MBL Returns

Fortunately, both these unique cars would eventually return to England, and continue to have an active competition history to this day. MBL, which Canadian drivers Bill Brack and Craig Hill had brought home in thirty-fourth place at Sebring in 1969, was used for promotional purposes in various dealerships in the USA until 1972. Having failed to sell the car in America, Bruce McWilliams then shipped it to England; Richard Martin-Hurst collected it from the docks and sold it, on his behalf, to Robert Brown in Lancashire who predominantly used it as a road car.

*The works mechanics find a distraction in the Nürburgring pits during the 1968 Marathon de la Route.*

## Richard Wileyman, Kit Edwards, MBL and KMO 386D

Richard Wileyman, the next owner of MBL, had seen Martin-Hurst's advertisement in 1972 but at the time could not afford it. Richard, who raced Minis, also owned another very interesting MGC, a Roadster, KMO 386D. This was a development car, one of fourteen pre-production MGCs built. Richard did a couple of Shanstone Car Club, Curborough sprints in it, but mainly used the car for towing the Mini to circuits, occasionally at a recorded 110mph (177km/hr). On the way to one meeting, he hit some road works at excessive speed, ripping the back bumper and tow bar completely off the car after all the bolts had sheared. He looked in his mirror to see the trailer, now detached from the C, still following him, so accelerated to get away from it. Fortunately the trailer stopped without damage. Richard later fabricated a more substantial tow bar that bolted directly to the chassis legs, rather than the bumper mountings.

KMO was built on 3 November 1966 and although it is chassis number 2, it is body number 1, which leads one to believe that the first MGC ever built utilized a modified MGB shell. First registered on 1 December 1966 to MG Cars Abingdon, the ownership was later changed to British Motor Holdings. Wileyman acquired it in 1967.

The car has many anomalies from the spec of a usual C, including 3.9 axle ratio, 1966-style MGB door handles and trim, non-reclining seats, single-speed wipers and a positive earth electrics with an alternator. Under the boot mat, current owner, Kit Edwards, found the car's factory build record. He believes that this car was used for cooling development, as the radiator had thermo couplers at top and bottom, as did the sump, and the top radiator fixings are missing. It seems that the radiator, which has now been rebuilt, originally had a special core.

Wileyman sold KMO 386D to Edwards in 1972; he used it as his daily transport and drove it in a few autotests and PCTs, for which he admits the MGC was totally unsuited. After taking it on honeymoon to Devon and Cornwall in 1976, Kit took the car off the road for a rebuild, but family and work meant this unique car would not reappear until 1992. Parts required came from a Unipart clearance sale, via a friend who worked there. The car is virtually as it was when built, with all its unique features still in place. Having run for a time with an engine from an Austin 3-litre, it now has its original, un-numbered 29G-series power unit back under the bonnet.

Wileyman paid £2,200 for MBL in 1974, deciding that, 'I was not going to miss it this time; at that figure it was an investment.' The sale included the spare engine and gearbox in their original factory crates, but Richard declined to pay an extra £200 for a set of J.A. Pearce knock-on alloys with racing tyres, the car coming on seventy-two-spoke wire wheels.

He collected it on 8 May 1974, and on 24 May, took part in the vehicle parade at MGCC Silverstone. The GTS was taken on a couple of family holidays: 'a bit noisy, a bit smelly but lots of fun to drive.' His only competitive outing was at the MGCC Wiscombe Park Hill Climb on 23 June 1974. He was involved in a three-way

*MBL 546E in the paddock at MGCC Wiscombe Park Hill Climb on 23 June 1974. This was Richard Wileyman's only competitive outing in the car.*

tussle for Class 7 with Jim Loveday and Mike Webb, who were sharing Jim's MGB. It was close, but after the second runs, Richard had to settle for third, having gone up in 52.63 seconds. Jim (52.47) won and Mike (52.53) was second. Richard was pleased, as the diff was wrong for the venue and he had to over-rev it in first out of Martini to the finish.

The MG Car Club were asked to provide a selection of interesting cars to take the drivers around Thruxton before the Easter Monday Formula 2 race, in 1975. Richard drove MBL and had Bang & Olufsen Team driver Bernard DeDriver as his passenger. During the lap he tried to make conversation with his celebrity, who had a moderate grasp of English. Bernard asked, 'Vat iz zis car?' Richard told him that it had been driven by Paddy Hopkirk, which produced absolutely no response; he then added that Timo Makinen had also raced it. Bernard's face broke into a broad grin, 'Aah Timo Makinen'. On arrival back in the paddock, Bernard was immediately surrounded by his group of twenty-year-old acolytes, pointed to the car and said something, then the group all looked up and mumbled, 'Aah Timo Makinen'.

When Richard originally bought MBL he had a car sales business and it was kept on the premises, but when he moved into plant hire he had nowhere to keep it. Thus, MBL ended up displayed at the Cheddar Gorge Motor Museum, which closed in 1979. This building, purpose built as a car museum, is now a branch of The Edinburgh Woollen Mill. The GTS had also lived in Richard's parents-in-law's garage, and during the final months of ownership it was displayed at Thornfalcon Garage in Somerset, which always had interesting cars in the showroom to attract customers.

On 10 October 1979, Colin Smith, an MG Triple M enthusiast, purchased MBL from Richard's advertisements in *Motor Sport*. By then the car had low oil pressure and he was advised that it would be safer to have it transported back to Suffolk rather than attempt to drive it. Having got the vehicle home, Colin instructed the then recently established Brown and Gammons to rebuild the engine and gearbox, and respray the car. Not being competition minded, Colin used MBL as a fast touring car and took it on camping trips to MGCC Silverstone. When Colin Pearcy acquired RMO, Smith took MBL over in order that the two sister cars could be compared. Smith sold his example at a 1985 auction, the car finding a new owner in David Collins. One source suggests an interim ownership by Michael Fisher.

## David Collins and Mick Darcey

Collins, who entrusted his acquisition to Graham Pearce of Bromsgrove MG, intended to race the car in historic events but never got round to it. In 1992, along with its sister car, RMO, it was track tested by Alec Poole for *Historic Race and Rally* magazine. Dave sold the car to Mick Darcey in 1995, about six months after Mick had bought RMO. Ron Gammons drove MBL to sixth place in the Coys, Abingdon Trophy Race in 1996, and in 1998, Malcolm Gammons won the Handicap Race in it at the same meeting. Mick will have selected outings in Class AB (for FIA cars) of the 2002 BCV8 Championship. He has previously raced his ex-works MGB GT, LBL 591E, in the series, winning the T & L Trophy for the highest-placed FIA car in 1996.

## RMO Returns

RMO 699F, which Paddy Hopkirk and Andrew Hedges brought home fifteenth overall (ninth Prototype) at Sebring, remained in America for somewhat longer. In July 1969, the Baker Motor Co. bought the car and put it up for sale. It took almost two years to find a buyer, then twenty-two-year-old Camran Ayoubpour purchased it on 8 April 1971. Camran worked in a local clothing store and managed to scrape together the required $4,500 with the aid of an HP loan of $2,200.

He later moved to California, put a personal number plate on the GTS and for a while it 'disappeared'. It seems the specially built Abingdon dual-circuit brake master-cylinder had broken

*Colin Pearcy races the ex-works Sebring GTS, RMO 699F, at the 1991 MGCC Snetterton meeting.*

and, having been told by his local MG spares dealer they were unable to replace it, the owner had pushed the car into a garage and forgotten about it. In 1986, he offered it to a local garage who contacted Julius Thurgood who, when he received the Polaroids, realized it was RMO, and purchased and returned the car to England. His friends at Moto-Build poured some oil down the bores, put new batteries on it and got the car to run.

## Colin Pearcy and Mick Darcey

Colin Pearcy became the new owner of RMO at the end of 1986. Following a rebuild by Roger Dowson Engineering, Colin, who had previously competed in the BCV8 Championship, returned to MG racing with RMO in 1988. It appeared at various historic meetings in the hands of Colin and Barry Sidery-Smith.

Mick Darcey now owns the car. Colin raced it for him in the Coys Historic Festival at Silverstone on 2/3 August 1996. He qualified the car on the inside of the third row, but made a good start and got into second place behind Stirling Moss in ex-works MGB, 6 DBL, closely followed by Barry Sidery-Smith in his Le Mans MGB and Tony Binnington in OMO 70. Colin

got by at Stowe but in doing so went wide, got two wheels on the grass and clipped the gravel trap, showering those behind with stones. He came through Luffield with one front wheel six inches in the air and managed to take the lead along the start finish straight.

In the closing stages, Barry got up to second and was slipstreaming the GTS at every opportunity. Colin was quicker down the straights, where Barry was keen to get a tow because when they got to the twisty bits his B handled much better, forcing Colin to take the GTS very wide. Colin won the Abingdon Trophy by 0.66sec, after twelve hectic laps, thus taking RMO's first outright win twenty-eight years after the car was first built. Mick Darcey drove it at the Coys Festival in 1998.

## John Chatham, VHY 5H

Peter Browning, who took over from Stuart Turner in 1967, intended the GTS to have its next outing in the Targa Florio, a tough road race in Sicily, and had lined up well-known Big Healey racer John Chatham to be one of the drivers. John remembers the phone call he received from Browning, asking if he wanted the good news or the bad news. Peter told him that

*Steve Hutchinson (L) and Mick Darcey (R) with their ex-works
GTSs RMO 699F and MBL 546E.*

*John Chatham gives VHY
5H a pre-Targa Florio
shakedown by racing it at
Thruxton in spring 1970.*

*There he goes! John Chatham during the 1970 Targa Florio.*

he no longer had the drive, to which John demanded, 'Who's bloody well got it then?' Peter replied no one had, as the project was being scrapped. The good news was that John would have the chance to buy everything that was left.

Chatham rushed up to Abingdon and spent a whole day inspecting the mass of remaining items on offer, and after discussion did a deal. He purchased the two remaining body shells, set of spare panels and all the other parts, including engines and gearboxes, that had not gone out to America for the Sebring race. Included were two alloy-block castings. Apparently, the factory had a number of MGC blocks cast in alloy, of which only two were any good; these arrived at Abingdon only days before the cars were due to be shipped out to America in 1968, too late to be used.

Encouraged by Peter, Chatham decided to enter the 1970 Targa Florio himself and built up a complete GTS, registered in his native Bristol in February 1969 as VHY 5H, taking the works body number as the chassis number. As there were no wheels amongst the spares acquired from Abingdon, John got some 8in JAP alloys and used Firestone semi-slick tyres, which he usually ran on his Austin Healey 3000.

To shake the car down, it was entered in a couple of races at Castle Combe, his local circuit. Satisfied all was well, he bought a new Vauxhall Ventura Estate car and used it to trailer VHY to Sicily, accompanied by Sprite racer Alan Harvey, his Targa co-driver, with mechanics John Horn and Jim Jewell. They caught the ferry across the Channel and drove to Paris, where Chatham took over the wheel until they reached the Alps, the first part of the non-stop journey where two slept in the back whilst the other two drove or navigated.

During scrutineering, the race officials told John that, in their view, his entry was not a GT car and insisted if it raced at all, it would have to be as a prototype. Knowing he had no chance of a win, John agreed to transfer to the Prototype Class and, eventually, the officials agreed to let it compete. Qualifying was dominated by the lightweight Porsche 980 Mark IIIs, that outclassed the five-litre Ferrari 512s to take the leading grid positions. Come the race, on 3 May, the cars started in order of cubic capacity, thus the Ferraris were on the front row. More to the point, John Chatham's three-litre MGC GTS was on the second row!

The start was delayed for some reason and, as a result, the GTS oiled a plug, completing most of the first lap of the forty-four-mile road circuit on five cylinders. The car came onto six just before John readied to turn into the pits for a plug change. 'Sod's Law,' commented John. Determined to enjoy himself, he powered into the corners, hanging the back out, to the obvious delight of the crowd. It was understood that there should be no overtaking in the villages. John recalls passing a slower Alfa, when all of a sudden the two of them were lapped by one of the leading Porsches, the air current nearly blowing the bottles off the roadside café tables. During the closing stages, John experienced brake problems and on reaching one corner was forced to use the Armco, protecting a long drop, to slow the car. He was suddenly horrified to see a girl sitting on the rails with her legs dangling over the side of the track. She threw herself backwards and broke a leg as a result of the fall.

After the finish, the local police began to express an interest in the incident, so the team quickly loaded up, took the first available boat from Palermo Harbour and sailed back to Naples to begin the long homeward journey. On arrival back to base, the Ventura was booked in to the Vauxhall dealers for its first service, the bemused mechanics pondering the 5,000 recorded miles and the list of warranty defects on the three-week-old vehicle.

## VHY Changes Hands

Shortly after returning from Sicily, John sold VHY 5H to Ian Perrett, who, at the time, was successfully campaigning his John Britten-built ex-Archie Phillips Midget in the hill-climb championship. Chatham had a customer for the Midget and persuaded Ian to give up what he felt was a championship win to acquire the GTS. Ian continued to do hill climbs in the new car and also entered the final rounds of the 1970 Modsports Race Championship. As a result, VHY appeared on the grid against Chatham in his subsequently built Modsports GTS at Thruxton on 14 November (where Ian came third in Class B, which Chatham won) and Brands Hatch on 6 December 1970.

Early in 1975, Cedric Brierley, another well-known racer of the era, who had competed in Elva Mk IV and V Sports Racing Cars in the early 1960s, acquired VHY. At the time, Brierley had a collection of interesting vehicles but admits that he never raced the GTS, eventually selling it to Rod Leach of Nostalgia in February 1977, the odometer recording 4,000 kilometres.

After a little refurbishment, the GTS was entered in the opening round of the HSCC-organized BAT Historic Championship at the JDC Silverstone meeting on 12 March 1977. Chris Drake, Rod's driver, found the car handled well despite the wet conditions, finishing third in the Group 4 Category. Rod enjoyed driving the car back from Silverstone until a half shaft broke fifteen miles from home, forcing him to trailer it the rest of the way. Rod, whose first car was an MGA Twin Cam, obviously had a great affection for the GTS, recalling, 'It had 202bhp, but the triple Webers were a pain. They used to pop and bang and you had to give it a good bootful to clear them!'

## Graeme Perkins and Tony Kember

The car was then sold to Ferrari and Porsche specialist Graeme Perkins, who had a showroom just off Berkeley Square. However, his everyday car was an MGC Roadster and he bought VHY, for

*Chris Drake on the grid at Silverstone Jaguar Drivers Club meeting on 12 March 1977. He finished third in Class.*

£5,000, partly as an investment and also because of his love of MGCs. The GT was kept in one of four Nissen huts on the outskirts of Harefield where he and his pals stored and tweaked their own cars. Graeme only used it on about four occasions; three of those were trips to the local pub, but the fourth and final outing was a little more memorable.

One weekend, an old friend arrived with a car-mad French journalist – apparently the journalist was most anxious to have a ride in Graeme's unique MG. The local enthusiasts had established their own test circuit around the country lanes of Harefield, and it was agreed that Graeme and his friend would take turns in taking the Frenchman on a 'lap'. Each trip saw the car going progressively faster with the drivers trying to outdo each other. Fourth time round saw Graeme's pal at the wheel and the locals, annoyed at having their Sunday afternoon peace shattered by the screeching of tyres and the roar of the open exhaust, shaking their fists at the passing vehicle. It was decided it was time to put the GT

back in the Nissen hut, where the very subdued Frenchman alighted after a trip he was unlikely to forget.

Whilst they were shutting the doors, the local policeman arrived and, as Graeme put it, they had their fingers well and truly slapped. When asked why he had not stopped them at the time, the policeman replied they were going too fast and all he saw was a flash of green. It was made clear that, if that car was ever seen on the road again, the proverbial book would be thrown at him. Graeme decided it was time to part with VHY and, having closed his own showroom, entrusted Nostalgia with the sale.

In April 1979, it found a new owner in Tony Kember, who kept the car for twelve years. He again obtained Group 4 papers from the HSCC. He considered that the class structure within the historic series put the GTS at a disadvantage, particularly as he was being lapped by Lola T70s after only five laps of Silverstone. Following two historic events, one on 1 August 1982, he confined his outings, when time and

money permitted, to MGCC BCV8 Championship rounds where, competing in the Modified Class, he found there was always someone to have a dice with.

Tony ran the car on Dunlop Green Spot tyres, using the original rims, but later, in an effort to find more grip, tried a lower-profile tyre on Revolution alloys. Towards the end of his ownership, a wet practice off at Silverstone's Becketts corner saw the GTS sustain heavy damage to the rear bodywork as the result of hitting the bank. Following repair, Tony decided, rather like Ian Perrett before him, that it perhaps had too many historic connections for an everyday racer and on 28 August 1991 sold it to Paul Jarrold, and bought a competition MGB to replace it.

### Paul Jarrold and Richard Hurl

Paul, a lifetime MG enthusiast, had, during the 1970s, owned various pre-war six-cylinder versions of the marque, including an F2 and two NDs. Having seen Tony's advertisement, he made enquiries and, realizing it was a rare vehicle, bought it. He did not compete in VHY,

just enjoyed driving it, describing the car as 'immense fun, if a bit uncivilized'. His early Sunday morning blast through the country lanes around Sevenoaks provided a therapeutic diversion from his hectic job in the city. Unhappy with the open air-intake, Paul got Doug Smith to make him a replica works grill, which was fitted to VHY. He drove it to MGCC Silverstone in 1992, the only time that all six cars ever appeared together.

Richard Hurl, the current owner, purchased from Rod Leach. In November 1992, Rod had taken the car in part exchange from Jarrold for an AC Ace. Having displayed the GTS at a number of shows, Richard was invited to enter it in the 1996 Coys' Festival at Silverstone. This was the trigger for him to enlist the help of Doug Smith, from MG Motorsport, to carry out a mechanical rebuild and it was Doug who drove in the race, recording eleventh place in the Abingdon Trophy Race. Doug raced the car again at the MGCC Silverstone International meetings in 1997, 1999 and 2000.

Satisfied that the GTS was once again in race order, Richard himself took the wheel at the MG

*Current owner Richard Hurl puts VHY through her paces at the MGCC Silverstone Sprint in 1977. Moments after this photograph was taken he hit the barrier at Copse.*

Car Club Silverstone Sprint on 15 June 1997. Having swapped ends during practice, as a result of the very efficient rear brakes, he used the gears to slow for Copse on his first timed run, but with the same effect, this time the car smote the Armco on the inside of the corner. A balance valve has now cured the problem and Richard still sprints VHY at MGCC Silverstone and Bentley Drivers Club Abingdon events.

## The Two Road Cars: VHW 330H and EHW 441K

British Leyland Motorsport Press Officer Alan Zafer bought the fourth shell. An Abingdon employee, probably Les Washbrook, built up a road GTS for him. Using a wrecked C for running gear and identity, the GTS became VHW 330H. Initially it utilized the engine from the 'donor car' complete with standard SUs. Later, looking for more power, Zafer bought a new iron-block and took the car to John Chatham, who built an engine to a much higher spec and also fitted some uprated components from his Abingdon batch. Meanwhile, SU in Acton made a balanced set of triple 2in carburettors.

As well as driving VHW as a fun, fast road car, Alan used it in a few sprints. He recalls a rocker arm breaking on the way to Mallory Park. He limped into a local garage, that happened to have an old Austin three-litre hearse standing out at the back. He was soon on his way with a rocker from the hearse, which, to his knowledge, is still on the car to this day. He also competed in sprints at Blackbushe Aerodrome. In the mid-1970s, Alan sold to Syd Beer; the car is still in his collection, having had just the two owners.

Chatham utilized the other body to build a road car, EHW 441K, for a Mr W. H. (Bill) Gardner, who used it until 10 August 1980, when the recorded mileage was about 30,000. This car ran on triple SU carburettors rather than Webers. Having always been fascinated by the GTS project, Edward Kirkland had asked Chatham if he knew the whereabouts of any of the cars and he was put in touch with Bill. Edward assisted with work on the car and was offered the chance to own it when it came up for sale.

Kirkland used the GTS as a fast road car, describing it as 'a joy to drive'; he competed in sprints at Colerne and Wroughton, and also did some demonstration laps at Castle Combe and Silverstone. Returning from Silverstone one day, he pulled up at a roundabout and looked in the mirror to see a large saloon car bearing down on him at great speed; it stopped with less than an inch to spare. He decided that the unique vehicle was not 100 per cent safe even on the road and, not wishing to see it damaged whilst in his hands, decided to sell.

Steve Bicknell had always asked for first refusal and a deal was done, Steve taking the car over on

14 February 1989. He put it on Goodrich 225 TA tyres, which he found made the steering much lighter. He says EHW had a distinctive creak, which he puts down to the body's bonded construction. It appeared at two MGCC Silverstones and, having done about 600 miles, Steve sold to Nigel Dawes in 1998.

In need of some refurbishment, Nigel decided to bring the car up to 'works' spec, John Chatham having a hand in the project and supplying some parts from his original consignment. Former BMC works driver Andrew Hedges then bought the vehicle and, following a Brown & Gammons make-over, re-registered the car LBL 547E, an ex-works number. He has discussed doing continental rallies in it with Clive Baker.

## The Chatham Modsports GTS

The 'sixth shell' is not entirely without foundation, given that, in 1970, John Chatham did build up a rather more radical Modsports MGC GTS. This had fibreglass wings moulded from the originals, but with even wider arches, and the all-alloy engine set back some four inches in the chassis. This car utilized the spare panels from the original GTS project but was built on the floor pan of an MGC Roadster, possibly a prototype shell, which Chatham acquired from Zafer in lieu of payment for work done on Zafer's own car. It incorporated many of the special Competition Department items such as high-ratio steering rack and up-rated torsion bars.

John campaigned it in Modsports races in 1970 and 1971. It was originally painted yellow, the livery of Tower Scaffolding, but later changed to black with orange stripes. The car performed well in the up-to-three-litre class, John beating the three-litre TVR Tuscan of Bob Haugh to take the Silverstone lap record at 65.4 seconds. Interestingly, John's very developed Big Healey's best time for the same circuit was 67 seconds.

Whilst his Healey alloy blocks gave no problems, Chatham says the MGC versions never had

*Perhaps the ultimate GTS? John Chatham's Modsports car at Thruxton in 1971.*

*Steve Bicknell races the 'Red Rooster', JHU 21L, at Castle Combe in 1987.*

sufficient oil pressure and also flexed. Both blocks threw number six con rod through the side, necessitating welding by a local specialist firm. On one occasion, he rang the company to arrange collection of the repaired block after such an incident, to be told they would get it out for him, ready for his visit the next day. The boy was given the job and left it out – literally. It was stolen overnight, presumably for scrap. Only one block remains and is still in the car.

The racer was also used for a few events in 1972. Having qualified second in the Modsports round at Thruxton on 9 July, John was looking forward to a good dice. Regrettably, Alison Davis in her Femfresh-sponsored Ginetta G15 tangled with him at the start and the GTS retired on the first lap, with a puncture from the G15's glass-fibre body. Eventually, John, tired of the continued engine problems, ceased racing the car; it was laid up and languished in a corner of his workshop, making occasional display appearances at MGCC Silverstone, until sold, fitted with aluminium front wings, to Mick Darcey in 1999. Having found the car ineligible to race because the engine had been moved, Mick will probably put it back in the standard position and hopes it will then be seen on the track once more.

## The Red Rooster, JHU 21L

Not strictly part of the GTS project, JHU was a very special one-off MGC Roadster that was also built by John Chatham. Known for making Healey 3000s handle, Chatham got hold of an MGC shell that was 'lying around at Abingdon', basically to see what he could do with it. He grafted on four fibreglass wings, moulded from one of the GTS cars, and added a fibreglass bonnet with alloy-skinned doors, scuttle and battery covers. Painted red with a red hardtop, he jokingly referred to his creation as 'The Red Rooster'. The three-litre engine had works crank, triple Webers and drove 14in by 8in J.A. Pearce alloy wheels through a straight-cut gearbox and LSD.

Having completed the project, John drove it on one of his trips to Abingdon to show Peter Browning, suggesting this was what BMC should have done with the MGC. Peter apparently told him that he agreed, but explained they were only the Competition Department and that, when it came to production models, no one listened to what they had to say. In any case, he had recently heard that the factory were about to discontinue the model, so John was too late.

Steve Bicknell, a friend of John's, did his first event in it, a hill climb at Wiscombe in 1978, taking a second in class. Having much enjoyed its use as a very fast road car for a while, John sold the unique MGC to Londoner Derek Grant, who liked the name so much that he put gold-leaf rooster logos on each side. Derek drove it on the road and competed at a number of race meetings, including Silverstone and Brands Hatch. John bought it back some years later and it found a new owner in Steve Bicknell.

Steve remembers losing it at Quarry during his first race, at Castle Combe in 1985. Deciding to join Chatham racing Big Healeys, Steve ran the C in the 1987 MGCC BCV8 Championship, whilst he finished building his race 3000. He used the year to learn his race craft, though he had to agree to compete for no points or prizes as the Rooster did not conform to the BCV8 regulations. Nevertheless, he had a most enjoyable year and still owns the car.

## 30 MGC and VVK 9H

Over the years, many GTS or Sebring replicas have been built, but the outstanding example is the car registered 30 MGC, completed by Doug Smith of MG Motorsport for Malcolm Young

in 1990. Malcolm had commissioned the project in 1988 having missed buying RMO at auction.

Malcolm's brief was for Doug to build him a near-exact replica of the original works Sebring cars and it was based on RMO, which Smith had access to. He purchased a LHD MGC GT shell and a works aluminium roof pressing from Beer. Apparently a tree had fallen on the GT when it was a current vehicle and the insurance company agreed to a re-shell; this was the slightly damaged original. The roof was to be replaced anyway, so it was ideal for the purpose. In the course of the project, Doug had certain brake and hub parts recast and machined to pattern.

30 MGC won the Cynthia Batley Trophy for the best MGC in the Silverstone International Concours in May 1990, and Malcolm took the class at the AMOC Goodwood Sprint in July (102.52sec). He also raced it at MGCC Silverstone in 1990 and 1991. The car is apparently now owned by Rodney Timson, husband of actress Penelope Keith.

VVK 9H was a race-spec copy of RMO, which Doug had built in 1988 when he worked for Colin Pearcy. Having acquired the real RMO, Colin wanted a look-alike that could be raced in earnest without the concern of damaging the historic original.

*Malcolm Young's 30 MGC at speed during a 1992 Goodwood test day.*

*Peter Hiley (80) leads a group of MGCC BCV8 cars in Doug Smith's unregistered replica GTS.*

An alloy-panelled GT that looked like a GTS, it lacked the fine detail of the original. The car also served as the prototype for Doug's modified torsion bars, which have done much to improve the handling and popularity of the MGC today. Although not a works-built car, it probably had more genuine works competition parts on it than the real ones. Gerry Marshall raced it at Oulton Park and Thruxton, and Colin had one outing in it at Donington Park. It was one of the BBC Top Gear Heritage Team Challenge contenders track-tested by Tony Dron for *Classic Cars* in June 1989. Up against MGBs, a Proteus C Type replica and TR4s, it came out on top. At the end of the year, Colin sold the car and it became part of the Carter collection.

## Was There One Other Works GTS?

Having spent many hours researching the GTS cars, I feel that I can not close this chapter with-

out airing the theory that maybe more than two lightweight cars were shipped out to Sebring. It has been suggested the third example was used as a practice car. So were there really six lightweight shells plus the Chatham Modsports car?

In late 1979 Graham Nashe-Wiseman was tipped off by a friend in America that what appeared to be one of the GTS cars had surfaced in San Jacinto scrap yard. In 1982, he returned from a trip to the States having shipped back eighty-six parts of what he believed to be RMO 699F, together with a very oil-stained British log book bearing that registration number. The intention was to rebuild the car on a budget with glass-fibre, rather than aluminium body panels.

On 24 May 1983, satisfied that this was the missing car, DVLA issued Graham with a replacement V5 Registration document for RMO 699F, recording the chassis number on the stamped plate, which was still attached to the bonnet slam

*One of the two road-going versions of the GTS that John Chatham built. EHW 441K pictured in the Silverstone paddock during Edward Kirkland's ownership. A GTS deserves to park anywhere.*

panel. In return he was required to surrender the original oil-stained cardboard log book, which was subsequently lost.

In 1986, Julius Thurgood shipped back the complete car, which bore the registration number RMO 699F, though it carried a chassis number two digits earlier than Graham's car. In March 1987, both vehicles displayed the same registration number. It was subsequently considered that this vehicle had greater claim to being the authentic RMO than Wiseman's almost-restored example and Graham reluctantly relinquished the registration. In the late 1980s,

Graham sold his car and it was later bought at auction in America by collector Derek Durst. This car is still believed to be in the USA.

Other theories are that the 'sixth' was written off testing in the desert, or that one shell was originally built up as the four-cylinder MGB GTS, MBL 546E, that Hopkirk and Makinen raced in the 1967 Targa Florio, with a separate body used for the later six-cylinder version. However, the records currently at Gaydon show only five were built and the former Abingdon employees of the time say they can only remember five.

# 10 Taming the MGB GT V8

It was well-known 1960s Mini racer Ken Costello who originally offered a V8-powered MGB for sale, in 1970, but it did not take British Leyland long to realize he was filling a real gap in the market, and by 1973 they were marketing a factory version. The official V8 eventually reduced the Costello production to a trickle, but not before Ken's outfit had produced about 200, a few of which were roadsters, whereas BL stuck to GTs on the grounds of strength.

## Ken Costello

Surprisingly, Ken only once raced a Costello, a 3.5-litre metallic-red roadster, which he competed in at Brands Hatch. He admits that it was really to satisfy himself as to how his creation would go round his local circuit, rather than a serious attempt to win.

## Bob Neville

The next milestone in racing V8s is down to Bob Neville, a former Morris Motors apprentice who, in 1973, was working in the Development Department at Abingdon. Bob, who had already raced a Mini, his own lightweight Midget and an Arkley, was now looking for something a little more powerful. Having previously been put off the idea of a racing MGC by Sid Enever, he decided that V8 was the way to go. Former fellow apprentice John Bilton, who navigated Alec Poole's Frogeye on the Welsh Rally, was now an executive with BL at Cowley and, as such, he could purchase parts at cost price. He had already expressed interest in getting involved with Bob's scheme so he ordered a GT shell that was taken

to Bob's workshop at Sutton Courtenay, which he shared with Mini racer John Watts, where work commenced.

Barry Jackson from the Development Department did the drawings, and Bob obtained fibreglass wings and arches from John Chatham, moulded from his GTS. Minilite were approached to supply wheels and provided 9in fronts and 10in rears, free of charge. Bob also had luck with an engine. Bill Shaw had raced a Rover 2000 Saloon for British Leyland and they had a 3,500cc V8 prepared for the car by Traco in America. During one outing, the heads had been damaged and the bottom end had been put on one side.

This engine was acquired from Alec Poole, who had bought the Rover. Bob stripped it down and sent the parts to Bassett Down Engineering in Wiltshire for machining and balancing, then entrusted the engine to Cliff Humphries from Competitions Department, who rebuilt it in his workshop at home. Cliff ported his own heads to complete the unit and 2in SU carbs were mounted on a special Development Department manifold. The car had uprated Armstrong front shock-absorbers and retained cart-springs at the rear, again with uprated levers and a specially fabricated anti-roll bar. This was later removed during testing, when it was found it reduced the suspension travel to about one inch. Mark Hale, from the Abingdon body shop, fitted the wings and carried out the other body modifications, including ducting to cool the brakes.

Bob debuted his V8 at the MG Car Club Twenty-Fifth Silverstone Festival on 24 May 1975, where it showed well in the MGB and MGC race, up against eventual winner Malcolm

*Bob Neville's V8 at Thruxton in 1976.*

Trewhitt in his MGC. However, it developed a slipping fan belt; that would become a problem with the prototype V8 road cars, which Bob eventually helped to cure. This outing marked the first appearance of a race-tuned MGB GT V8 at an MG Car Club event, Bob finishing second in class, fifth overall, as the result of finally losing the fan belt. He had two other outings and finished a Thruxton Modsports race early in 1976.

The regulations for Group 5 Sportscars had just been announced and it was decided to rebuild the V8 to comply, and to enter some international races. Keen to attract a large grid for the Silverstone round, Pierre Aumonier, from the BRDC, had offered start money. A great deal of work was required to convert to Group 5,

most done by Derek Worthington at Roger Heavens' workshop. This was in the yard at the back of the family pub, 'Mister Warrick Arms' in Ock Street, Abingdon. Within two minutes walk of the factory, the Warwick was frequently used by both Competition and Development staff to take visitors to lunch. Roger, who was often seen behind the bar, raced a Chevron at the time. Derek, his mechanic, latterly manager of Xtrack, was to be Bob's co-driver.

The roll cage had to be upgraded and the car fitted with a long-range tank and Rellumit refuelling system, the filler neck coming out of the tailgate window. Throttle cables were doubled up and Hale enlarged the brake ducts still further. John Bilton was to be time keeper and the pit crew, most of whom were Abingdon employees, worked under the direction of Mike Ticehurst of Motor Race Engineers, Bourne End. A tyre contract had been negotiated with Dunlop.

The car was ready for the third round of the Group 5 World Sportscar Championship at Silverstone on 29 May 1976. However, the scrutineers were not happy about the filler neck, necessitating an all-nighter to encase it in a fire wall. Neville and Worthington qualified twenty-fourth, in reality using the session to get a race set-up. Come the race, the car was soon working through the field and, after three hours, it looked as if, barring no major problems, they were in with a chance of finishing in the points. But the brake pads wore out during the last half hour and it would not have been time effective to pit for replacements. Bob, who was at the wheel, reduced his pace accordingly.

They finished, coming home eighth, scoring two World Championship points and beating the Mass/Ickx Porsche, which was tenth. Bob was delighted; he says it brought it home to him when he saw his car standing in Parc Fermé two places in front of the Porsche that had been driven by two such formidable names in long-distance racing. As a result, MG was joint fourth in the Championship. These were the last international points scored by MG as a marque of BMC or British Leyland. Bob now has the gouged brake-pad backing plate from the car on his desk as a paperweight.

Following the success, John Bilton approached Alan Edis to see if Leyland would back the project, which would obviously provide further good publicity for MG. Having just axed the Jaguar Coupé project and with GT V8 production being scaled down to free engines for the

*Parc Fermé, Silverstone 29 May 1976. Neville's V8 after it scored the last World Championship points for MG under the Leyland regime.*

Rover 3500, he was told the answer was no. Bob is sure their times at Silverstone would have got them an entry at Le Mans and wonders if they shouldn't have gone ahead as privateers.

He had one final outing in the V8 at Snetterton in June; here his luck did not hold good and he retired with a broken half-shaft. In fairness, the car was still in long-distance trim and really too heavy for a ten-lapper. It returned home and stood in his shed. He subsequently sold the car to Malcolm Beer who used it to great effect in the MG Car Club BCV8 Championship between 1977 and 1997. Soon after Silverstone, Bob was approached by Stratstone, a large London Leyland Cars distributor, to get involved in their own V8 project, initially as a test driver but later in a racing role.

## The Stratstone V8

In 1976, Tim Goss was working for Leyland Cars when he negotiated with MG for Ginetta G4 racer Mike Gidden to purchase, for £250, a USA-spec orange MGB GT rolling shell that was surplus to requirements. The concept was to build a Modsports V8 that conformed to FIA regulations as well, so it could also be used for occasional World Sports Car Championship rounds. Chas Beattie was commissioned to build the car, which ended up as a very radical lightweight version, resplendent in its dark blue Stratstone livery.

It had coil-sprung trailing-link rear suspension, whilst at the front Beattie did away with the heavy sub-frame, replacing it with a redesigned

*Not much room! The engine bay of the Stratstone MGB GT V8.*

*The Stratstone car on display outside the sponsor's showroom.*

space frame with McLaren wishbones and brakes. Tim had negotiated a sponsorship deal with Stratstone and through them obtained a V8 engine. This was rebuilt by Weslake Engineering in Rye, who bored it to 3.9 litres. With Isky cams and a Holley carburettor it obtained a power output of around 400bhp.

Goss competed fairly successfully in 1977 Modsports races at Brands Hatch, Thruxton and Silverstone, and also recalls, as a member of the MGB team, leading the 1977 Donington Six-Hour Relay race until being pushed into the sand trap by a Porsche. He lost time whilst the car was dug out but still won the Driver of the Day Award, possibly as the result of his spectacular cornering, the car over-steering because the front spoiler came off in the accident. Mike Gidden and Bob Neville joined Tim for the World Sports Car Round at Silverstone on 15 May, but the car retired from the Six-Hour Race as the result of the engine maladies that had plagued it during practice.

Tim and Bob came home sixteenth in the Brands Hatch Six-Hour Race, round 7 of the World Championship for Makes, on 25 September. The race was held in appalling wet conditions; Clerk of the Course, Peter Browning, stopping it for safety reasons after thirty-seven laps. A completely new race was eventually started, for a reduced duration of two and three quarter hours, on a drying track. At the finish, Tim had to be lifted out of the car and resuscitated after driving the final hour with exhaust fumes leaking into the cockpit. The car had covered eighty laps, compared to 103 of the winning Porsche 935 driven by Mass/Ickx, an excellent showing, given that all but six of the twenty-two-car entry were Porsches.

The V8 was advertised in *Autosport* at the close of the season and sold to Richard Scantlebury. Subsequently, Jim Smiley the MD at Stratstone agreed to back Goss and Neville running a Triumph Dolomite in endurance races and, the following year, making an attack on the emerging British Touring Car Championship.

## Richard Scantlebury

Richard Scantlebury ran the V8 in British club races during the 1978 season. Richard changed the colour to what he describes as refrigerator white and had 'Vote Conservative' and 'Maggie for PM' sign-written on the back. One racing correspondent wrote of 'the V8 scything through the back markers, or should it be back benchers!'

On 28 August, Richard beat the Aston Martins of David Ellis and Dave Read, to win the All Comers Race at Mallory Park – earlier in the programme he had beaten Malcolm Trewhitt's MGC to win the MG Car Club Race. Having set a blistering pole position lap of 77.37mph (124.51km/hr) at the 17 September MGCC Brands Hatch meeting, Richard howled away

*The Stratstone V8 creeps up on one of the Porsches.*

from the line and took the lead, only to melt from the contest at the bottom of Paddock Hill Bend, on lap four, when a broken Panhard rod forced retirement. The race was eventually won by Terry Osborne's MGB, with Alan White taking the Modified V8 Class in his recently rebuilt example.

Eventually, continual use took its toll on the front suspension, a broken wishbone forcing another retirement. Richard then had the set-up rebuilt by Arch and saw the rest of the season through with no further problems. Moving house in 1979 necessitated selling the V8 to a hill climber. Richard later heard that the car had been damaged and does not know if the former Stratstone MGB GT V8 was ever rebuilt.

## Peter Robertson's Rallycross V8

Probably one of the most unusual V8s was the Rallycross example of Pete Robertson. He had seen a similar beast, driven by Richard Stock, at a Long Marston Rallycross meeting in 1980 and decided it was cheaper to build himself an MGB GT V8 than to get a Ford BDG for his Twin Cam Escort. In 1982, his neighbour sold him a B GT rolling shell for £150 and by the time he had sold off the interior, doors and wings, which were replaced with fibreglass, the shell had cost him nothing. Modified Escort bubble arches were fitted to cover the tyres, in accordance with the regulations. A 'cut and shut' Ford Capri fibreglass front spoiler replaced the original heavy BMC front-panel assembly. He retained the aluminium bonnet and also the metal tailgate, to keep weight over the back axle.

The power unit came from a 1968 Rover 3-Litre Coupé, which was rebuilt and tuned, by changing the cam and working the heads, to run on a Holley carb. Pete made his own manifold and exhaust system that ran through the passenger foot well. Initially the car was completed using a Wolseley-110 back axle, up-rated front lever arms and a Morris 1800 radiator mounted in the back.

Pete had obtained permission from Lord Rockingham's estate manager to test his cars at nearby Rockingham Airfield, now the site of the new Rockingham Raceway. He used the largely intact perimeter road and ploughed through the old allotments when he needed a rough section. Initial running of the V8 revealed a floppy front end and severe overheating problems. Back to the drawing board.

The radiator was changed for a four-core version fed by 2½in bore pipes – air was ducted in behind the doors and sucked out by two fans through large vents in the tailgate. Telescopic shock absorbers were added to the front suspension, retaining the lever arms as the top link. Following early outings, the back axle was changed for the modified Jaguar E Type axle from Stock's car, which had been broken for spares. Pete substituted single shock absorbers for the doubles and fabricated a ladder frame from 2in-square tubing to bolt the whole assembly onto the shell.

Subsequent modifications included fitting a Rover 2600 five-speed gearbox, which had closer ratios than one from a 3500, and throwing away the lever arms, using Mini top mounts to locate the telescopics, later upgraded to gas-filled units. The Holley carburettor was changed to four Weber IDAs. With a little over 300bhp at his disposal, Pete had to develop his flamboyant driving style to get the car round corners. Early on, he had found that attempts to steer produced terminal understeer, so he put it into the bend sideways, then used the throttle to bring the back round. Well-known Mini exponent Tom Airey had christened the bonnet power bulge for the Webers 'the coffin' and asked Pete how he managed to see over it. He replied that he didn't need to, as the car was always sideways!

Being an American car enthusiast, Pete used Cyclone 15in dished and finned wheels, like the ones on the Dodge Charger 444 in the TV series Dukes of Hazard. At one meeting, an eagle-eyed scrutineer suggested that they did not look very strong. Pete produced a magazine photograph showing the Dukes' car about to land from six feet in the air. The wheels were not queried again. Hubs were machined so all four wheels had five bolt fixings. He hand-cut his own

*Pete Robertson's Rallycross V8 throws up the mud. The massive duct in the window is to funnel air into the radiator, that was mounted in the luggage compartment.*

Dunlop slick tyres, on the outside only, with negative camber all round the tread that gave grip on the rough allowing the smooth slick section to take over when on the tarmac.

The car had 8½in-wide rims on the front and 9in rears. Despite the scrutineers' concerns, Pete found he could beat the inevitable dents out of the rims cold. When competing in the Star Tyres Championship he ran 7in Wolfrace wheels with the obligatory 185 remoulds all round, which gave excellent grip – the front would lift off the line. They shredded after three meetings. Being the only MGB in the sport, the car was always noticed and Pete had some enjoyable dices, especially with Tony Proctor's V6 Capri and Rob Gibson's Porsche.

In his final season, 1985, with proliferation of the four-wheel-drive super cars, Pete was looking for still more power and decided that the bottom end was not strong enough for a wilder cam, which would also result in loss of low-down power. He felt that the way to go was to supercharge. A Wade unit was obtained from APS who also provided shims, which, along with machining the piston crowns, would reduce the compression ratio. Just to make sure, the crank was changed and fitted with four-bolt main caps. The pulleys were arranged so the Wade was 50 per cent over-driven, usually running a boost of 7 or 8psi, but he had been known to turn it up to approaching 20psi.

When fired up, the engine cracked like a

*Pete Robertson's MG and Will Gollop's Saab lead a Ford Escort and a Vauxhall Chevette, cars that were more usually seen in Rallycross.*

dragster. First time out at Croft, the car went off the line like a scalded cat, but stopped after twenty-five yards when the engine detonated. Pete later discovered he had actually been running a 10.5 to 1 compression ratio instead of the intended 8 to 1. £50 bought another Rover 3-litre engine and, with even more piston machining, the compression ratio was reduced to the correct figure.

Peter ran the car until 1985, won several B finals, came third in A finals at Croft, Cadwell Park and Lydden, and won the Driver of the Day Award three times. Deciding he could no longer afford to stay competitive against the big money four-wheel-drive brigade, Pete retired from Rallycross. Having spoken to Barry Sidery-Smith, who explained that the V8 would not comply with the BCV8 Championship Regulations owing to the extent of its modifications, Robertson, who felt disinclined to de-modify the car, eventually broke it and sold the bits. He defected to circuit racing, running a Rover SD1 in the BRSCC Slick 50 Road Saloon series. Had he known then what he knows now, he might have persevered a little longer with the MG. He could have used the crank shaft from a 350 Chevrolet and stretched the engine to five litres. Would it have held together? Who knows?

# 11　The MGC

Arguably the most unloved MG of its time – the contemporary road testers certainly showed it no mercy – today, the MGC has acquired cult status. Only 4,542 Roadsters and 4,457 GTs were made, so they are obviously more rare than an MGB. Despite their understeering characteristics, blamed on that heavy straight-six engine and the torsion-bar suspension, a few hardy drivers took it by the scruff of its neck and taught it manners on the race track.

## Ted Reeve

Driving his well-thrashed Lotus Cortina to an appointment in Worthing, chartered surveyor Ted Reeve called in to the local BMC dealers for a brochure on the recently announced MGC. The salesman told him there was no such car, but proffered the MGB leaflet! Some weeks later, he took the now smoking Cortina to Colchester on another job and spotted a blue MGC GT in a showroom. He called in, did a deal and collected AEV 153F on his way home. Despite its bad press, Ted found the car handled well and drove it as fast as he could, 'as one did'.

*Ted Reeve (15) rounds Copse in the pouring rain at the Eight Clubs Silverstone meeting in May 1968. As well as providing his daily transport, the MGC GT was also used for sprints, rallies and even the occasional Autocross meeting.*

*Having dropped the clutch at 6,500rpm, Malcolm Trewhitt (80) smokes the tyres as he pulls off the Silverstone start line.*

Having competed in the Cortina it was not long before Ted was using the C in all manner of motor sport events, including races at Silverstone, and he suggests that he was one of the first drivers to race this new model.

## Malcolm Trewhitt

Yorkshire farmer, Malcolm Trewhitt, started his motor sport sprinting various examples of the MGB. When the MGC was announced in 1967, he liked the idea of the extra horsepower and, in 1969, went to his local dealers and bought a brand new example, with wire wheels and overdrive, for £1,650. Having barely run it in, YWT 666G replaced his MGB on the hills. Driving to meetings he towed the racing wheels and tyres

behind in a small camping trailer. He had to run the car in standard trim for the first year, in order not to invalidate the warranty, but once it was out of guarantee, he began the ongoing tuning process, which would continue for the next seven years.

The car was taken to the legendary Downton Engineering in Wiltshire where, using parts they had in stock along with some that Malcolm had bought from John Chatham, they converted the C to half race-spec. Downton's bill was £1,500 plus the Chatham parts. It now had triple 45s, and was running a 9.4 to 1 compression ratio. Malcolm still drove to events but found he was only getting about 20mpg (12 litres/100km).

In 1971, it went back to Downtons for Barry

Haig to give it the full race treatment. The cam was up-rated to a 649 and the engine had everything that went with it, including enormous 2in Chevvy inlet valves. Barry used to wait until the early hours to road test the C, which was now without tax or MOT. With nothing below 4,500 rpm it had to be trailered to meetings and the only car available at the time was Malcolm's father's 1,300cc VW Beetle. He recalls a Sprint outing at RAF Kemble near Cirencester when they arrived home in North Yorkshire thirty-six hours after they had set out.

For the slicks, the car now had 10in-wide J. A. Pearce Magna wheels, purchased at a cost of £165 for four, suitably covered by wide arches. The C was always run as a road-derived car and the regulations stated that arches could only be 2½in wide. Malcolm got round this by cutting the arches high into the wing so that at their widest they were still only 2½in out from the position of the original arch. Just one scrutineer queried this and put him in another class. Straight-cut gears and a ZF limited-slip differential strengthened the drive train, and the overdrive unit was fitted with uprated Jaguar parts.

To get off the line, Malcolm dropped the clutch at 6,000rpm and hoped it all stayed together. The clutch certainly did, as it had been upgraded to one usually found on a 4.2-litre Jaguar. Maximum torque was at 5,200rpm and the red line was at 7,000, but it would take occasional bursts of 7,200rpm. Malcolm wrecked two diffs and about six gearboxes over the years – strangely it was not first but third gear that always stripped, usually every tooth, as the result of the power, 240bhp at the flywheel. He always used the 4.22 diff ratio, which meant he only ran out of revs at the end of the back straight at Silverstone, just before Woodcote.

Axle tramp was prevented by two very strong adjustable anti-tramp bars. They were so effective that, after each outing, Malcolm had to beat the floor straight with a seven-pound hammer. Vanderville engine bearings were always used and would last a season; when they became unobtainable they had to rebuild twice a year and once had to grind the crank ten thou.

Malcolm had his most successful outings at the MGCC Silverstone meeting on two consecutive years, winning two races one year and three the next. He arrived late for another Silverstone race and, despite his protestations that he was two seconds a lap quicker than anyone else, had to start at the back of the grid because he had practised out of session. On the line, the starter pointed out that he had ten laps to hit the front; unconsoled, Malcolm told the two drivers on the penultimate row that he was coming through and they had better make room, which they did. He cut his way through the grid, followed by Derek Grant in his Chatham-built MGC, and was second at the end of lap one. He went on to win the race with Grant second.

When Downton closed down, Malcolm managed to buy the MGC manifold and exhaust system jigs from the scrap dealer who cleared the premises. The car was then entrusted to Rally Equipe in Bolton. Noted as Mini specialists, they soon got to grips with the MGC and, having obtained Malcolm's consent, copied and marketed some of his special modifications. Set up on Harry Ratcliffe's rolling road at British Vita, the engine produced maximum power with 165 main jets in the Webers. Concerned it was running too lean and would burn out the valves and pistons, Malcolm played safe and used 175s. Fuel consumption at racing speeds was a meagre 10mpg (23.5 litres/100km)!

Malcolm's most exciting race was the one he had with Keith Ashby's Midget at Mallory Park. The C led off the line but the Midget managed to get in front coming out of Gerrards. By braking later at the Esses, the C would get a nose in front; keeping ahead through the Hairpin, Malcolm would engage overdrive third, halfway out, and it would kick in as he came out of the Elbow. Thus he would head the field over the line again. This continued for all ten laps, resulting in Malcolm taking his first outright win.

By 1977, the only thing left to do was reduce the weight – the vehicle had ended up weighing 56lb (25.4kg) more than a standard car. Malcolm stripped it down to attend to this detail, but illness prevented him completing the job and eventually the car was sold, as it stood, to Chris Green.

Achievements have included winning the prestigious MGCC Banana Trophy, for the fastest MG at the club's sprint, three times, and second in the 1971 MGCC North East Centre Speed Championship, scoring equal points with winner Ernie Foster. He scored many race wins and top three places and, as a noted trier, suggests that one in three of his races ended in the barriers, as the result of his do-or-die efforts.

Having retired from racing for medical reasons in 1978, Malcolm, a former amateur steeplechase jockey, runs a riding centre and now gets his kicks on horseback at 40mph.

## Chris Green

Yorkshire garage owner Chris Green had built a Sebring MGC GT replica and considered entering it in the Pirelli Marathon, but discovered it would be ineligible. When Malcolm phoned and offered him YWT 666 G, he decided to buy it, put the car back in standard trim and enter that in the rally. In order to lose the wide arches, he had to replace all four wings and the JAPs were changed for standard-width Minilite wheels. The

head and carburettors were swapped for standard items.

Chris and his navigator, John Hampshire, experienced overheating problems on the event. It got so hot when it reached the top of the Stelvio Pass that one of the Special Tuning alloy rocker spacers expanded so much that the push rod came out from beneath the tappet. Ex-works mechanic, Den Green, who was manning the emergency repair van, tried to lever it back without success and suggested that they would have to take the head off. Chris was so frustrated that he kicked the front wheel and it popped back in of its own accord! Having lost over a day because of their problems, the pair, running as car 113, were classified fourteenth in Class, sixty-seventh overall in the 1989 Marathon, with total penalties of twenty-seven hours fifteen minutes and fifteen seconds.

## Doug Smith

Having spent his formative years with Colin Pearcy and the late Martin Dell, often joining them for visits to 1970s race meetings with Colin's father, it is hardly surprising that long-time MGC enthusiast Doug Smith would get

*Chris Green converted Malcolm Trewhitt's MGC, YWT 666G, into a rally car and finished sixty-seventh overall in the 1989 Pirelli Marathon.*

*Doug Smith's first MGC, FUD 226G, racing at Zolder in 1994.*

drawn to motor racing. Doug's first C was a factory-built rally MGC GT assembled at Abingdon for one of the employees. The Tartan Red car, FUD 226 G, had a special wiring loom and twenty-two-gallon fuel tank, but unfortunately, Doug did not realize the significance until after he had removed them from the car.

Doug bought FUD to replace his wife Maggie's Mini in 1975. John Chatham converted it to Sebring spec in 1976 and Smith got Minilite to cast him a set of 8in wheels in magnesium. When it needed an engine rebuild in 1984, Colin persuaded him that, whilst he was about it, he might just as well up-spec the whole car and take it racing. Many is the time Doug was soaking in the bath after a hard day's work, as a contracts

manager for Pearcy's construction company, and hearing the sound of Colin working in his garage on the car.

Doug competed in the MGCC BCV8 championship from 1984 to 1995, when he sold the car to German MG collector Dietter Rohl. In 1987, he made a concerted effort to race in every round of the championship and it proved to be his most successful season. Going to the last round at Oulton Park, Malcolm Beer, Tony Price and Doug all had a mathematical chance of winning the series; Doug came third but won Class C for modified MGCs, scoring 120 points. He also won class C in 1986.

The heavy car was well suited to the Brands Hatch Grand Prix circuit and would straight-line

*Vic Young's MGC (79) in full flight at Silverstone in March 2000. The car is fitted with the narrow version of the Sebring-style wheel arches.*

Dingle Dell on the kerbs with ease. Doug recalls putting it on the front row on 23 July 1986, alongside the V8s of Terry Smith and Colin Pearcy, with the other V8s on the second row behind him. Doug loved the BCV8 annual visit to Zolder; he invariably did well there.

By 1990, Doug's part-time business selling MGC spares was consuming more and more hours, so that year he set up MG Motorsport at Bovingdon in Hertfordshire, on a full-time basis. As well as selling spares, he now builds, race prepares and repairs MGs, specializing in MGCs. He has also built several FIA Spec MGBs which he has raced and then sold on. One such B, GMF 806, was sold to a Belgian and Doug's crew acted as mechanics for him when he entered the first historic 24-hour race at Paul Ricard.

Happy to go to the track to watch one of his cars, or someone he knows, compete, Doug finds a whole day's spectating boring and usually heads for home immediately after the finish of the race he has gone to see.

## Peter Hiley and Jason Bull

In 1995, Doug Smith and Vince, his mechanic, built what he describes as his ultimate MGC GT racer, again Sebring-like in appearance. Everything non-essential was left off and the weight pared down to 18cwt (900kg), 7cwt (350kg) below the kerb weight of a standard C GT. The car was built right to the limit of the BCV8 regulations. Doug raced the new car for a while, but decided he was not doing it justice. Having adjourned to the pub after one race meeting, he and Vince mulled over various names of drivers they thought would do well in the car. As a result Peter Hiley got a phone call and drove it in the

1996 BCV8 Championship. Doug had experimented, taking the engine out to 3.4 litres, but this proved to be the car's Achilles' heel.

Now back to 3 litres the car is in good form in the hands of its new owner, ex-kartist Jason Bull, the original capacity engine producing 300bhp at the flywheel, more power than the unreliable enlarged version. In his first race at a damp Silverstone in 1999, Jason came third overall to the V8s of Williams and Collis. Jason's was the highest-placed MGC in the 2000 BCV8 Championship.

## Vic, Ian and Andy Young

Computer expert Vic Young also has a great working knowledge of MGCs, having competed in CGTs since 1975. He drove his first example, a blue car, 9588 K, in sprints and had his maiden race at the first BCV8 Championship visit to Brands Hatch in September 1977. Vic pragmatically states that he started his racing days at the back of the grid, then graduated to being a mid-field runner, but nowadays is at the back once more, where he still thoroughly enjoys his racing.

In the early days, his was the only C on the BCV8 grid and therefore won the award for the best-turned-out example. He recalls many good midfield dices with Rod Gill's MGC Roadster and Colin Cork in his white V8. Racing has always been a family affair: Vic drove his wife and sons Andy and Ian to 1970s race meetings in the GT with a trailer tent behind. He would often finish second in his race at MGCC Silverstone on Saturday, then polish the car up and come second in the Sunday concours, before driving it home again.

In 1974, Vic bought a second CGT, a primrose-yellow example, 8 GBP, which he stored away for several years (so his wife did not find out he had two) before bringing it home to rebuild. Once completed, it replaced the blue one as his race car. This later made way for his current white car, BCG 384G. Over the years, Vic had a hand in organizing the re-manufacture of several obsolete spare parts for the MGC.

*Andy Young tries the two-wheel approach at Snetterton in 1998.*

*An MGC with a difference: Paul Campfield's Roadster (98) has a full race V8 engine under the bonnet. Here he leads Warwick Banks (95) and Derek Stewart at Snetterton in 1992.*

To mark son Ian's twenty-first, he was given 9588 K and his brother Andy was presented with 8 GBP when he became of age. Both continue the family tradition and compete in the BCV8 series. Vic has competed in the Brighton Speed trials for twenty-five years and took the MG Trophy in 2000; Ian won the award in 1998 and 1999. Vic is building himself a new GT to race for 2002, likewise Andy, to preserve his twenty-first birthday present. This brings the number of Cs in the household to six!

# Bibliography

The majority of the information in this book has been obtained by speaking to the people involved at the time but the following publications have been used for the verification of certain facts:

Allison, Jeff and Dunbar, Roger A., *The Cars Just Happen . . . The Story Of Frank Nichols and Elva Cars*

Allison, Michael and Browning, Peter, *The Works MGs* (Haynes Publishing, 2000) ISBN 0 85960 603 2

Baggott, John, *Mighty Midgets & Special Sprites* (The Crowood Press Ltd, 1998) ISBN 1 86126 106 3

Filby, Peter, *TVR Success Against The Odds* (Motorbooks International, 1976) ISBN 0 905064 08 9

Knowles, David and the MG Car Club V8 Register, *MG V8 Twenty One Years On . . . From Introduction to RV8* (Windrow & Greene Ltd, 1994) ISBN 1 872004 89 X

Laban, Brian, *MGB The Complete Story* (The Crowood Press Ltd, 1990) ISBN 1 85223 358 3

Lawrence, Mike, *AZ of Sports Cars Since 1945* (Bay View Books, 1991) ISBN 1 870979 23 0

Price, Bill, *The BMC/BL Competitions Department* (Foulis, 1989) ISBN 0 85429 677 8

Robson, Graham, *The Mighty MGs* (David & Charles, 1982) ISBN 0 7153 8226 8

Walklett, Bob, *Ginetta The Inside Story* (Bookmarque, 1994) ISBN 1 870519 28 0

Wimpffen, Janos L., *Time and Two Seats – Ten Decades of Endurance Racing* (American Motor Sport Research Group, Washington, 1999) ISBN 0 967252 0 05

# Index

Adams, Graeme 86
Aitchison, Keith 140
Aitken, Mike 149
Aley, John 141
Alison, Derek 145
Alman, Peter 33
Armstrong, Ray 91
Ashby, Jill 50
Ashford, Roy 11, 19–21, 23, 77
Ashworth, Dr Mark 56, 65, 80–83, 86
Axon, Phil 35, 37
Ayoubpour, Camran 158–159

Baker, Clive 47, 166
Baker, Gil 137
Baker, Ken 124–125
Baker-Carr, Robert 150, 152
Baldet, Andre 43–44, 125
Ballisat, Keith 136
Bamford, Anthony 16, 32–34
Banks, Warwick 43–46, 84, 92–94, 111
Barnard, Tony 60, 128
Barwell Racing 12, 15, 116, 124, 126
Baynham, Jim 99–101, 109
Beadnell, Bob 63
Beer, Adrian 68–69
Beer, Malcolm 62, 64, 66–68, 73, 76, 85, 86, 88, 94, 95, 168, 174, 184
Beer, Syd 66, 67, 165
Begbie, Rod 151
Belsey, John 144
Bentley, Andy 94
Bentley, Roche 99
Beresford, Dave 52
Beresford, Jonathan 53
Bergonzi, Lew 95, 98
Berridge, Bob 63, 65
Bianchi, Tony 153–154
Bicknell, Steve 165–166, 168
Bilton, John 171–173

Binks, Godfrey 147
Binnington, Anthony 11, 23, 26–27, 38, 84, 86, 149, 151, 159
Binnington, Tim 26
Bird, Mike 127
Birrell, Bob 57
Blyth, Charles 147–149
Bolton, Peter 136
Booth, Ken 137
Boothby, Fred 57, 152
Boothby, James 145, 152
Bowler, Bernie 70
Boyce, Dr Tom 28–31
Brack, Bill 156
Brierley, Cedric 162
Britten, John 32, 142, 162
Brown, Gerry 25–26, 120
Brown, Peter 16, 32–34
Brown, Robert 156
Browning, Peter 36, 41, 42, 159, 161, 167, 175, 188
Buchanan, Charles 99
Bucknum, Ronnie 9
Bull, Jason 186
Bunce, Don 11, 12–13, 32, 38, 47, 115, 118, 142
Burgess, Peter 52, 94
Burrows, Graham 147
Burton, Arnold 150

Cakebread, Andy 96–98
Cakebread, Brian 96–98, 121
Campbell, Mike 129, 141
Campfield, Paul 68, 86
Campling, Paul 80
Cannon, Mike 35
Carlisle, Christabel 39–40
Carpenter, Terry 24
Carter, John 73
Chalk, Mike 80, 83–84
Chandler, Mike 132, 134

Chatham, John 159–162, 165, 166–168, 171, 181
Chowne, Peter 80
Chudecki, Paul 15
Clark, Peter 150
Clarkson, Roy 101
Classey, John 132–133
Clayden, Roy 78
Claydon, Tony 148–150
Cleverdon, David 37, 91
Cobban, Gordon 118
Cochrane, Norman 127
Cocker, Jeremy 50
Colbrook, Jim 24
Collins, David 158
Collis, Peter 93–96
Conn, Norman 63
Costello, Ken 47, 171
Cotton, John 23–24
Cottrell, Peter 130, 134–135
Council, Gordon 47
Cox, Jim 14
Crawford, Alistair 50–51

Dalziel, Ken 116
Darcey, Mick 158, 159, 167
Davis, Darryl 102–104, 107
Davis, Grahame 95, 102–104
Davis, Rae 59–60, 87, 102
Dawes, Nigel 166
Dawkins, Charles 11, 34–37, 58
Day John, 77
Dell, Jenny 129
Dell Martin, 80, 183
Delmar-Morgan, Jeremy 48–49
Dence, Adrian 140
Dent, Angus 60–61
Dent, Ruth 60–61
Denton, Jean 15, 27–31, 32, 47, 142
Denton, Tony 28, 47
Dignan, John 53–56

Dignan, Pauline 53–56
Dignan, Peter 55
Dilley, Ray 16–18
Dobbs, Joan 64
Downton Engineering 20, 25, 35,
    181, 182
Drake, Chris 162
Dron, Tony 169

Eade, Rod 34–37, 58
Edwards, Kit 157
Edwards, Roger 12, 148
Elford, Vic 33
Elliott, Henry 42
Ellis, Nigel 131
Ellison, David 135
Elva Courier 123–129
Emsley, Phil 114
Enever, Roger 18, 34, 42, 46–47, 142,
    147, 171
Enever, Syd 11, 14, 30
Entwhisle, Mike 82
Entwhistle, Tommy 31, 137–139, 140,
    145, 147
Everingham, Peter 57

Fall, Tony 33, 34
Fangio, Juan Manuel 120
Fawkes, Bev 131
Fenemore, David 151
Flaherty, Jack 40
Fletcher, Rivers 132
Fowler, Trevor 125
Frankel, Andrew 122
Franklin, David 11, 23, 56, 75, 76–78
Franklin, Deborah 56, 77
Friese, Bernard 129

Gammons, Malcolm 158
Gammons, Ron 118, 158
Gardner, Bill 165
Garner, Mark 107–108, 109
Garratt, Peter 129, 146
Garton, Mike 30–31
Gaston, Mike 140
Gaston, Paddy 137, 139–141, 152
Gates, Maurice 127
Gathercole, David 112
Gear, Geoff 73–75, 84, 100
Gidden, Mike 174–176
Gilbern GT 1800 129–134

Gilbern V8 GT 134–135
Ginetta, G11 135–136
Gladwin, Danny 125–126
Goddard, Jimmy 150
Godrez, Perry 84
Goodwin, Natalie 30
Gordon, Robbie 31–32, 147, 152, 153
Goss, Tim 174–176
Gott, John 11, 12, 24, 31, 142, 152
Grant, Derek 168, 171, 182
Grant, Rob 150
Gravett, Robb 86–87
Gray, Bernard 131–132
Green, Chris 183
Green, Den 183
Griffiths, Doc 26
Grub, Ben 153
Gurrier, Keith 58, 73, 85–86

Haig, Rob 83
Halford, Brian 94
Hall, Peter 91
Hart-Banks, Suzie 92–93
Harvey, Alan 161
Harvey-Bailey, Roddy 32
Harwood, Ian 100
Hatcher, Chris 107
Hawkins, Paul 36
Haynes, Annette 127
Haynes, John OBE 126–127
Hayter, Jackie 50, 53
Heavens, Roger 172
Hedges, Andrew 14, 40–43, 48, 158,
    166
Herd, Robin 77
Hewitt, Bill 84, 104–105
Hewitt, John 22, 37, 80, 81, 83, 84,
    99, 104–105
Hibberd, Michael 87, 104
Hiley, Peter 90, 185–186
Hill, Craig 156
Hill, Graham 9, 115
Holmes, Andy 96
Hooper, Phil 144
Hopkirk, Paddy 6, 40, 46, 48, 117,
    156, 158, 170
Horn, Richard 87, 105–106
Hounslow, Alec 140
Howard, Paul 142–144, 149
Howe, Anson 151
Humphries, Cliff 171

Hunisett, Roy 14
Hurl, Richard 164–165
Hutcheson, Alan 9, 10, 34, 40–43,
    124–125

Ickx Jackie, 36, 173, 176
Ingall Martin, 133–134
Isherwood, Kelly 114

Jackson, Peter 31–32
Jardini, Gerard 144
Jarrold, Paul 164
Jarvis, Dave 99, 101–102
Jones, Graham 83
Jones, Liz 40
Jordan, Nigel 13–14

Kember, Tony 163–164
Kenny, Tom 135–136
Kirkland, Edward 165
Konig, Gabriel 15, 28, 142, 148

Lambert, Barbara 57–59, 61, 66
Lambert, Brian 37, 57–59, 66, 70
Lambert, Mark 59
Lanfranchi, Tony 146–147
Langton, Amanda 154
Leach, Rod 162
Lees, Nick 150–151
Leithead, Stan 151
Lewis, Mike 32, 152–153
Lewis, Steve 111
Lilley, Arthur 146
Lilley, Martin 146, 147, 149
Lodge, John 70, 76, 77–80, 85
Longden, Andrew 48–49
Longman, Richard 23
Longton, Dr Rod 13, 22, 32, 59,
    62–66, 70, 82, 87, 122, 142, 144
Loveday, Jim 20, 24–25, 35, 37, 158
Luff, Bob 22, 59, 63, 64–66, 68,
    69–70, 72
Lutz, Ron 123

Mahon, Laurence 43
Makinen, Timo 48, 156, 158, 170
Mallock, Arthur 139, 141
Mansell, Geoff 91–92
Marriner, Neville 15, 84, 100
Marshall, Gerry 13, 15, 18, 104, 105,
    116, 140, 141, 146–147, 148, 169

Martin-Hurst, Richard 156
Massey-Crosse, Ian 137
Mayman, Pauline 40
McCarthy, Roy 18, 59, 75, 87–88, 91–92, 94, 106, 129
McCarthy, Russell 88–90, 96
McCarthy, Spencer 88–90, 96
McCluggage, Denise 40
McDonald, John 140
McHardy, Alistair 137, 140, 144–145
McMahon, Derek 43
McWilliams, Bruce 156
Miles, Alan 129
Milligan, Dr Spike 99
Mills, Alan 58–59
'Mister Warrick Arms' Abingdon 49, 172
Mitchell, Terry 9
Monk, Rod 151
Moore, Don 31, 43–46
Moyer, Geoff 15

Nashe-Wiseman, Graham 169–170
Neilson, Andrew 43
Neville, Bob 42–43, 66, 171–176
Newcomer, Tom 137
Nichols, Frank 123
Nicholson, Bill 10–11, 13, 20, 23, 25, 29, 30, 32, 36, 43–44, 47, 69, 78, 84, 125, 128, 147, 148, 152
Nicoll, Norman 151
Nightingale, Terry 18

O'Neill, Chris 77
Osborne, Terry 21–23, 37, 63, 73, 177
Osborn-King, Roger 70, 72–73
Osteen, Dick 123

Page, Andy 34
Palmer, Jack 64, 65
Palmer, John 65
Palmer, Jonathan 121
Palmer, Peter 99
Parker, Dave 94
Parker, Dr Terry 131, 133
Parkinson, Graham 34
Parkinson, Jim 40
Pearcy, Colin 15, 22, 38, 73, 76, 77, 79, 80, 84–86, 87, 93, 116, 122, 158, 159, 168, 183–184

Perkins, Graeme 162–163
Perrett, Ian 162
Pertwee, Jon 134
Petch, Nigel 106–107
Phillips, Archie 63
Pierpoint, Roy 44
Pigott, Terry 51–52
Pinkerton, Robin 153
Playfoot, John 128
Polak, Francis 47
Pollard, Peter 31
Polley, Ian 25, 37, 77
Pond, Tony 75
Poole, Alec 11, 42, 46–47, 158, 171
Poole, Arnie 42–43
Price, Tony 65, 105, 111, 184

Ralph, John 43
Ransom, Tim 67, 73, 85
Ratcliffe, Harry 182
Reader, Howard 149
Redman, Brian 36
Reece, Brian 11
Reeve, Ted 180–181
Rhodes, John 43–46, 48
Richards, Gerry 93
Richardson, Ken and Paul 138
Richardson, Martin 83
Richardson, Paul 80
Ripley Carl, 128
Robertson, Peter 177–179
Rodman, Paul 82
Rosner, Emil 130, 132, 133
Rule, Phil 102
Ryder, Les 11–12, 128, 147, 148

Sagerman, Gerry 139
Sanderson, Ninian 136
Scantlebury, Richard 176–177
Schlagenhauf, Karl 152
Schmitt, Bernd 151, 152
Schneider, Ivan 137
Scott, Derek 137
Scott, Dr Paul 130–131, 134
Scott, Sheila 29
Senna, Ayrton 105
Shaerf, Robbie 72
Sharp, John 11, 14–15, 125, 138
Sharp, Peter 131–132
Shaw, Martin 87
Shellard, Rob 23, 43, 117

Sidery-Smith, Barry 12, 15, 22, 37, 43, 59, 62, 63, 65–66, 69, 78, 82, 84, 86, 87, 92, 94, 98, 115–122, 153, 159, 179
Sidery-Smith, Pam 116, 117, 118, 153
Siffert, Jo 36, 56
Simpson, Peter 139, 140, 147
Slotemaker, Rob 136
Smith, Alan 134
Smith, Chris (Gilbern) 131, 132, 133
Smith, Chris (Westfield) 37, 57
Smith, Colin 158
Smith, Doug 79, 91, 168, 183–185
Smith, Giles 129
Smith, Les 100
Smith, Terry 67, 73, 75–76, 77, 78, 84, 85, 185
Smith, Victor 62, 77, 118
Sprinzel, John 14
Staniforth, Alan 50
Stephenson, Roy 152
Stewart, Tom 53
Stock, Richard 177
Stuart, Derek 65
Sullivan, Peter 80
Sutton, Mike 134
Swift, Glyn 84

Tadman, John 71–72
Target, John 18, 26
Tatton, Peter 146
Taylor, Anita 43–46
Taylor, Huw 108–110
Taylor, Neil 109
Taylor, Trevor 43–46
Thomas, Kitty 132
Thompson, Phil 87
Thomson, Jonathan 146
Thornley, John 27
Thurgood, Julius 18, 100, 102, 159, 170
Tilley, Dave 63
Tolhurst, Josie 154
Trace, Jeremy 125–126
Trace, John 125–126
Trewhitt, Malcolm 171–172, 176, 181–183
Tudor-Owen, Jenny 15–16, 32, 115

Turner, Stuart  17, 32, 40, 155
TVR 1800S  145, 148
TVR Grantura  136–152
TVR Vixen  149

Unger, Ernie  124

Valentine, Sean  108–110
Vernaeve, Julian  47, 119
Vernon, John  80

Wadsworth, Howard  133
Walden, Richard  78, 79
Walker, Phil  110–112
Walkinshaw, Tom  75–76, 78
Walklett, Bob, Douglas, Ivor and
    Trevers  135
Walton, Mike  48–49
Wansbrough, David  31, 32,
    148

Ward, Joe  151–152
Warrard, Michael  14, 145
Webb, Michael  25, 158
Wellman, Tommy  42
Wheeler, Mary MBE  129,
    145–146
Whiffen, Gerald  42
Whistlecroft, Denis  153
White, Alan  177
Wileyman, Richard  157–158
Wilkinson, Ray  132
Willard, Graham  96
Williams, Bernard  139
Williams, Keith  94, 96
Williams, Steve  64, 68, 72–73, 88
Williams, Tony  43
Wilson, Ken  134–135
Wilson-Spratt, Douglas  31, 32, 152,
    153
Wilson-Spratt, Tony  154

Windmill and Lewis  19
Wingfield, John  139, 141
Wiseberg, Adam  80
Wood, Paul  51
Wood, Tommy  136–137
Woolcott, Nigel  112–113
Worswick, Ted  32, 150
Worthington, Derek  172
Worts, Richard  12, 13, 115
Wright, Brian  116
WSM MGB  152–157

Yeoman, Alan  10
Yhapp, Freddie  15
Young, Andy  86, 186–187
Young, Ian  187
Young, Malcolm  116, 168
Young, Vic  77, 186–187

Zafer, Alan  165, 166